God, Politics, Economy

The book intervenes into the contemporary debate on religion, politics, and economy, focusing on the field of formation which emerges as these seemingly autonomous spheres encounter one another.

Empirically, it concentrates on examples from literature, theatre, and cinema, as well as a case study of the recent revolts in Turkey where a 'moderate' Islamic government is in power. Theoretically, its focus is on the contemporary 'return' of religion in the horizon of the critique of religion, seeking to articulate an affirmative politics that can re-evaluate the value of dominant values in religious governance and governance of religion.

Bülent Diken teaches Social and Cultural Theory at Lancaster University, Department of Sociology.

Routledge Advances in Sociology

1 **Virtual Globalization**
Virtual spaces/tourist spaces
Edited by David Holmes

2 **The Criminal Spectre in Law, Literature and Aesthetics**
Peter Hutchings

3 **Immigrants and National Identity in Europe**
Anna Triandafyllidou

4 **Constructing Risk and Safety in Technological Practice**
Edited by Jane Summerton and Boel Berner

5 **Europeanisation, National Identities and Migration**
Changes in boundary constructions between Western and Eastern Europe
Willfried Spohn and Anna Triandafyllidou

6 **Language, Identity and Conflict**
A comparative study of language in ethnic conflict in Europe and Eurasia
Diarmait Mac Giolla Chríost

7 **Immigrant Life in the U.S.**
Multi-disciplinary perspectives
Edited by Donna R. Gabaccia and Colin Wayne Leach

8 **Rave Culture and Religion**
Edited by Graham St. John

9 **Creation and Returns of Social Capital**
A new research program
Edited by Henk Flap and Beate Völker

10 **Self-Care**
Embodiment, personal autonomy and the shaping of health consciousness
Christopher Ziguras

11 **Mechanisms of Cooperation**
Werner Raub and Jeroen Weesie

12 **After the Bell**
Educational success, public policy and family background
Edited by Dalton Conley and Karen Albright

13 **Youth Crime and Youth Culture in the Inner City**
Bill Sanders

14 **Emotions and Social Movements**
Edited by Helena Flam and Debra King

15 **Globalization, Uncertainty and Youth in Society**
Edited by Hans-Peter Blossfeld, Erik Klijzing, Melinda Mills and Karin Kurz

16 **Love, Heterosexuality and Society**
Paul Johnson

17 **Agricultural Governance**
Globalization and the new politics of regulation
Edited by Vaughan Higgins and Geoffrey Lawrence

18 **Challenging Hegemonic Masculinity**
Richard Howson

19 **Social Isolation in Modern Society**
Roelof Hortulanus, Anja Machielse and Ludwien Meeuwesen

20 **Weber and the Persistence of Religion**
Social theory, capitalism and the sublime
Joseph W. H. Lough

21 **Globalization, Uncertainty and Late Careers in Society**
Edited by Hans-Peter Blossfeld, Sandra Buchholz and Dirk Hofäcker

22 **Bourdieu's Politics**
Problems and possibilities
Jeremy F. Lane

23 **Media Bias in Reporting Social Research?**
The case of reviewing ethnic inequalities in education
Martyn Hammersley

24 **A General Theory of Emotions and Social Life**
Warren D. TenHouten

25 **Sociology, Religion and Grace**
Arpad Szakolczai

26 **Youth Cultures**
Scenes, subcultures and tribes
Edited by Paul Hodkinson and Wolfgang Deicke

27 **The Obituary as Collective Memory**
Bridget Fowler

28 **Tocqueville's Virus**
Utopia and dystopia in Western social and political thought
Mark Featherstone

29 **Jewish Eating and Identity Through the Ages**
David Kraemer

30 **The Institutionalization of Social Welfare**
A study of medicalizing management
Mikael Holmqvist

31 **The Role of Religion in Modern Societies**
Edited by Detlef Pollack and Daniel V. A. Olson

32 **Sex Research and Sex Therapy**
A sociological analysis of Masters and Johnson
Ross Morrow

33 **A Crisis of Waste?**
Understanding the rubbish society
Martin O'Brien

34 **Globalization and Transformations of Local Socioeconomic Practices**
Edited by Ulrike Schuerkens

35 **The Culture of Welfare Markets**
The international recasting of pension and care systems
Ingo Bode

36 **Cohabitation, Family and Society**
Tiziana Nazio

37 **Latin America and Contemporary Modernity**
A sociological interpretation
José Maurízio Domingues

38 **Exploring the Networked Worlds of Popular Music**
Milieu cultures
Peter Webb

39 **The Cultural Significance of the Child Star**
Jane O'Connor

40 **European Integration as an Elite Process**
The failure of a dream?
Max Haller

41 **Queer Political Performance and Protest**
Benjamin Shepard

42 **Cosmopolitan Spaces**
Europe, globalization, theory
Chris Rumford

43 **Contexts of Social Capital**
Social networks in communities, markets and organizations
Edited by Ray-May Hsung, Nan Lin, and Ronald Breiger

44 **Feminism, Domesticity and Popular Culture**
Edited by Stacy Gillis and Joanne Hollows

45 **Changing Relationships**
Edited by Malcolm Brynin and John Ermisch

46 **Formal and Informal Work**
The hidden work regime in Europe
Edited by Birgit Pfau-Effinger, Lluis Flaquer, and Per H. Jensen

47 **Interpreting Human Rights**
Social science perspectives
Edited by Rhiannon Morgan and Bryan S. Turner

48 **Club Cultures**
Boundaries, identities and otherness
Silvia Rief

49 **Eastern European Immigrant Families**
Mihaela Robila

50 **People and Societies**
Rom Harré and designing the social sciences
Luk van Langenhove

51 **Legislating Creativity**
The intersections of art and politics
Dustin Kidd

52 **Youth in Contemporary Europe**
Edited by Jeremy Leaman and Martha Wörsching

53 **Globalization and Transformations of Social Inequality**
Edited by Ulrike Schuerkens

54 **Twentieth Century Music and the Question of Modernity**
Eduardo De La Fuente

55 **The American Surfer**
Radical culture and capitalism
Kristin Lawler

56 **Religion and Social Problems**
Edited by Titus Hjelm

57 **Play, Creativity, and Social Movements**
If I can't dance, it's not my revolution
Benjamin Shepard

58 **Undocumented Workers' Transitions**
Legal status, migration, and work in Europe
Sonia McKay, Eugenia Markova and Anna Paraskevopoulou

59 **The Marketing of War in the Age of Neo-Militarism**
Edited by Kostas Gouliamos and Christos Kassimeris

60 **Neoliberalism and the Global Restructuring of Knowledge and Education**
Steven C. Ward

61 **Social Theory in Contemporary Asia**
Ann Brooks

62 **Foundations of Critical Media and Information Studies**
Christian Fuchs

63 **A Companion to Life Course Studies**
The social and historical context of the British birth cohort studies
Michael Wadsworth and John Bynner

64 **Understanding Russianness**
Risto Alapuro, Arto Mustajoki and Pekka Pesonen

65 **Understanding Religious Ritual**
Theoretical approaches and innovations
John Hoffmann

66 **Online Gaming in Context**
The social and cultural significance of online games
Garry Crawford, Victoria K. Gosling and Ben Light

67 **Contested Citizenship in East Asia**
Developmental politics, national unity, and globalization
Kyung-Sup Chang and Bryan S. Turner

68 **Agency without Actors?**
New approaches to collective action
Edited by Jan-Hendrik Passoth, Birgit Peuker and Michael Schillmeier

69 **The Neighborhood in the Internet**
Design research projects in community informatics
John M. Carroll

70 **Managing Overflow in Affluent Societies**
Edited by Barbara Czarniawska and Orvar Löfgren

71 **Refugee Women**
Beyond gender versus culture
Leah Bassel

72 **Socioeconomic Outcomes of the Global Financial Crisis**
Theoretical discussion and empirical case studies
Edited by Ulrike Schuerkens

73 **Migration in the 21st Century**
Political economy and ethnography
Edited by Pauline Gardiner Barber and Winnie Lem

74 **Ulrich Beck**
An introduction to the theory of second modernity and the risk society
Mads P. Sørensen and Allan Christiansen

75 **The International Recording Industries**
Edited by Lee Marshall

76 **Ethnographic Research in the Construction Industry**
Edited by Sarah Pink, Dylan Tutt and Andrew Dainty

77 **Routledge Companion to Contemporary Japanese Social Theory**
From individualization to globalization in Japan today
Edited by Anthony Elliott, Masataka Katagiri and Atsushi Sawai

78 **Immigrant Adaptation in Multi-Ethnic Societies**
Canada, Taiwan, and the United States
Edited by Eric Fong, Lan-Hung Nora Chiang and Nancy Denton

79 **Cultural Capital, Identity, and Social Mobility**
The life course of working-class university graduates
Mick Matthys

80 **Speaking for Animals**
Animal autobiographical writing
Edited by Margo DeMello

81 **Healthy Aging in Sociocultural Context**
Edited by Andrew E. Scharlach and Kazumi Hoshino

82 **Touring Poverty**
Bianca Freire-Medeiros

83 **Life Course Perspectives on Military Service**
Edited by Janet M. Wilmoth and Andrew S. London

84 **Innovation in Socio-Cultural Context**
Edited by Frane Adam and Hans Westlund

85 **Youth, Arts and Education**
Reassembling subjectivity through affect
Anna Hickey-Moody

86 **The Capitalist Personality**
Face-to-face sociality and economic change in the post-communist world
Christopher S. Swader

87 **The Culture of Enterprise in Neoliberalism**
Specters of entrepreneurship
Tomas Marttila

88 **Islamophobia in the West**
Measuring and explaining individual attitudes
Marc Helbling

89 **The Challenges of Being a Rural Gay Man**
Coping with stigma
Deborah Bray Preston and Anthony R. D'Augelli

90 **Global Justice Activism and Policy Reform in Europe**
Understanding when change happens
Edited by Peter Utting, Mario Pianta and Anne Ellersiek

91 **Sociology of the Visual Sphere**
Edited by Regev Nathansohn and Dennis Zuev

92 **Solidarity in Individualized Societies**
Recognition, justice and good judgement
Søren Juul

93 **Heritage in the Digital Era**
Cinematic tourism and the activist cause
Rodanthi Tzanelli

94 **Generation, Discourse, and Social Change**
Karen R. Foster

95 **Sustainable Practices**
Social theory and climate change
Elizabeth Shove and Nicola Spurling

96 **The Transformative Capacity of New Technologies**
A theory of sociotechnical change
Ulrich Dolata

97 **Consuming Families**
Buying, making, producing family life in the 21st century
Jo Lindsay and JaneMaree Maher

98 **Migrant Marginality**
A transnational perspective
Edited by Philip Kretsedemas, Jorge Capetillo-Ponce and Glenn Jacobs

99 **Changing Gay Male Identities**
Andrew Cooper

100 **Perspectives on Genetic Discrimination**
Thomas Lemke

101 **Social Sustainability**
A multilevel approach to social inclusion
Edited by Veronica Dujon, Jesse Dillard, and Eileen M. Brennan

102 **Capitalism**
A companion to Marx's economy critique
Johan Fornäs

103 **Understanding European Movements**
New social movements, global justice struggles, anti-austerity protest
Edited by Cristina Flesher Fominaya and Laurence Cox

104 **Applying Ibn Khaldūn**
The recovery of a lost tradition in sociology
Syed Farid Alatas

105 **Children in Crisis**
Ethnographic studies in international contexts
Edited by Manata Hashemi and Martín Sánchez-Jankowski

106 **The Digital Divide**
The internet and social inequality in international perspective
Edited by Massimo Ragnedda and Glenn W. Muschert

107 **Emotion and Social Structures**
The affective foundations of social order
Christian von Scheve

108 **Social Capital and Its Institutional Contingency**
A study of the United States, China and Taiwan
Edited by Nan Lin, Yang-chih Fu and Chih-jou Jay Chen

109 **The Longings and Limits of Global Citizenship Education**
The moral pedagogy of schooling in a cosmopolitan age
Jeffrey S. Dill

110 **Irish Insanity 1800–2000**
Damien Brennan

111 **Cities of Culture**
A global perspective
Deborah Stevenson

112 **Racism, Governance, and Public Policy**
Beyond human rights
Katy Sian, Ian Law and S. Sayyid

113 **Understanding Aging and Diversity**
Theories and concepts
Patricia Kolb

114 **Hybrid Media Culture**
Sensing place in a world of flows
Edited by Simon Lindgren

115 **Centers and Peripheries in Knowledge Production**
Leandro Rodriguez Medina

116 **Revisiting Institutionalism in Sociology**
Putting the "institution" back in institutional analysis
Seth Abrutyn

117 **National Policy-Making**
Domestication of global trends
Pertti Alasuutari and Ali Qadir

118 **The Meanings of Europe**
Changes and exchanges of a contested concept
Edited by Claudia Wiesner and Meike Schmidt-Gleim

119 **Between Islam and the American Dream**
An immigrant Muslim community in post-9/11 America
Yuting Wang

120 **Call Centers and the Global Division of Labor**
A political economy of post-industrial employment and union organizing
Andrew J.R. Stevens

121 **Academic Capitalism**
Universities in the global struggle for excellence
Richard Münch

122 **Deconstructing Flexicurity and Developing Alternative Approaches**
Towards new concepts and approaches for employment and social policy
Edited by Maarten Keune and Amparo Serrano

123 **From Corporate to Social Media**
Critical perspectives on corporate social responsibility in media and communication industries
Marisol Sandoval

124 **Vision and Society**
Towards a sociology and anthropology from art
John Clammer

125 **The Rise of Critical Animal Studies**
From the margins to the centre
Nik Taylor and Richard Twine

126 **Atoms, Bytes and Genes**
Public resistance and techno-scientific responses
Martin W. Bauer

127 **Punk Rock and the Politics of Place**
Building a better tomorrow
Jeffrey S. Debies-Carl

128 **Bourdieu's Theory of Social Fields**
Concepts and applications
Mathieu Hilgers and Eric Mangez

129 **Global Management, Local Resistances**
Theoretical discussion and empirical case studies
Edited by Ulrike Schuerkens

130 **Migrant Professionals in the City**
Local encounters, identities and inequalities
Edited by Lars Meier

131 **From Globalization to World Society**
Neo-institutional and systems-theoretical perspectives
Edited by Boris Holzer, Fatima Kastner and Tobias Werron

132 **Political Inequality in an Age of Democracy**
Cross-national perspectives
Joshua Kjerulf Dubrow

133 **Social Networks and Music Worlds**
Edited by Nick Crossley, Siobhan McAndrew and Paul Widdop

134 **Gender Roles in Ireland**
Three decades of attitude change
Margret Fine-Davis

135 **(Sub) Urban Sexscapes**
Geographies and regulation of the sex industry
Edited by Paul Maginn and Christine Steinmetz

136 Advances in Biographical Methods
Creative applications
*Edited by Maggie O'Neill,
Brian Roberts and Andrew Sparkes*

137 Social Cohesion and Immigration in Europe and North America
Mechanisms, conditions and causality
*Edited by Ruud Koopmans,
Bram Lancee and Merlin Schaeffer*

138 Digital Publics
Cultural political economy, financialization and creative organizational politics
John Michael Roberts

139 Ideology and the Fight Against Human Trafficking
Reyhan Atasü-Topcuoğlu

140 Rethinking Serial Murder, Spree Killing, and Atrocities
Beyond the usual distinctions
*Robert Shanafelt and
Nathan W. Pino*

141 The Re-Use of Urban Ruins
Atmospheric inquiries of the city
Hanna Katharina Göbel

142 Reproductive Tourism in the United States
Creating family in the mother country
Lauren Jade Martin

143 The Bohemian Ethos
Questioning work and making a scene on the Lower East Side
Judith R. Halasz

144 Critical Theory and Social Media
Between emancipation and commodification
Thomas Allmer

145 Socio-Cultural Mobility and Mega-Events
Ethics and aesthetics in Brazil's 2014 World Cup
Rodanthi Tzanelli

146 Seeing Religion
Toward a visual sociology of religion
Edited by Roman Williams

147 European Citizenship and Social Integration in the EU
Jürgen Gerhards and Holger Lengfeld

148 International Migration and Ethnic Relations
Critical perspectives
Edited by Magnus Dahlstedt and Anders Neergaard

149 Stigma and the Shaping of the Pornography Industry
Georgina Voss

150 Religious Identity and Social Change
Explaining Christian conversion in a Muslim world
David Radford

151 God, Politics, Economy
Social theory and the paradoxes of religion
Bülent Diken

God, Politics, Economy
Social theory and the paradoxes of religion

Bülent Diken

LONDON AND NEW YORK

First published 2016
by Routledge
2 Park Square, Milton Park, Abingdon, Oxon OX14 4RN

and by Routledge
711 Third Avenue, New York, NY 10017

First issued in paperback 2018

Routledge is an imprint of the Taylor & Francis Group, an informa business

© 2016 Bülent Diken

The right of Bülent Diken to be identified as author of this work has been asserted by him in accordance with sections 77 and 78 of the Copyright, Designs and Patents Act 1988.

All rights reserved. No part of this book may be reprinted or reproduced or utilised in any form or by any electronic, mechanical, or other means, now known or hereafter invented, including photocopying and recording, or in any information storage or retrieval system, without permission in writing from the publishers.

Trademark notice: Product or corporate names may be trademarks or registered trademarks, and are used only for identification and explanation without intent to infringe.

British Library Cataloguing-in-Publication Data
A catalogue record for this book is available from the British Library

Library of Congress Cataloging in Publication Data
God, politics, economy: social theory and the paradoxes of religion / edited by Bülent Diken. -- 1 [edition].
    pages cm
Includes bibliographical references.
1. Religion--Philosophy. 2. Religion and politics. 3. Political theology.
4. Religion and state. 5. Religion--Economic aspects.
6. Economics--Religious aspects. I. Diken, Bülent, editor.
  BL51.G6845 2015
  201'.7--dc23
                                        2015024863

ISBN 13: 978-1-138-59638-2 (pbk)
ISBN 13: 978-1-138-01467-1 (hbk)

Typeset in Times New Roman
by Integra Software Services Pvt. Ltd.

To the memory of my friend Besim Sağırkaya

Contents

Acknowledgments		xvi
	Introduction: profanation versus sacralization	1
1	Religion as superstition	12
	Excursus I: Voltaire's *Mahomet* as despot	29
2	Love, love of God, intellectual love of God	41
	Excursus II: *The Devils*, possession, and truth-telling	57
3	From political theology to politics	70
	Excursus III: the emancipated city: notes on the Gezi revolts	88
4	Capitalism as religion, religion as capitalism	103
	Excursus IV: the map, the territory, and the impossibility of painting a priest	118
	Instead of conclusion: from four religions to four truth procedures	131
	References	141
	Index	148

Acknowledgments

I am very grateful for discussing this book with Niels Albertsen, Arthur Bradley, Michael Dillon, and Carsten Bagge Laustsen. Thanks for the inspiring comments and ideas. Thinking with them always turns into a pleasure.

I have had the opportunity to discuss parts of the book with some colleagues at Lancaster University: Bruce Bennett, Graeme Gilloch, Mark Lacy, and John Urry. Many thanks!

Some colleagues at Mardin Artuklu University, Department of Architecture, have provided me with wonderful insights during the writing process. Sincere thanks especially to Ezgi and Tayfun Gürkaş, Zeynep Sayın, Bülent Tanju, and Uğur Tanyeli.

I am also very grateful to Sümer and Olga Gürel, Ebru Thwaites, Craig Hammond, Burak Güray, Nayanika Mookherjee, Işıl Baysan Serim, Şengül Güneş, İhsan Metin Erdoğan, Murat Utkucu, and Diana Stypinska: I have greatly benefited from their insightful critique.

Bülent Diken
2014 December

Introduction
Profanation versus sacralization

> If you have to suffer martyrdom, and if all the universe has to be destroyed in the process, still, still, still, O Christian, you shall reign as a king and set your foot on the neck of old bosses!
>
> (Lawrence 1931: 15)

A resentful will to power which is ready to sacrifice *this* world in order to achieve a final victory in an imaginary *other* world: this is, according to D. H. Lawrence's *Apocalypse*, the real message of Christianity as a 'popular religion'. But Lawrence insists that this popular religion must be distinguished from what he calls 'thoughtful religion' (Ibid. 9). For there are 'two kinds of Christianity': the one focused on love, on the command 'Love one another!', the other focused on power and glorification (Ibid. 11). It is easy to recognize Nietzsche's signature in this juxtaposition of Christ as an exceptional, mystic, amorous personality and Christianity as organized religion as an instantiation of will to power grounded in herd mentality and the belief in immortality, in (the last) judgment: 'there has been only one Christian, and he died on the Cross' (Nietzsche 1969: 151).

Significantly, what the Christian 'herd' wants is power. But not only pacts with existing powers; indeed, Christianity invented a new image of power, the ultimate power, power of God, which can judge all other powers (see Deleuze 1998: 39). Thus it invested its desire on a 'postponed', other-worldly triumph (Lawrence 1931: 32). The idea of postponement is substantial in two respects. First, it signifies a break 'with the elegant immanence of Christ, for whom eternity ... could only be experienced in life ("to feel oneself in heaven")' (Deleuze 1998: 41–42). Second, and equally importantly, the management of the postponed victory, of the long march to salvation, remarks the birth of governmentality, of account-keeping and 'reckoning up sins throughout the ages' (Lawrence 1931: 57). The real significance of the Apocalypse, its modernity, lies in its setting up of an apparatus of power and glorification, its 'demented installation of an ultimate judiciary and moral power' (Deleuze 1998: 45–46). This apparatus is the cornerstone of Christianity which is opposed to Christ, who systematically renounced the desire for power and thus 'betrayed' the love of power in his disciples. 'So it betrayed back again: with

2 Profanation versus sacralization

a kiss' (Lawrence 1931: 18). In a sense, therefore, Judas is the ultimate figure of Christianity; in truth 'it is Christianity that becomes the Anti-Christ' (Deleuze 1998: 38).

Hereby we have the major interrelated themes of this book: sovereignty (politics), governmentality (economy), glory (the spectacle), and betrayal (revision). But unlike Lawrence, who thinks with Nietzsche and operates in terms of two opposed senses of religion, focusing on the uncanny disparity between them, my intention here is to turn to Spinoza. It is commonly held that Spinoza operates with three understandings of religion: religion as 'superstition' (which is similar to Lawrence's 'popular religion'); religion as the 'universal faith' based on love of God and love of neighbor (which is, again, reminiscent of Lawrence's 'thoughtful religion'); and the 'true religion' grounded in the 'intellectual love of God'. In addition, I argue that Spinoza's thought opens up the space for a fourth understanding of religion, which can accommodate instrumental reason. With Benjamin (1996) I will call this fourth understanding of religion 'capitalism as religion'. What is important for me in this differentiation is how, and through which trajectories, these four conceptions of religion relate to and distance themselves from each other.

The book is a series of forays into the problem of religion in modernity. What has enticed me to this theme is the intriguing lack of critique and bluntness with which the 'return of religion' is taken for granted today. I deal with this 'return' at the intersection point of religion, politics, and economy, focusing on the field of formation, intervention, and intelligibility which emerges as these seemingly autonomous spheres encounter, problematize, define, and invent one another. I also seek to problematize the return of religion through another return, by revitalizing the critique of religion. In this sense the book aims at articulating an affirmative perspective that can re-evaluate the value of values that present themselves in the intersection of political theology, religion, and capitalism today.

This necessitates a genealogical re-reading of political theology and economic theology as well as their secular forms, politics and economy. To be sure, the paradigmatic theorist in this context is Carl Schmitt who has claimed that 'all significant concepts' of modern political theory are merely 'secularized theological concepts' (1985: 36). Modern politics consists in re-instating the essentials of theology in a modern context, translating 'devil' into 'enemy' for instance, 'miracle' into 'decision', and so on. Even modern revolts and revolutions, in this prism, bear the mark of theology; 'Prometheus arises in the shadow of Christ' (Taubes 2009: 89).

This book can be read as a critique of this theological reductionism. Political theology has always been a political theory of power. The history of religion demonstrates the way in which a *political* theory of power and government has emerged in the guise of *theology*. Only, power was disguised in the claim that it comes from God (see Dillon 2011 and 2012). In this sense one could claim that, contra Schmitt, all concepts of theology are political. If, in this prism, modern political theory has any significance, it is its attempt to profane the religio-theological mindset. As evidenced again and again, this mindset is deeply rooted in our culture and still defines the human condition today. Its strength is what proves, from the standpoint of this book, why profanation is a significant category.

Classical sociology grounded religion in 'sacred' things, 'things set apart and surrounded by prohibitions' (Durkheim 2001: 46). In its originary sense 'sacred' meant removing things from the domain of free use and commerce so that they could not be sold or bought nor held as private property, that is, to 'consecrate' them for specific use in the religious domain; 'profane' in turn indicates returning that which is sacred to free use, making it common again (Agamben 2007: 73). It is thus separation (of the sacred and the profane) that is the paradigm of religion, and not, as the term 'religio' suggests, their relating together. 'Religio' is what seeks to keep the profane and the sacred distinct; profanation is what ignores and thus neutralizes this separation by 'playing' with the sacred, putting it into new, 'inappropriate' uses, and thus freeing humanity from the domain of the sacred, without necessarily abolishing it (Ibid. 76). Free play, after all, is an expression of the useless, of God's anti-utilitarian 'childlikeness' (Nietzsche 1967: 410). In this sense, as free play, profanation is the core of the critique of religion, the 'first premise of all criticism' (Marx 1957: 41).

God is created in the image of man. Religion posits that the reverse is the case. And the more this reversal is ascertained the more it seems that we are indebted, that we owe everything, to God (see Feuerbach 1989). Any affirmative critique of religion, therefore, must be able to deal with this alienating reversal and show that what is considered 'sacred' by religion – friendship, love, human togetherness ... – is in its origin 'profane', part of life. Insofar as its immanent source is external to religion, insofar as religion is an apparatus of capture, sacralization is not an inevitable process; the profanation of the immanent nucleus of religion is always possible. What is at stake here is the nonidentity of religion and faith. Not all faith is religion and not all religion is faithful.

Herein lies the significance of Spinoza for the book. Spinoza was the philosopher who engaged with profanation most consistently and most radically. The crucial Spinozist question is therefore whether thinking and action are oriented toward transcendence or immanence, toward a vertical plane, where all 'organization ... comes from above' (Deleuze 1988: 128) or whether '[w]e head for the horizon, on the plane of immanence' (Deleuze and Guattari 1994: 41). 'Whenever there is transcendence, vertical Being, imperial State in the sky or on earth, there is religion' (Ibid. 43). The vertical plane of transcendence is a theological plane for there is always a hidden steering at work, a creator God, an evolution in the supposed depths of nature, or a society's organization of power (Deleuze 1988: 128). But if we, on the other hand, 'head for the horizon', there will be nothing beyond, and everything will be a common plane of immanence. Not every gift comes down to us from above.

> Perhaps this is the supreme act of philosophy: not so much to think THE plane of immanence as to show that it is there, unthought in every plane, and to think it in this way as the outside and inside of thought, as the not-external outside and the not-internal inside – that which cannot be thought and yet must be thought, which was thought once, as Christ was incarnated once, in order to show, that one time, the possibility of the impossible. Thus Spinoza is the Christ of the philosophers, and the greatest philosophers are hardly more than apostles who distance themselves from or draw near to this mystery.
>
> (Deleuze and Guattari 1994: 60)

Of course the conception of profanation has mutated extensively since Spinoza's time. I deal with this. However, what I am interested in is not primarily the conceptual history of profanation but rather the possibilities which profanation offers. It is because of the possibility of profanations that modern political theory cannot be reduced to theology. After all, modern political theory has emerged from the crisis of theology. The Enlightenment is grounded in the desire for profanation, in the critique of religion. I am tempted to revisit, in this context, Foucault's essay 'What Is Enlightenment?' in which he refuses the standard blackmail of the Enlightenment – that one should be either for or against it – and emphasizes instead that Enlightenment must be thought of as a process. Enlightenment is basically an attempt to answer the Kantian question: What have we become, and who are we now? (Foucault 1997: 305).

> The critical ontology of ourselves must be considered not, certainly, as a theory, a doctrine, nor even as a permanent body of knowledge that is accumulating; it must be conceived as an attitude, an ethos, a philosophical life in which the critique of what we are is at one and the same time the historical analysis of the limits imposed on us and an experiment with the possibility of going beyond them.
>
> (Ibid. 319)

If what we are is a genealogical construction, we can also refuse to be captured by the categories instituted by those genealogies that have produced us. Enlightenment means that it is possible to refuse what we are. In this sense, any critical task 'entails faith in Enlightenment' (Ibid.), the idiomatic meaning of which is a refusal, to refuse being ruled by a system. But refusal in the name of what? Foucault's first intimation of an answer to this question is the concept of 'political spirituality' (Foucault 2005). But, crucially, the 'spirituality' at issue here is neither reducible to religion nor religious in its essence. Political spirituality is a profane concept that works as a certain defense of the Enlightenment rather than as a wholesale rejection. Referring to a set of practices that arise when a truth is obscure to the subject, political spirituality is what enables the subject to access truth and to criticize power in order to be governed less. Therefore it is grounded in truth-telling, in what the ancient Greeks called *parrhesia*:

> a kind of verbal activity where the speaker has a specific relation to truth through frankness, a certain relationship to his own life through danger, a certain type of relation to himself or other people through criticism (self-criticism or criticism of other people), and a specific relation to moral law through freedom and duty.
>
> (Foucault 2001: 19)

Parrhesia is not only a theoretical pursuit but also a 'practice' (Ibid. 106) that shapes the critical relations between the self and the society and between the self and truth. It relates to moral subjectivity, to the style of life which the self should invent in order to stay in tune with the demands of truth. Thus *parrhesia* often appears in the form of a 'spiritual exercise' (Ibid. 165).

As such, *parrhesia* was a widespread philosophical practice in the ancient Greek culture. From Euripides' tragedies to the Epicurean, Stoic and Cynic texts, one meets it as a *techne* to deal with epistemological, personal, and political situations. Consider the Cynic *parrhesia*, a politically radical, radically political version of *parrhesia* which the Cynics practiced in public preaching and in personal encounters. The Cynic preaching was typically focused on issues such as freedom, the ascetic enunciation of luxury as a way of putting a distance to wealth and power, and the political criticism of public institutions. It often reverted to scandalous behavior in order to problematize established opinions, existing institutions, and collective habits. The basic Cynic idea is that a person is 'nothing else but his relation to truth', a relation which is always reflected in one's style of life (Ibid. 117, 120). Hence the famous image of Diogenes: the dog-like truth-teller living in a barrel, insisting that the most important thing in life is freedom of speech, *parrhesia*, a freedom which must be protected from the influence of wealth and power at any price: 'for if I should be bribed too, there would be none left to rail upon thee' (Shakespeare 1970: 665). Recall Diogenes' famous, probably mythical, encounter with Alexander:

> This encounter ... does not take place in the privacy of Alexander's court but in the street, in the open. The king stands up while Diogenes sits back in his barrel. Diogenes orders Alexander to step out of his light so that he can bask in the sun. Ordering Alexander to step aside so that the sun's light can reach Diogenes is an affirmation of the direct and natural relation the philosopher has to the sun, in contrast to the mythical genealogy whereby the king, as descended from a god, was supposed to personify the sun.
>
> (Foucault 2001: 121)

The dialogue between Diogenes and Alexander is not a dialogue between equals in terms of power; Diogenes takes a risk. But in another sense, too, the dialogue is unequal: it is Diogenes who is the master of truth, making Alexander feel inferior to him. In this sense the encounter amounts to a struggle between political power and *parrhesia*, the power of truth-telling (see Ibid. 124, 133). The Cynic teaching demanded a public, spectacular, provocative – and courageous – way of life in order to make its teaching accessible to everyone. Therefore the idea that a philosopher's life should be exemplary and heroic is important in understanding the Cynic *parrhesia* as a public activity.

Interestingly, Foucault mentions at one point the Cynics' 'resemblance to the early Christians' (Ibid. 116). Christians took over from the Cynics the practice of preaching, a form of truth-telling which involves the idea that truth must be told to everyone (Ibid. 120). Most importantly, the Cynic asceticism played a decisive role in early Christianity. (Just as the *parrhesiastes*, the truth-teller, must be alert to self-delusions and demonstrate steadiness of mind, stay close to himself rather than being moved by passions, in the Christian spirituality one must fasten one's mind to God. Thus the Christian devil represents the danger of self-delusion and the instability of mind.) In this sense Foucault historicizes religion. Theology is a phase in history, not an absolute beginning. There is always already something else before that. However, the capturing of *parrhesia* by early Christianity, thereby the transfer of Greek-pagan competencies to monotheistic religions, did not take place without revision. There are significant differences between the two kinds of asceticism.

> the Greek conception of *askesis* differs from Christian ascetic practices in at least two ways: (1) Christian asceticism has as its ultimate aim or target the renunciation of the self, whereas the moral *askesis* of the Greco-Roman philosophies has as its goal the establishment of a specific relationship to oneself – a relationship of self-possession and self-sovereignty; (2) Christian asceticism takes as its principal theme detachment from the world, whereas the ascetic practices of the Greco-Roman philosophies are generally concerned with endowing the individual with the preparation and the moral equipment that will permit him to fully confront the world in an ethical and rational manner.
>
> (Foucault 2001: 144)

While the Greek *parrhesia* assumes the possibility of a different (bettered) world, the Christian *parrhesia* is directed at a totally other, metaphysical world (Bernauer 2004: 85). And in contrast to the emphasis on freedom in the Greek *parrhesia*, Christianity aligned *parrhesia* with obedience. Truth was to appear now not as free speech but as 'obedience to a god who is conceived of as a despot, a master for whom one is slave and servant' (Ibid.).

But what is sacralized can be profaned. If *parrhesia* is captured by religion it can be re-appropriated. With Foucault, therefore, we can imagine a profaned form of political spirituality which is not reducible to revealed religion, according to which truth can only be a mystery. If truth is opaque it is not because it is a mystery but because it is a function of veridical operations that pertain to the governmental machine (technologies of truth, apparatuses of truth-making). It is these operations that make the truth opaque; their insistence on transparency is the means by which the truth is obscured. The spectacle dazzles.

Profanation thus involves turning 'the criticism of heaven into the criticism of the earth' (Marx 1957: 50). Herein lies, too, its intrinsic relation to the critique of religion. To be sure, religion might express real suffering and real protest against suffering, but religion is always 'the sign of an oppressed creature, the heart of a heartless world, just as it is the spirit of a spiritless situation' (Marx 1957: 42). Religion has historically justified slavery, serfdom, and the condition of the modern proletariat, preaching 'the necessity of a ruling and an oppressed class' (Marx 1847). It has 'transferred' social, economic, and political problems 'to heaven', and moralized 'cowardice, self-contempt, abasement, submission, dejection' (Ibid. 83). It has, in one word, functioned as the 'opium of the people' (Marx 1957: 42).

I agree with this verdict, which is why I seek to re-actualize the critique of religion in the face of the contemporary 'return of religion'. However, 'opium' seems to have a paradoxical status, for Marx describes philosophy as the 'head' and the proletariat as the 'heart' of emancipation in the same essay. Any true political intervention must be able to link together the head and the heart, strategy and intoxication. This brings us to another ancient Greek concept, *kairos*, which is closely associated with *parrhesia* (see Foucault 2001: 111). As a strategic decision that aims to 'seize' the moment, *kairos* is the moment of opportunity, which can be seized by an untimely intervention into the course of time on the basis of reading the symptoms, the signs, available in a given situation. However, the decision-making at work here is not merely a strategic, rational act; while one 'seizes' the moment, one must also be 'seized' by the moment. Confronted with the potentiality of the event, the promise of the new, one must be able to affirm this potentiality. In this sense *kairos* is an act which forms one's ethos, an ethical act: being in the moment, one is formed by the moment. To use Nietzsche's phrase, you become what you are in *kairos*. Then, the moment of the event is not only something to be seized strategically in a calculating manner but also something one must 'become worthy' of (Deleuze 1990: 148). In this sense, *kairos* necessitates an intoxication which results from being 'seized' by the moment. In kairological time one 'is always in the position of deciding and being decided' (Dillon 2008: 13). Therefore the problem of *kairos* is never merely an epistemological problem. *Kairos* requires fidelity, too; it demands an appropriate response from the subject, which is, paradoxically, constituted in the very moment of response. Thus what is really at stake in *kairos* is to interweave 'seizing' with 'being seized', strategic timing of the event with fidelity to the event, for without such fidelity 'the very opening of the world itself is endangered' (Ibid. 13–14).

So the 'intoxicated' actor – opium – is as necessary as the strategist. Only when people invest their desire in an event, only when they have a desire to become part of it, to seize and to be seized by an event, can they 'see' the event.

Therefore, asserts Walter Benjamin, any radical politics must 'win the energies of intoxication' (1979: 236). Only a politics that can accommodate intoxication can go beyond the domain of pragmatic calculations and 'interweave' the two dimensions of *kairos*, strategy and intoxication. However, strategic thinking can be linked to intoxication not necessarily as a religious experience ('the opium of people') but as a 'profane illumination' taking place in a materialist context (Benjamin 1979: 227). Faith and fidelity are not necessarily grounded in religion. We do not need religion to have belief. We can have values without religion.

Written in this spirit, the book has the following formal structure.

Chapter 1 deals with two conceptions of religion: religion as superstition and as 'universal faith'. Both are grounded in what Spinoza calls 'imagination', which proceeds from passions rather than reason. Superstition, in this respect, signifies an impossible attempt at imagining God, that which cannot be imagined. It goes hand in hand with a series of theological and political mystifications such as envisioning God through anthropomorphic and monarchic attributes (as a despot, law-giver, merciful, just and so on). The universal faith, on the other hand, only demands love – loving God and one's neighbor – excluding all public or private rituals which institutionalize religion. The notion of universal faith incorporates universality or commonality to religious imagination. However, as is the case with superstition, the universal faith calls for obedience rather than reason and remains pivotal for voluntary servitude. By way of this discussion, the chapter moves to the understanding of religion in Marx and Nietzsche, where religion characteristically has an imaginary status and the notions of creation, free will, revelation, and chosen people are regarded as 'fiction' or 'illusion'. Yet, neither Marx nor Nietzsche dismisses illusion as such, for insofar as it expresses the creation of values, illusion is necessary. What matters is rather the critique of illusion as ideology (Marx) or as a reactive force that must be overcome (Nietzsche). Finally, the chapter relates religion as superstition to economic theology taking its point of departure in the ancient Greek concept *oikonomia* and its genealogical link to the concept of despotism.

Excursus I fleshes out the relation between economic theology, despotism, and superstition by focusing on an early modern fiction, Voltaire's controversial play *Mahomet*. What is interesting in this play is the parallel drawn between two concepts, despotism and Islam. I discuss what is at stake in this association as well as its political implications. I argue that just as despotism signifies not merely another form of politics but, above all, the lack of political form as such, Islam in the play becomes a stand-in for the ground zero of religion, that is, superstition. Approaching this topic through a double reading of social theory and fiction, the excursus shows in what way Voltaire's take on Islam might bear significance today.

Chapter 2 returns to the three levels of knowledge in Spinoza: imagination, reason, and intuition. Since it is imagination that defines religion as superstition and obedience, the question becomes how to denounce illusions. This task invites the involvement of reason. With reason, at the level of the second kind of knowledge, things are no longer regarded as contingent but as part of a relational network that one can understand rather than imagine. And ultimately, with the third and highest form of knowledge, intuitive knowledge, one attains the knowledge of eternity, of the virtual, perceiving things as singularities which directly express their virtual cause, God. The active joy that arises here is what Spinoza calls the 'intellectual love of God'. As such, the idea of God is the basis for what Spinoza calls the 'true religion', the third understanding of religion in our context. However, the 'true religion' must not be confused with the 'universal faith'. Religion as universal faith only appeals to obedience on the basis of moral concepts such as sin. But the 'true religion' is an appeal to freedom grounded in an *intellectual* love, an active joy that arises from reason. With the third kind of knowledge, the intellectual love of God replaces love as obedience, as voluntary servitude. I return to the concept of profanation at this junction, for with the intellectual love of God, true religion and non-religion (atheism) come to coincide. Profanation obliterates theology by obliterating the distinction between theology and philosophy. I discuss this by showing how Spinoza 'profanes' religion and the religious categories such as the soul, immortality, salvation, and blessedness, redefining both love and God in immanent terms, as profane relations. This is coupled with a reading of Badiou's Paul in the horizon of profanation, arguing that Badiou's re-appropriation of the religious-transcendental lexicon opens up the religious imagination to reason and the promisory aspect of religion (salvation) is re-inscribed in the democratic-communist tradition. Finally, the chapter turns to the concept of secularization, differentiates it from profanation, and considers the relation between secularization and economic theology.

Excursus II thematizes superstition and faith through an allegorical reading of Ken Russell's film *The Devils*. The contrast between the function of love of God in mysticism and in the governmental economy of the church is central here. Mysticism, in this context, signifies unmediated love of God and excludes economic theology and governmentality. The mystic believes that God can be known directly in the union of the soul with the divine. This is why mysticism has often been excluded and labeled as 'heresy', and the mystic claim to be possessed by God is countered with the charge of possession by the devil. I discuss the political implications of this contrast focusing on the function of 'love of God' in mysticism and of pastoral power in the governmental economy of the church. Crucially, love is originally a universal, immanent impulse, which is captured by religion. Thus it can always be profaned. Religion cannot fully appropriate or exhaust the virtual potentiality of faith. By the same token it is possible to distinguish religion and faith. One can attain a 'political spirituality' outside the religious domain.

10 *Profanation versus sacralization*

Chapter 3 confronts the consequences of the previous discussions and asks whether it is possible to move from political theology to politics. Following Spinoza, one could say that just as imagination can perfect itself by ascending to the intellectual love of God, political theology can transform itself into democracy. But the transition from passion to reason, from nature to the city, is not a pure break. There is always a remainder: passions. The chapter projects the distinction between passion and reason onto the distinction between two cities: the 'despotic city' founded on superstition, and the 'free city' founded on reason. It asks how despotism can be avoided. Should religion determine politics or the other way around? Or should the powers of the state and the church be separated? The chapter deals with these questions through a discussion of Spinoza's absolute democracy which makes use of religion at the level of the universal faith, without allowing it to determine politics otherwise. The outcome of this is threefold: first, in the transition from political theology to politics the transcendent aspect of the law is profaned. Second, this profanation is synonymous with the proliferation of the 'true religion'. Third, this is also a process of democratization in which religious heteronomy is superseded by the autonomy of the actors, promoting agonistic respect and thus peace and security. To end with, the chapter considers democracy as a concept that has always been subject to corruption and revision.

Excursus III deals with the 2013 revolts in Turkey as a paradigmatic case of the tension between religious governance and governance of religion. It depicts the revolts as a political event, as an attempt at inventing a link between the particular and the universal. To start with I briefly discuss the history of Turkish republicanism and the transformation of its relation to secularism, economy, and the state. Then I turn to the political dimension of the revolts, focusing on the iconic figures of subjectivity that emerged during the events. In this respect the practical and theoretical tension between mobility and immobility is emphasized, arguing that it is what constitutes the background for the de-stabilizing aspects of the revolts in relation to both *Islamic* neo-liberalism and *neo-liberal* Islam. This is followed by an examination of the reactionary views of the revolts combined with a critique of their political–theological leitmotivs. The pivot around which these moves are undertaken, and the terms of the discussion determined, is the concept of event.

Chapter 4 is an attempt at rethinking the structural link between capitalism and Christianity. It is normally held that secularization brings with it disenchantment. But theology persists as an active force in modern capitalism. In discussing this, the chapter takes its point of departure in Nietzsche's conception of the guilt–debt nexus in the genealogy of morality. Seen in the prism of guilt, capitalism has not only found support in religion but it is itself a religion. It posits an infinite debt to capital, from which everything appears to emanate and to which everything returns. Interestingly in this respect, Spinoza emphasizes in *Ethics* that money can appear as 'cause', that is, as

God, for it provides a short-cut to everything. Developing this idea, the chapter adds to the framework of the book a fourth form of religion, capitalism as religion, which signifies the perversion of reason into instrumental reason. I argue that in the framework of the capitalist religion, democracy is de-limited to liberal democracy and universalism only applies to the logic of God-capital. Here 'common' and 'profane' do not coincide. On the contrary, something profane (capitalism) is elevated to the level of the sacred.

Excursus IV develops the discussion of capitalism as religion by analyzing Michel Houellebecq's latest novel, *The Map and the Territory*. The idea that serves as its meta-plot is the total subsumption of society under capital. In the late-modern world Houellebecq describes, capital tends to replace, like a map, the actual experience of life, the territory. In this world, in which everything is re-modeled according to the logic of businesses, capitalism progressively takes the place of religion. In this sense *The Map and the Territory* distils the relationship between religion and capitalism anew, and this relationship, together with the political questions it invites, is the leitmotiv for my considerations here.

The final pages of the book, *Instead of conclusion*, sum up the four different definitions of religion I operate throughout the book in a diagrammatic form, arguing that these ideal–typical conceptions of religion can overlap with one another. For instance, other understandings of God can be present in a capitalist social formation in spite of the dominance of the capitalist cult. Following this, I return to the theme of profanation, discussing the sense of profanation in a contemporary philosopher, Badiou, who often recasts theological figures (Paul, for instance) in terms of his philosophical framework as well as making use of theological categories by profaning their content, which is legible even in his early work (see for instance Badiou 2009a on 'aporias of the creation', 'logic of heresies', 'theory of incarnation' ...). Then I compare the two different styles of profanation in Spinoza and Badiou, articulating a relation between their non-theological uses of theological concepts, which is a useful resource for thinking about the relation between philosophy, politics, and religion. The complex elements in this articulation are the different understandings of religion in Spinoza and the different truth procedures in Badiou. I claim that Badiou's truth procedures could be perceived as the Spinozist diagram's re-entry into itself.

1 Religion as superstition

> Is there any more dangerous seduction that might tempt one to renounce one's faith in the gods of Epicurus who have no care and are unknown, and to believe instead in some petty deity who is full of care and personally knows every hair on our head and finds nothing nauseous in the most miserable small service?
>
> (Nietzsche 1974: 224)

> Not all belief is reducible to superstition but what is considered to be 'religion' is often sheer superstition, the origin of which is our irrational, imaginary fears and unrealistic hopes. If people did not need to hope or fear, they would not become superstitious. But most people are neither so powerful nor so fortunate, and they often believe what they hope for and have difficulty to believe what they fear, often misjudging the real reasons that cause hope or fear in them.
>
> (Spinoza 1993a: 3, 115)

Superstition is grounded in what Spinoza calls 'imagination', in treating nonexisting things as if they exist (Ibid. 55). Since imagination proceeds from emotions, not from reason, superstition arises as a consequence of being subjected to one's passions. This subjection consists in inadequate, inconsistent, and vague ideas acquired on the basis of the perception of phenomena through chance encounters, without being able to see the causal network behind them (Ibid. 54–61). Concomitantly, within Spinoza's hierarchy, imagination is considered to be the lowest kind of knowledge in relation to the other two kinds, reason and intuition.

But superstition is not only an epistemological matter. There is an intrinsic relation between superstition and despotism. The church and the state invest religion with 'pomp and ceremony', ruling the multitude by superstitious fantasies which lead it to glorifying its 'kings as gods' or debasing them equally irrationally (Spinoza 1951a: 5, 7). The elementary mystification of superstition in this context consists in imagining God through human attributes, as a willing God in charge of judging what is happening in a passive nature (Spinoza 1993a: 81). But God is not a personal power; he does not respond to human needs and prayers, rewarding and punishing humans for their deeds. Since the judgments of God surpass our comprehension, mankind 'cannot imagine God' (Ibid. 74).

Superstition is an attempt at imagining what is unimaginable. In this pursuit it mystifies not only the existing world (by juxtaposing it to an imaginary world) but also religion itself. Thus Spinoza initially distinguishes between superstition and what he calls 'universal faith'. The 'universal faith' is 'common to all' and consists in seven fundamental dogmas that are 'absolutely required in order to attain obedience to God' (Spinoza 1951a: 186). Its first dogma is that there exists a Supreme Being, a sovereign and omnipresent God, who loves justice and charity. Second, this God is One, for the love of God emanates from his superiority over all else. Third, God is also omnipresent; nothing is concealed from him and everything is directed by his judgment. Fourth, God has supreme dominion over all things and must be obeyed by all while he himself does nothing under compulsion but directs everything by his absolute fiat and grace. Fifth, the worship of this God consists only in the practice of justice and love towards one's neighbor, that is, by one's way of life. Sixth, only those who worship and obey God in practice are saved. And finally, God expiates the sins of those who repent (Ibid. 187).

Crucially, if faith is defined in this way, questions such as what God really is (spirit, fire, light, thought ...), in which way he is omnipresent (potentially or essentially ...), how he sets forth laws (in the manner of a sovereign or in the form of eternal truths), or whether paradise and hell are natural or supernatural constructions, cease to be relevant – such questions have 'nothing to do with faith' and everybody may think about them as they like (Ibid. 187). Every person adapts the seven dogmas of faith to her way of thinking, to her 'opinions' (Ibid. 188). This adaptation does not need reasoning because faith does not require truth or reason. For faith, the piousness of the dogmas is more important than their truthfulness (Ibid. 185). Hence the 'best faith is not necessarily possessed by him who displays the best reasons, but by him who displays the best fruits of justice and charity' (Ibid. 188). One is faithful through obedience alone:

> the Word of God has not been revealed as a certain number of books, but was displayed to the prophets as a simple idea of the mind, namely, obedience to God in singleness of heart, and in the practice of justice and charity.
>
> (Ibid. 9)

The 'universal faith' demands worship, but this worship consists only in love, in loving God above all things and in loving one's neighbor as oneself (Ibid. 187). Since the core of religion in this sense is love, 'obedience' is obedience to the law of love. Otherwise there is no demand in the universal faith for public or private 'ceremonies' which institutionalize religion as a means of salvation (Ibid. 9, 61). In fact, the Divine Law 'excludes ceremonies' (Ibid. 70). Ceremonial practices only refer to 'temporal bodily happiness', to

14 Religion as superstition

the establishment, preservation and confirmation of the society, and in this sense they are necessary; they function as the medium through which the universal faith is 'accommodated' or 'adapted' to existing opinions (Ibid. 9, 78). But they are not part of the Divine Law (Ibid. 69, 71, 73). According to Spinoza, the Christian rites such as baptism, festivals, public prayers were instituted only as 'external signs' of universal faith, without any sacredness in themselves and anything to do with blessedness. Such ceremonies

> were ordained for the preservation of a society, and accordingly he who lives alone is not bound by them: nay, those who live in a country where the Christian religion is forbidden, are bound to abstain from such rites, and can none the less live in a state of blessedness.
>
> (Spinoza 1951a: 76)

But from where did the prophets receive the Divine Law? They received the revelations through imagination, that is, 'beyond the boundary of the intellect' (Ibid. 25). Imagination is more successful than reason in constructing ideas through words and figures. Yet, it is also 'fleeting and inconstant'; thus the power of prophecy is rare and exceptional (Ibid. 25–26). Further, imagination, in contrast to clear and distinct ideas, cannot provide any certainty of truth but needs some extrinsic sign 'as we may see from Abraham, who, when he had heard the promise of God, demanded a sign, not because he did not believe in God, but because he wished to be sure that it was God Who made the promise' (Ibid. 28). In this sense imagination, or prophetic knowledge, is inferior to natural knowledge, which does not need signs (Ibid. 28). When one thinks with signs, one sees mysteries beneath every event, even beneath natural phenomena. As such, prophecy is grounded in the lack of knowledge, in images (Ibid. 33, 40). An image is an inadequate idea, that is, 'an idea that cannot express its cause' (Deleuze 1992: 148). Inadequate ideas merely indicate, as 'signs', impressions or passive affections that make things known to us only through their effects, without revealing their causes. We perceive or imagine something without understanding what lies beneath. Thus imagination is not really knowledge; 'it is at best recognition' (Ibid. 147). 'Truth', on the other hand, 'needs no sign' (Spinoza 1993b: 233).

Objectification, appropriation, reversal

Following Spinoza, Feuerbach conceptualizes the 'illusion' at the heart of superstition as that which mystifies the essence of religion (Feuerbach 1989: xvii). All religion is a testimony to the fact that human beings are emotional and sensuous beings, that they are 'governed and made happy only by images, by sensible representations' (Ibid. 75). Divinity itself is imagination made objective: mankind creates an image of God from its own thinking power and recognizes this subjective image as if it were an objective reality. The notion of 'God' is therefore necessarily anthropomorphic for whenever we talk about

God we basically transfer some human characteristics (love, will, reason) to an abstract being.

God consists in 'objectification', the projection of human qualities, which are infinite in principle, onto a divine being, the 'object' of religion that appears as a Person, as the Lawgiver, the Good, the Just, the Merciful, and so on. Since God is created in the image of man, and since all the characteristics of God are in reality human characteristics, Feuerbach claims that in reality there can be no opposition between man and God – for knowledge of God is nothing else than humanity's self-knowledge. Through the notion of God we only externalize, give objectivity to our own knowledge of ourselves, our own essence; we should therefore recognize in God ourselves. In this sense atheism is 'the secret of religion' (Ibid. xvi).

All divine predicates are abstracted from mankind and the essence of religion is this abstraction, that is, sacralization or appropriation of the world of humans. Crucially, however, this truth, that which we call divinity, is in fact the divinity of the human nature, hidden to religion itself. Religion is necessarily blind to its own principle, imagination. Thus the humans who have given objectivity to themselves do not recognize the 'object', God, as their own nature (Ibid. 13).

> But here it is also essential to observe, and this phenomenon is an extremely remarkable one, characterising the very core of religion, that in proportion as the divine subject is in reality human, the greater is the apparent difference between God and man; that is, the more, by reflection on religion, by theology, is the identity of the divine and human denied, and the human, considered as such, is depreciated. The reason of this is, that as what is positive in the conception of the divine being can only be human, the conception of man, as an object of consciousness can only be negative. To enrich God, man must become poor; that God may be all, man must be nothing. But he desires to be nothing in himself, because what he takes from himself is not lost to him, since it is preserved in God. Man has his being in God; why then should he have it in himself? Where is the necessity of positing the same thing twice, of having it twice? What man withdraws from himself, what he renounces in himself, he only enjoys in an incomparably higher and fuller measure in God.
> (Feuerbach 1989: 25–26)

What we have here is a reversal: no longer recognizing themselves in divinity, the believers are trapped in the illusion that the human is created in the image of God. And the more this reversal is ascertained the more it seems that we are indebted, that we owe our best qualities, everything, to God. As if everything emanates from God. This illusory process, in which God and mankind are increasingly isolated from and juxtaposed to each other, is what Feuerbach calls religious alienation.

Vis-à-vis this alienation, it is necessary openly to admit that the only essence the human being can imagine, believe, desire or think is 'the essence of human nature itself' (Ibid. 270). This is the only affirmative critique one can direct towards religion. What is depicted in religion as the first (God) is in fact second (to human). It is life itself that is divine; what is considered 'sacred' by religion – friendship, love, human togetherness ... – are all parts of life, while religion regards them as commandments of a distinct, transcendent being, God. Religion 'consecrates' life, what is common to humans (Ibid. 271). And by making us forget this process, in which it appropriates and sacralizes common notions such as friendship, love, solidarity, reason, and so on, religious alienation makes human togetherness more difficult, not easier, for it deprives human beings of the power of real life, the genuine sense of truth and love, as if they are merely appearances and would only ever come to them for God's sake. Paradoxically, therefore,

> Wherever morality is based on theology, wherever the right is made dependent on divine authority, the most immoral, unjust, infamous things can be justified and established. [...] To place anything in God, or to derive anything from God, is nothing more than to withdraw it from the test of reason, to institute it as indubitable, unassailable, sacred, without rendering an account why. Hence self-delusion, if not wicked, insidious design, is at the root of all efforts to establish morality, right, on theology.
> (Feuerbach 1989: 274)

Insofar as religion consists in sacralization of the commons, critique consists in demystifying the illusion which enables this process. The task of critique is 'simply to destroy an illusion' (Ibid. 278) by inverting the religious relations – elevating what religion subordinates to the level of a means to the level of the primary. This task was to be joined by two significant figures inspired by Feuerbach: Marx and Nietzsche, who both sought to destroy the religious illusion, the illusion that we are indebted to God, by focusing on economy, albeit in different ways.

Debt, error, and the necessity of illusion

'Metaphysical need of man' – this is what Schopenhauer claims in *The World as Will and Representation*: religion provides for human beings explanations of their existence and supports for their morality (1957: 361). Nietzsche strongly rejects this idea. The origin of religion is not metaphysical need: 'what first led to the positing of "another world" in primeval times was not some impulse or need but an *error* in the interpretation of certain natural events, a failure of the intellect' (Nietzsche 1974: 196). This error is based, first, on the 'corruption' of reason: mistaking causes for consequences. When religious imperatives dictate certain things in order to attain happiness ('do this and this ... and you will be happy!'), they merely perform a reversal, that is, they depict happiness as a consequence of some dictated virtues whereas those virtues are in reality consequences of happiness (see Nietzsche 1969: 47–48). Second, religion is characterized by 'false causality' in the sense that it seeks the causes of things and actions in the consciousness, in the motives of 'free' subjects, denying material causalities (Ibid. 48). Third, religion explains what is hostile to us through 'imaginary causes' (like 'evil spirits'). And finally, religion's error is based on the notion of 'free will', a notion 'fabricated' by monotheistic religions to make humanity 'accountable' to a transcendent God and to subject its guilt to God's judgment and punishment (Ibid. 53).

The consequence of these errors is nihilism: religion produces an 'anti-natural' illusion which is in conflict with life. By contrasting it to another 'true' world, religion judges *this* world as value-less and treats it 'as a mistake ... which one *should* rectify' (Nietzsche 1996: 96). But what is the value of religion's 'highest values' in terms of life? Feuerbach had said that it is not God that has created the human beings; rather, the human beings have created God in their own image. Nietzsche adds that it is a certain kind of human beings who have achieved that (see Hass 1982: 150). Two concepts, *ressentiment* and bad conscience are crucial here.

Ressentiment builds upon a fiction, the fiction of a force that can be separated from what it can do. The illusion at work here is that a force can refrain from causing effects, from exerting itself (e.g. a bird of prey that does not prey on lambs). Coupled with the notion of 'free subject' this illusion maintains the belief that '*the strong may freely choose to be weak*, and the bird of prey to be lamb – and so they win the right to blame the bird of prey for simply being a bird of prey' (Nietzsche 1996: 30). And finally, in a moment of moralizing, *ressentiment* reverses the values and derives a morality in which the weak is depicted as superior: the lamb is good because it is eaten. Because the forces are projected onto subjects, the subjects take the blame. Thus the weak can also seem as if he has a force which he does not use, because he is 'good' (see Deleuze 1983: 122–24). Thanks to this self-deception of powerlessness, the weakness of the weak can appear as 'a free achievement, something willed, chosen, a *deed*, a *merit*' (Nietzsche 1996: 30). Herein lies, too, the creativity of *ressentiment*, a creativity that consists in translating impotence into 'goodness', fear into 'humility', submission into 'obedience' (Ibid. 14).

But if *ressentiment* is a passive emotion, how can any action result from it? How can the subject of *ressentiment* attain a will? In this context the figure of the priest, one of the main protagonists in Nietzsche's genealogy of religion, is crucial. According to Nietzsche, the 'noble' class is not monolithic, that is, it contains competing subgroups, the most important of which are the 'warriors' and the 'priests'. The 'priests' are those defeated by the powerful 'warriors', thus developing a sense of impotence (see Ibid. 16–22). However, this impotence is repressed and is turned into *ressentiment*. Concomitantly, their hatred, lust for power and feelings of revenge become 'more dangerous' (Ibid. 18). The recognition of his weakness in realizing his values does not result in the priest's reconciliation with his situation but, on the contrary, feeds his will to power (see Reginster 2006: 253–54). And in the crowd he finds what he needs: the reactive forces. The priest finds in the *ressentiment* of the masses the means by which he can negate the existing, sensual world in the name of a true, other world. In turn, the crowd finds in the priest, in his will to power, a means by which they can raise themselves from the impotent state of *ressentiment*. In this sense, the priest is the figure who gives *ressentiment* a form and sediments the desire for revenge further by reversing values (Deleuze 1983: 126). He preaches that 'the miserable alone are the good; the poor, the powerless, the low alone are the good. The suffering, the deprived, the sick, the ugly are the only pious ones, the only blessed, for them alone is there salvation' (Nietzsche 1996: 19). Hence the image of the other, heavenly world – a happier world, in which the powerful cannot exert their force on the weak, pain and suffering cease to exist – a world tailored to the abilities of the weak.

The most crucial turn in Nietzsche's genealogy concerns bad conscience, the process in which pain is interiorized as feelings of guilt, fear and punishment (Ibid. 116–19; see also Deleuze 1983: 129). In Nietzsche, punishment is basically a form of compensation, similar to the repayment of a debt (Nietzsche 1996: 44). It is based on 'the idea that any damage somehow has an *equivalent* and really can be paid off, even if this is through the *pain* of the culprit' (Ibid. 45). Punishing the offender, inflicting pain on him, functions as a compensation for the damage done to the offended, the assumption being that the damage can be paid off through this suffering. As such, the relationship between damage and pain mirrors the contractual link between the creditor and the debtor where, in order to guarantee repayment, the debtor promises to the creditor something he possesses, his body, his wife, his life … (Ibid. 45). But this process of repayment is never direct. Rather, the equivalence between the debt and the corresponding punishment is established in the form of 'pleasure' – the pleasure of violation, of doing something evil for the pleasure of it (such as humiliation, torture), so that the suffering of the debtor compensates for the loss of the creditor (Ibid. 46). This mechanism of compensation is also the anthropological background for festivals. 'No festivity without cruelty' (Ibid. 48).

Nietzsche's point is that this process is not based on reactionary forces. Despite the amount of the external violence and pain, the debt-punishment nexus did not cause *ressentiment*, allowing for the debtor to be liberated from debt through actual repayment (see Deleuze and Guattari 1983: 191). But with monotheistic religions, punishment has been internalized in the form of guilt or bad conscience (or sadness in Spinoza), and debt has become infinite, that is, impossible to pay. In this sense the origin of religion is in the economic relationship between the debtor and the creditor.

But how has debt become an infinite debt to the divinity? In sociological terms, the relationship between the debtor and the creditor has gradually evolved into the relationship between existing generations and their ancestors. Each generation recognizes a debt, a legal obligation towards the earlier generations in the conviction that it is only thanks to their sacrifices and efforts that the society exists. Thus the debt continually accumulates; sacrifices, festivals, temples, tributes of veneration, and above all, obedience increase. Suspicion, fear, follows: does one ever give them enough? The fear of ancestors and the cognizance of owing debts to them inescapably increase as the power of the living generation increases – 'ultimately, the forefather is necessarily transfigured into a *god*' (Nietzsche 1996: 69–70). Gods, in other words, do not originate from piety but from fear (Ibid. 70).

Ultimately, with the foundation of the state, sovereign power over life and death has taken the place of primitive rituals of inscription. Punishment has ceased to be a festive occasion and turned into the vengeance of the despot. Debt has become an infinite debt to the despot, a debt of existence, which has assumed a juridical form in the law (Deleuze and Guattari 1983: 213). And since the will of the despot's subjects is repressed, *ressentiment* was born. Hence, within the matrix of debt, there is a direct correspondence between the limitless vengeance of the despot and the never-ending *ressentiment* of the subjects (Ibid. 215). In the end, every despotic gesture, every command, produces *ressentiment* (see Canetti 1962: 305).

Decisive in this regard is the parallel between the despotic rule and the idea of transcendence. Every despotic formation contains within itself an element of theocratic origin that generates the 'divine right' of kings (Balibar 1998: 48). In this sense 'despotism' has prepared the way for the movement towards universal divinities, for monotheistic religions and thus for further accumulation of guilt (Nietzsche 1996: 70). In particular, the advent of the Christian God brought with it the 'uttermost sense of guilt' (Ibid. 71). Indeed, with Christianity, guilt and duty are turned against the debtor himself, to God, in the sense that God himself is included in guilt:

> ... the horrific and paradoxical expedient in which tortured humanity has found a temporary relief, that stroke of genius on the part of *Christianity*: God sacrificing himself for the guilt of man, god paying himself off, god as the sole figure who can redeem on man's behalf that which has become irredeemable for man himself – the creditor sacrificing himself for his debtor, out of *love* (are we supposed to believe this? –), out of love for his debtor! ...
>
> (Ibid. 72)

So, once we move from 'pre-history' (primitive society) to 'history' (the state and the church), debt is transformed, and we are confronted with an impossible debt, a debt that cannot be repaid. Consider the notion of 'original sin': when one is born in debt (creation, Christ/God's self-sacrifice for humans' sins) the debt becomes eternal and infinite. It can only be countered by the idea of 'eternal punishment'. And when this paradox of debt (the more you pay the more you owe) coincides with the nihilistic negation of this world in favor of the other, heavenly world, life becomes subjected to an infinite economy of good and evil (rather than good and bad).

Significantly in this respect, the movement of history for Nietzsche is not necessarily progressive. Thus the advent of monotheistic religions signifies a regress rather than progress. Their history designates, above all, the movement of a reversal, the triumph of reactive, life-negating forces over active ones. The transition from *ressentiment* to bad conscience, which transforms the debtor–creditor relation into a relationship in which the freedom of the debtor is gradually diminished, is the sign of this reversal. First, *ressentiment* and its accusation, then, its insertion into culture and society through the most primitive relation, that between the debtor and the creditor, and finally, the internalization of *ressentiment* in the form of bad conscience: 'History thus appears as the act by which reactive forces take possession of culture or divert its course in their favour' (Deleuze 1983: 139). In this process (finite, repayable) debt becomes an (infinite, unpayable) debt to reactive instances, that is, to the state, to God, and to society.

> Examine what Christianity calls 'redemption': It is no longer a matter of discharge from debt, but of a deepening of debt. It is no longer a matter of suffering through which debt is paid, but a suffering through which one is shackled to it, through which one becomes a debtor forever. Suffering now only pays the interest on debt; *suffering is internalized, responsibility-debt has become responsibility-guilt.*
>
> (Ibid. 141)

It is a process, in which real redemption, irresponsibility becomes progressively impossible. Nietzsche's critique of monotheistic religions maintains that illusion is indispensable to this process. Religion mystifies and justifies will to power through deceptions and self-deceptions. This is the case even when people honestly believe in religion and act accordingly. Therefore only 'atheism might redeem humanity entirely from [the] feeling of indebtedness towards its origins, its *causa prima*' (Nietzsche 1996: 70). Importantly, however, this does not mean that a world devoid of illusions is the best possible world. Illusions are necessary to live. Indeed, life is interpreted through images (see Nietzsche 1995: 2–3). All values are necessary illusions or fictions to live, to interpret life. Only, illusions must not, as monotheistic religions do, be treated as truths. 'Truths are illusions which we have forgotten are illusions' (Nietzsche 2006: 117). In this regard Nietzsche echoes Spinoza: 'the mind does not err from the fact that imagines, but only insofar as it is considered as wanting the idea which cuts off the existence of those things which it imagines as present to itself' (Spinoza 1993a: 56).

Following this, the significant question is not only whether religion is an illusion; what is decisive is whether religious illusions affirm or negate life.

> What sets *us* apart is not that we recognize no God … but that we find that which has been reverenced as God not 'godlike' but pitiable, absurd, harmful, not merely an error but a *crime against life*. … We deny God as

God. ... If this God of the Christians were *proved* to us to exist, we should know even less how to believe in him.

(Nietzsche 1969: 162–63)

Considering that he finds an affirmative God in Dionysus, Nietzsche cannot be considered an atheist who does not recognize a multiplicity of senses in religion (see Deleuze 1983: 143). Along the same lines, the fact that the origin of the monotheistic 'holy God' is *ressentiment* must not, in itself, lead to 'deterioration of the imagination'; there exist 'nobler' ways of inventing gods than the negation of the world and the self-degradation of humanity (Nietzsche 1996: 73). The ancient Greeks, for instance, utilized their gods to keep 'bad conscience' at bay and to enjoy their freedom of soul in ways opposed to Christianity.

> The Greeks ... have themselves *admitted* as much as the reason for a great deal of what is bad and disastrous – foolishness, *not* sin! [...] Thus the gods at that time served to justify man even to a certain extent in wicked actions, they served as the cause of evil – at that time they did not take upon themselves the execution of punishment, but rather, as is *nobler*, the guilt ...
>
> (Ibid.: 74)

'Every selection', every value judgment, 'implies a religion' (Nietzsche 1996: 74). In this sense, Nietzsche not only historicizes the religious illusions by showing their contingency, he not only demystifies them by showing their genealogical origin, he also wants values/gods fit for this world. Thus his antithesis to Christ is not the Anti-Christ but Dionysus.

And what is an illusion that knows that it is an illusion if not the artistic fiction? Art tells the truth of the social world in the guise of fiction. This is why, for Nietzsche, the artistic 'will to illusion' is more profound, more divine, than the will to truth. It is art that is the main antidote to the problem of nihilism (Nietzsche 1967: 452). It is the only activity that can replace *oikonomia*, 'God's art' (see Mondzain 2005: 13, 115).

Ideology

Marx, too, interrogates religion as illusion, maintaining that religion enables the illusory perception of real history in line with a transcendent standard. In this regard he follows Feuerbach: by creating the illusion of the other-worldly domain, religion mystifies *this* world: the historical, real life-production. Hence his metaphor for religion: 'the illusory sun which revolves around man as long as he does not revolve round himself' (Marx 1957: 42). Accordingly, the criticism of religion is what 'disillusions', brings back to reason the alienated self-consciousness and self-feeling of man (Ibid. 41). But the criticism must not be confined to the realm of consciousness. One must focus on the material world that prepares the conditions for the emergence of religious consciousness. 'It is not consciousness that determines life, but life that determines consciousness' (Marx and Engels 1998: 42). The 'phantoms' formed by the religious imagination are merely sublimations of material life-processes that are bound to material premises.

> *man* is no abstract being squatting outside the world. Man is *the world of man*, the state, society. This state, this society, produce religion, *a reversed world-consciousness*, because they are *a reversed world*. Religion is the general theory of that world, its encyclopedic compendium, its logic in a popular form, its spiritualistic *point d'honneur*, its enthusiasm, its moral sanction, its solemn completion, its universal ground for consolation and justification. It is the *fantastic realization* of the human essence because the *human essence* has no true reality. The struggle against religion is therefore mediately the light against *the other world*, of which religion is the spiritual *aroma*.
>
> (Marx 1957: 41–42)

The task of critique is to ascertain the 'truth of this world', to fight the world that needs religious illusions as well as illusory ideas. Only when human problems are unmasked in their holy forms can the criticism of heaven be turned into the criticism of this world, the criticism of theology become the criticism of actual politics (Ibid. 50). Only through this profaning path can the criticism of religion arrive at 'the categorical *imperative to overthrow all relations* in which man is a debased, enslaved, abandoned, despicable essence' (Ibid. 50).

Marxism perceives religion as ideology par excellence. Religion consists of an imaginary representation of mankind's real conditions of existence, an alienated description of an alienating reality. Significantly, however, religion as ideology does not simply provide an imaginary, i.e. distorted, representation of the actual world. To say this would mean reducing ideology to false consciousness. More importantly, ideology constitutes the imaginary relationship of individuals to that world (see Althusser 2008: 39). As an ideology in this sense, religion has a material existence; it exists in an apparatus and its practices (see Ibid. 40). The church, for instance, is never merely a spiritual entity. Likewise, religious ceremonies and rituals are as much about the organization of material life as spiritual life. It is only by means of this material apparatus that religion can turn individuals into religious subjects subjected to God. Althusser's discussion of the formal procedure at work here (Ibid. 51–57) is worth re-visiting:

The religious ideology addresses itself to the individual in order to tell her or him that God exists and s/he is responsible to God's call. In this, the individual is 'interpellated', transformed into a subject free to obey or disobey the call. In the same movement the subject recognizes itself as a subject as well as its proper place, a place designated for it in the socio-symbolic order. However, there can be a multitude of subjects constituted this way only if there is an absolute and unique Subject, God, that is, interpellation takes for granted the existence of God as an absolute, big Other. Subjects are subjected to this Subject; they become subjects through this subjection. In this sense the subjects and the Subject need each other.

> Better: God duplicates himself and sends his Son to the Earth, as a mere subject 'forsaken' by him (the long complaint of the Garden of Olives which ends in the Crucifixion), subject but Subject, man but God, to do what prepares the way for the final Redemption, the Resurrection of Christ. God thus needs to 'make himself' a man, the Subject needs to become a subject, as if to show empirically, visibly to the eye, tangibly to the hands ... of the subjects, that, if they are subjects, subjected to the Subject, that is solely in order that finally, on Judgment Day, they will re-enter the Lord's Bosom, like Christ, i.e. re-enter the Subject.
> (Althusser 2008: 53–54)

This duplication, which is constitutive of all ideology, is specular in nature, a mirror-structure, in which the absolute Subject occupies the center. It is around this center, which functions as the guarantor of recognition, that ideology interpellates individuals into subjects, 'subjects the subjects to the Subject', while making it possible for the subjects to contemplate their own image in the Subject (Ibid. 54). As the subject recognizes itself as a subject through this process, it also misrecognizes in this very form of recognition the reproduction of the real social and economic relations that surround it. As such, ideology is synonymous with ignorance or misrecognition (Ibid. 56–57).

Then, the driving force in religion is a specular void. As an image, 'God' is nothing, with no actual being and no positive attribute. It can only be known through its effects. Hence Althusser's emphasis on the double body of the ideological Subject can be taken as a reference to the centrality of Christological assumptions within political theory. For in political theory the Christological duality is translated into the two bodies of the king: a God-made and thus mortal body subject to all susceptibilities that come by nature and accident, and another, man-made and thus immortal body politic which is faultless and immune to the defects of nature such as infancy or old age (Kantarowicz 1985: 18, 436). The political subject is constituted in relation to a sovereignty which is incarnated in the king, a subjection, in which the king's immortal body functions like a '*deus absconditus*', a hidden or absent God, which is knowable by the human mind only in its effects, and which, therefore, attracts everything towards itself like a void (Ibid. 12; see also Foucault 1977: 28).

It is easy to identify the same specular logic in Hobbes's *Leviathan*. The subjects create the sovereign through the social contract, by transferring their rights to him, yet, it appears as if everything emanates from the sovereign, as if the sovereign, like the sun, were the hidden source of all visibility. Thus, although in the absence of the sovereign some subjects shine more, some less, in his presence the subjects are all equal: 'they shine no more than the Starres in the presence of the Sun' (Hobbes 1985: 238). All subjects have the same relation to the sovereign, just as all humans are related to God in the same way.

The subjects create the sovereign in their own eyes; their own sight is embodied in Leviathan and reflected back at them as something alien, as a sovereign gaze. That is, the belief in God's or the king's 'reality' is an ideological effect of the subject's own vision, own power. However, this *imaginary* figure of belief is paradoxically more dazzling and blinding than any actual reality. For this reason, it can give rise to a linguistic, *symbolic* chain in which the name (God/sovereign) occupies a central place as a master signifier, as a sign recognized by the subjects as an arbitrary will. Faced with this absolute and unique figure, the One, the multitude of the subjected subjects are equal in obedience; they all obey and serve the One. It is in this process, in which fascination (with the image) and obedience (to the sign) mutually form and reinforce each other, love and fear feed upon each other, that the subjects create the Subject while imagining that the Subject creates them. And this interplay of the image and the sign, of belief and obedience, can be held together by ideology thanks to a void (the nonexistence of God): the real that maintains the link between the imaginary and the symbolic (see Grosrichard 1998: 81–83).

Understood in this way, the notion of the Son in Althusser's example is crucial; since God's absolute power cannot be given in person, the Son comes to stand in for the master signifier in actual reality. This split is a structural necessity. The invisible, fictive source of power (God), and its visible manifestation or exercise (the Son), do not coincide. What is hidden in the relationship between the Father and the Son is a deeper genealogical relationship between theology and economy, which brings us to the concept of despotism.

The despot and economic theology

In its origin, in ancient Greece, the rule of the despot, *oikonomia*, designated a specific power relation that takes place in the household, in the domestic sphere. 'Political' power, in contrast, was seen as something that pertains to the city/polis, as a relationship between free men concerning the common good. In the household, the despot governs three kinds of subjects: his children, his wife, and his slaves. Aristotle draws a parallel between the power relation between the despot and his children on the one hand and that between the king and his people on the other. The defining aspect of this parallel is that both relations are to the benefit of the ruled (people/children). To his wife, the despot relates as husband; not force but equality determines the terms of this 'democratic' relation which is beneficial for both parties. And finally, to his slaves the despot relates as a tyrant or as a master, and since slaves are not free this relation is only to the benefit of the master.

On this account, the existence of the slave, that is, the process of 'primitive accumulation', is the main reason why *oikonomia* cannot be political. Insofar as the despot is engaged with governing the slaves, he is an apolitical figure.

> But there is also a form of knowledge belonging to the master, which consists in the use of slaves: a master is such in virtue not of acquiring, but of using slaves. This knowledge belonging to the master is something which has no great or majestic character: the master must simply know how to command what the slave must know how to do. This is why those who are in a position to escape from being troubled by it delegate the management of slaves to a steward, and spend on politics or philosophy the time they are thus able to save.
>
> (Aristotle 1995: 20)

Going to the polis to engage with philosophy or politics, the despot can be a master in absentia, while the steward/overseer governs the working slaves in the *oikos*. What we get here is effectively a pairing: the absent despot and the present overseer governing in his name. This paradigmatic pairing of sovereignty and governmentality is significant because, with Christianity, the Greek term *oikonomia* has moved into the theological field, signifying a celestial design, the 'divine plan of salvation' (Agamben 2011a: 20). As such, *oikonomia* is the concept that links together the absent God and his earthly overseer. It is the theological answer to the question of what is to be done in a world ontologically created by God and which must be redeemed by the praxis of a separate person, the Son. This means that the economy (the praxis which is to be followed to reach the goal of salvation) has no foundation in ontology (in creation). However, praxis (the Son) must be related to ontology (God); God and his government of the world must be brought together. Hence the significance of the concept of 'free will'. Through this concept, which is 'in agreement with the theological *oikonomia*' (Ibid. 56), the Trinitarian theology has sought to overcome the Gnostic split between two gods, and to unite God's creation with the government of the created world, to reconcile a transcendent God who is inoperative in relation to the existing world, and a savior/redeemer as the ruler of the world. In this sense Christian theology is not only political but also economic-managerial from the start (Ibid. 66).

Here we also arrive at the point at which political and economic theology intersect: glory. It is only through the specular notion of glory that being and economy, sovereignty and governmentality appear to coincide. Power needs the spectacle. Acclamations, protocols, ceremonies, exclamations of praise, often accompanied by ritually repeated bodily gestures, are indispensable to power because they form a public opinion and express consensus (Ibid. 169–70). In its Judaic origin, glory signifies the manifestation, the becoming visible, of God as a consuming (thus dazzling and blinding) fire. As such, it is an 'objective' aspect of the divine. At the same time, however, there is a 'subjective' dimension: the glorification of this divine reality by God's subjects, by human praxis: 'glorification stems from the glory that, in truth, it founds' (Ibid. 199). In this sense, glory, the spectacle, is what establishes the link between the Kingdom and *oikonomia*, between sovereignty and governmentality. 'The economy glorifies being, as being glorifies the economy' (Ibid. 209).

Crucially, however, this relation between ontology and praxis, sovereignty and governmentality, does not constitute a dialectic that results in a synthesis. Rather, it constitutes 'a bipolar machine, whose unity always runs the risk of collapsing and must be acquired again at each turn' (Ibid. 62), or a disjunctive synthesis, in which the two poles can neither be united nor fully separated. The King/God reigns but does not administer, the task being beyond his dignity. At the same time, however, his power cannot be separated from him, that is, the two poles are not completely unrelated either; they operate together, within the same system (Ibid. 79). The functioning of the governmental machine depends on both the disjunction between being and praxis, and the attempts at suturing it. Central here is the reciprocity between the two poles.

This reciprocity ceases on one occasion only: after the Last Judgment. Glory, in this context, designates the post-governmental condition of the blessed, the Sabbath, characterized by the total absence of activity and work, of government (Ibid. 239). In other words, glory stands in for a void, for an inoperativity, at the center of the bipolar machine. Hence:

> The apparatus of glory finds its perfect cipher in the majesty of the empty throne. Its purpose is to capture within the governmental machine that unthinkable inoperativity – making it its internal motor – that constitutes the ultimate mystery of divinity.
>
> (Ibid. 245)

There is perhaps no better place to investigate this mystery, the inoperativity that constitutes 'the political substance of the Occident' (Ibid. 246), than Orientalist fantasies. For three reasons. First, as is well-known, fantasy is the instrument through which the Occident disavows its own excesses. The way 'they' are defined always reveals a repressed and thus unsayable truth about 'us'. In this sense there is a structural necessity that pertains to all Orientalism: the image of (Oriental) despotism as a perversion of (Western) sovereignty is precisely what sustains (Western) sovereignty. Second, and less obvious, the 'Orient' offers an occasion, a scenario, in which the two poles of the bipolar machine, sovereignty and economy, appear to coincide. The concept of Oriental despotism is particularly significant in this respect for the economic relation is, in its origin, a despotic relation. And third, a similar coincidence takes place in theological terms in the context of Islam. Thus the role which the concept of Islam plays in relation to the Trinitarian theology is comparable, if not identical, to the role which the concept of despotism plays in relation to political philosophy (see *Excursus I*).

'Despotism' has become the 'specter' it is during the Enlightenment (Grosrichard 1998: 3). As already mentioned, despotism was originally defined not in terms of political power, the polis, but in terms of domestic power, the *oikos*. In this sense despotism cannot refer to a political category. But a displacement occurs in eighteenth-century Europe, when despotism starts to signify the perversion of regal power (the king ruling his 'people' as if they were his 'slaves'). As such, 'despotism' connotes a political way to de-politicize (or pervert) politics. Crucially, in the same period, the concept of despotism becomes the cornerstone in Orientalism, which perceives the Orient as a space of perversion: the despot as the sole owner of all enjoyment, including the multitude of harem women (Ibid. 141–46). It is a space in which everything exists for the despot, whose power terrifies his powerless subjects who are reduced to nothing, to slaves, and motivated by fear rather than free will (Ibid. 36–40). Accordingly, the relationship between the West and the Orient is not seen merely as a differential relationship, as a difference, between two elements within the same space. The Orient rather signifies a ground zero. Hence the castrated eunuch, not the woman, is the emblem of the Orient. Despotism is not merely a political form such as monarchy, tyranny, and democracy, but rather an *a*political 'formlessness' (Grosrichard 1998; Boer 1996: 46). It is a discursive representation of a space that cannot be represented.

> Despotism, then, appears very much as the negation of all forms of *government*, but this is all the better to highlight the kernel of *political power*, which is always masked and covered up in existing governments ...
> (Grosrichard 1998: 51)

Despotism is the phantasmatic background of all power relations. One can make sense of this background in two different ways. First, in specular terms: the despot exercises his power through the gaze, he is the one who sees all; obedience, in turn, is blind. If the despot ever shows himself, this takes the form of a calculated spectacle (Ibid. 56–59). And second, the despot is the master through the letter, his word, which can create or annihilate its subjects. Thus everything he says, regardless of how meaningless it is, is an order-word, a command, and the more arbitrary it is, the more it is obeyed by his slave-subjects. This is why there can be no dialogue, hence no misunderstanding, and therefore no revolt in despotism. The despot can only be 'echoed' (Ibid. 61–62). In this economy, the despot is the central 'void' in a desert-like smooth space in which all commands flow from him while all wealth, all enjoyment, move directly towards him (Ibid. 67). While his name functions as the efficient cause of everything that happens, his gaze is perceived as the ultimate object of desire, of 'love', that both discloses and hides the central void into which everything disappears (Ibid. 70).

Significantly, in terms of both the image and the sign, the despotic power is not shared; it is only transmitted in a mechanical fashion through the hierarchy of the seraglio. The vizier, the highest official in the sultan's court, is particularly interesting in this respect, for his role is comparable to that of the 'overseer' in Aristotle and the 'Son' in the Trinity. The Ottoman vizier has power through the sign, the 'name' of the despot, and his task is to incarnate and to transmit it instantaneously, without the intervention of his own subjective judgment. He is chosen by the despot in an arbitrary way. He can also fall from grace at any time, equally arbitrarily. Thus he must always be careful not to annoy or displease the despot. It is therefore essential for him to know what the despot desires. His 'existence' in the socio-symbolic system depends on this. Yet he is per definition ignorant of the despot's arbitrary desire. He can only know with absolute certainty what the despot desires when he is sentenced to death. Otherwise the vizier remains in doubt. And in doubt the only way for him to sustain his existence is to give the despot the opportunity to love himself through his vizier. Thus he constantly flatters, glorifies the despot's image, which, as in all flattery, produces in the despot both a momentary feeling of lack (the despot cannot really take the vizier's flattery seriously if the vizier really counts as nothing) and a gain in enjoyment, a surplus of *jouissance*. This surplus, which flows towards the despot, is countered with another flow, the surplus power of the vizier as a gift of existence (Ibid. 73). And paradoxically, in the long run, the despot becomes less and less capable of exercising his power as he progressively abandons himself to his *jouissance* (Ibid. 75). While the vizier actually governs, the absent despot enjoys.

> A despot who erases himself, absents himself in his stupid *jouissance*, and a vizier who merges with the pure signifier which constitutes him ... – this is the basic dyad which is constitutive of despotic power.
> (Grosrichard 1998: 81)

The pairing of the (imaginary) figure of the despot with the (symbolic) position of the vizier links love and belief (fascination with the image of the despot) with fear and obedience (to the sign). In the process, the absent despot's name becomes more and more fear-provoking; the void becomes all the more powerful. So there are not two economies, one despotic and one religious, but rather two interchangeable languages to describe the same process that maintains power.

Excursus I
Voltaire's *Mahomet* as despot

> The action I have described is terrible; I do not know whether horror was ever carried farther on any stage. A young man born with virtuous inclinations, seduced by fanaticism, assassinates an old man who loves him; and whilst he imagines he is serving God, is, without knowing it, guilty of parricide: the murder is committed by the order of an impostor, who promises him a reward, which proves to be incest.
>
> (Voltaire 1742)

This is the plot of Voltaire's controversial play of 1741, *Mahomet*. The setting is a city under siege, Mecca 630 AD. The military force of Mahomet is at the gates. The leader of the defending Meccans is Zopir. Both sides are ready to fight and the terms of the war are being discussed under a ceasefire.

In the first act we meet Zopir talking to one of his senators, telling him that he will never 'bend the knee' to Mahomet. He cannot worship, he says, a 'proud hypocrite' whom he himself banished from Mecca. Here Zopir is presented as a friend of 'freedom' and Mahomet as an 'impostor' and a 'conqueror' before whom nations bend and masses turn into fanatics, 'a band of wild enthusiasts, drunk with furious zeal'. Mahomet is a 'tyrant' who can bring nothing but slavery, a false prophet who can promise nothing but a false religion. His 'fancied miracles' only amount to superstition. How could Zopir, a defender of liberty, make peace with a traitor, even if he threatens to lay the city waste? Kingdoms, after all, 'are lost with cowardice alone'. Of course obstinate resistance might bring with it devastation, too: 'Then let us perish, if it be our fate'.

Next it transpires that one of Mahomet's demands is to marry Palmira, a former citizen of Mecca, enslaved and brought up by Mahomet, but now a prisoner of war in Zopir's Mecca. In her beautiful sight Zopir is saddened: 'Shall beauty's charms be sacrificed to bribe a madman's frenzy?' Throughout her stay in Mecca, Palmira has scarcely felt the yoke of slavery and she feels indebted to Zopir for that. However, she also wants to return to Mahomet's camp. Mahomet has been a 'father' to her and her soul 'looks up to Mahomet with holy fear, as to a god'. Thus she refuses Zopir's proposal. 'I am not mistress of myself, and how can I be thine?' To this Zopir replies:

> Deluded mortals!
> How blind ye are, to follow this proud madman,
> This happy robber, whom my justice spared,
> And raise him from the scaffold to a throne!
>
> (Act I, Scene II)

However, Zopir does not grant Palmira to Mahomet. She is a 'treasure' for him, which it is too difficult to part with. But this makes Mahomet only more eager and more determined. The object of desire is the other's desire. Thus Mahomet's obsession with Palmira plays a crucial part in the siege. Indeed, when his general Omar arrives at Zopir's camp to bring the terms of peace, the message from Mahomet condenses into one single demand:

> Name your conditions, and the terms of peace;
> Set your own terms on fair Palmira; take
> Our treasures, and be happy.
>
> (Act I, Scene IV)

Zopir is not prepared to accept this condition for peace. In an attempt at discussion with Omar, whom he knows from earlier days (they fought on the same side against Mahomet before Omar decided to serve Mahomet), Zopir appeals to reason. He encourages Omar to be honest and look at Mahomet 'with the impartial eye of reason', to consider him 'as a mortal'. But Omar cannot be rational; he insists on admiring, believing, and obeying Mahomet. Faced with Omar's inflexibility, Zopir states his own: 'if he e'er, re-enters Mecca, he must cut his way through Zopir's blood'.

In the following act we realize that Palmira is in love with Seid, another slave-disciple of Mahomet. Seid, too, very much like Palmira and Omar, sees not a man but a god in Mahomet and considers him his master.

> My ever-honored father, and King,
> Led by that power divine who guided thee
> To Mecca's walls, preventing your commands
> I came, prepared to live or die with thee.
>
> (Act II, Scene III)

For all his obedience to Mahomet, though, Seid means next to nothing to Mahomet. For the more Mahomet watches the affection between Palmira and Seid, the more he is obsessed with Palmira. Thus he confesses to Omar:

> Thou knowest the reigning passion of my soul;
> Whilst proud ambition and the cares of empire
> Weighed heavy on me, Mahomet's hard life
> Has been a conflict with opposing Nature,
> Whom I have vanquished by austerity,

And self-denial; have banished from me
That baleful poison which unnerves mankind,
Which only serves to fire them into madness,
And brutal follies; on the burning sand
Or desert rocks I brave the inclement sky,
And bear the seasons' rough vicissitude:
Love is my only solace, the dear object
O fall my toils, the idol I adore,
The god of Mahomet, the powerful rival
Of my ambition: know, midst all my queens,
Palmira reigns sole mistress of my heart:
Think then what pangs of jealousy thy friend
Must feel when she expressed her fatal passion
For Seid.

(Act II, Scene IV)

Captivated by jealousy, Mahomet makes a plan: he will turn Seid into an assassin and send him to Mecca to become Zopir's hostage. As a hostage, he might find an occasion to kill him. He knows that Seid is young and inexperienced; he is 'superstitious, bold, and violent, but easy to be led ... obedient' (Act II, Scene V). He has 'all the warmth of wild fanaticism' (Act III, Scene V). And so, as the assassination is planned, Mahomet's carnal desire, his 'fatal passion', is hidden beneath the mask of justice and divine authority. Precisely at this point, another secret is revealed: Palmira and Seid are siblings. In fact, they are Zopir's children, whom Mahomet had kidnapped in their infancy and turned into slaves. Zopir's 'children', in other words, are Mahomet's 'slaves' who call Mahomet 'father'. The truth is obscure both to the real father and to the children.

In the final act, the fanatic Seid assassinates Zopir. Herein lies the tragic aspect of the play as well: Seid, seduced and enslaved by a false 'father', kills his real father who loves him. He becomes a murderer because he imagines he is serving God while acting by the orders of an impostor, who promises him an incestuous reward, his own sister.

However, at the moment of the murder, the truth is revealed. Phanor, a senator and a friend to Zopir, tells Palmira and Seid that they are Zopir's children. Zopir, too, hears this in his final moment. Tellingly, Seid is arrested in the end for the murder of Zopir by Mahomet's own authorities. With this arrest, the despotic face of Mahomet is masked. Then Mecca is conquered, and Palmira is seized. But she, too, wakes up from her intoxication, recognizing Mahomet as an 'execrable tyrant' (Act IV, Scene VI), and renounces Islam. She expresses her hope that 'a God more just' than Mahomet's will arrive. But until then: 'let Mahomet reign here in peace: this world was made for tyrants' (Act V, Scene IV). She commits suicide. And so, having lost his object of desire, Mahomet is confronted with his own abyss:

> She's gone; she's lost; the only dear reward
> I wished to keep of all my crimes: in vain
> I fought and conquered; Mahomet is wretched
> Without Palmira: Conscience, now I feel thee,
> And feel that thou canst rive the guilty heart.
> O thou eternal God, whom I have wronged
> Braved and blasphemed; O thou whom yet I fear,
> Behold me self-condemned, behold me wretched,
> Even whilst the world adores me: vain was all
> My boasted power: I have deceived mankind;
> But how shall I impose on my own heart?
> A murdered father, and two guiltless children
> Must be avenged: come, ye unhappy victims,
> And end me quickly!—Omar, we must strive
> To hide this shameful weakness, save my glory,
> And let me reign o'er a deluded world:
> For Mahomet depends on fraud alone,
> And to be worshipped never must be known.
>
> (Act V, Scene IV)

Mahomet and Zopir: the despot and the king

It is 'surprising', as Grosrichard (1998: 107) remarks, that at a time when Orientalists were busy trying to understand the 'truth' of Islam and were inclined to see it as another global religion on a par with Judaism and Christianity, Voltaire insists on depicting Islam merely as superstition, reducing Mahomet to a false prophet masking imperial ambitions with divine rhetoric. Voltaire's Mahomet readily confesses that he is driven by passions, by envy, vanity, and, most importantly, 'ambition', which Spinoza defines as an excessive desire for power and glory (1993a: 136). Voltaire's Mahomet, in other words, is all too human:

> I have ambition, Zopir; where's the man
> Who has it not? But never citizen,
> Or chief, or priest, or king projected aught
> So noble as the plan of Mahomet;
> In acts or arms hath every nation shone
> Superior in its turn; Arabia now
> Steps forth; that generous people, long unknown
> And unrespected, saw her glories sunk,
> Her honors lost; but lo! The hour is come
> When she shall rise to victory and renown ...
>
> (Act II, Scene V)

What, then, are the instruments with which to rise to 'victory and reknown'? Mahomet reveals that they are twofold: to promise and to threaten. Only by these means, he imagines, can he let his God alone be worshipped, and those who won't love his God will be taught to fear him (Act II, Scene III). Hence 'men must either be deceived, or forced into obedience' (Act V, Scene I). They must be taught to 'tremble and obey in humble silence' (Act II, Scene V) so that their obedience is blind. If Mahomet is blinded by his passions, he can only be followed blindly, like Seid does.

> The multitude are ever weak and blind,
> Made for our use, born but to serve the great,
> But to admire, believe us, and obey.
>
> (Act I, Scene IV)

This 'despotic' relation is qualitatively different from other forms of politics. And it is this difference that highlights the difference between Zopir and Mahomet, between the king and the despot. As previously mentioned, the concept of despotism is an instrument through which the Occident disavows its excesses. Its function is that of the real that returns in the guise of a fiction, as that which cannot be integrated into the socio-symbolic reality and therefore can only be experienced as an excessive, uncanny spectrality (see Žižek 2002a: 19). In this particular sense Orientalism is not simply a distortion of reality (Orientalism 'fictionalizing' the Orient) but also a symptom that reveals how the reality (of Western political power) itself is mistaken for fiction (as Oriental despotism). Fictionalizing the despot hides the fact that the tendency of despotism necessarily exists in every power relation, that the 'abuse of power' is not only a contingent aspect of power that depends on the power holders' intentions or qualities but the 'natural modality' of all power (Grosrichard 1998: 50).

It is, against this background, easy to understand why Zopir emphasizes Mahomet not only as his enemy but 'the foe of all mankind' (Act II, Scene IV). And why, when Mahomet announces his aims – banishing idolatry and building a theocratic state beneath 'one king, one prophet, and one God' (Act II, Scene V) – Zopir gestures towards an enlightened, non-despotic form of government:

> Canst thou change the hearts of men,
> And make them think like thee? Are war and slaughter
> The harbingers of wisdom and of peace;
> Can he who ravages instruct mankind?
> If in the night of ignorance and error
> We long have wandered, must thy dreadful torch
> Enlighten us? What right hast thou to empire?
>
> (Act II, Scene V)

This polarization between the imposter despot and the just king continues until the end of this crucial scene, illuminating Mahomet's purpose as enslaving mankind with an air of glory. In turn, Zopir makes it clear that there can be no compromise between Zopir and Mahomet, politics and despotism: 'Can Mahomet and Zopir / E'er be united? Say, what god shall work a miracle like that?' (Act II, Scene V). Even their gods are different: Mahomet's God is 'interest'; Zopir's 'justice' (Act II, Scene V).

Mahomet and Seid: the impostor and the fanatic

The relationship between Seid (the multitude) and Mahomet is a despotic relationship. Its principle is straightforward: while it is 'the voice of God' that expresses itself in Mahomet, Seid silently obeys his commands (see Act IV, Scene III). The multitude are born to obey Mahomet, to whom God has delegated his sovereign power, and to whose indulgence the multitude 'owe' their beings (Act V, Scene IV).

It is significant that Voltaire's Seid does not know who his real father is. He is a figure without a father. Like the Janissaries in the Ottoman army, Mahomet's 'children' are orphans who misrecognize him as their father. On the basis of this ideological misrecognition, they fraternize around the same father, the despot-Mahomet, towards whom their love flows (see Grosrichard 1998: 86). The figure of the despot emerges as a specular illusion in the gaze of the multitude, the soldier/orphan children of the despot, who adore the glory of the despot which is in reality an effect of their own glorification. In this sense, the relation between Mahomet and his 'children' is based on 'voluntary servitude' (La Boétie 1942). Hence the despotic paradox: the more the multitude obeys the despot, the more it gets accustomed to the idea of subjection, and the more despotism is naturalized. The problem with despotism is not only that it can mobilize the masses effectively and quickly; the problem is that subjects desire it; they 'love' power, the very thing that dominates them (see Foucault 1983: xiii).

It is this enigmatic desire for repression that Seid incarnates in relation to Mahomet. He is dazzled by what he sees in Mahomet as a spectacle. Since Mahomet is an impostor, Seid's belief in Mahomet is merely an illusion, a belief in an imaginary being. And Mahomet is aware of this, that he can only reign over 'a deluded world' (Act V, Scene IV). He knows that he 'never must be known' (Ibid.). His power can disintegrate at the moment it is unmasked as illusion. Then, if despotic power is based on ignorance, if only blind obedience can feed it, superstition is indispensable to despotic power. And 'the superstitious man is governed by the fanatic and becomes fanatic' (Voltaire 2011: 239).

Fanaticism, for Voltaire, operates along two axes: the fanaticizer and the fanatic (see Appelbaum 2011) – on the one hand the cynical manipulator (Mahomet), on the other the inexperienced, youthful Seid, who admires Mahomet. In other words, 'fanatics are led by scoundrels who supply the weapons' (Voltaire 2011: 137–38). As an effect in this sense, fanaticism is grounded in imagination and passion. Concomitantly, Voltaire defines fanaticism in dramatic terms (Appelbaum 2011: 3). There is a theatrical, scenic element to fanaticism because what defines the 'fanatic' in Voltaire is the discrepancy between presentation and representation: the fanatic is present in a world while he mentally belongs to another. Certain of his beliefs, he seeks to become the instrument of an absolute authority, of a transcendent master, be it God or a King or a Chief, to make the existing world fit into his ideals (see Colas 1997: 5–6). The fanatic is one who doesn't like the existing world and perceives no problem in destroying it, even though that implies his own destruction as well. In the primordial scene, which Girard (1986) describes, the society is constituted on the basis of the lynching mob, whose mimetic desire, whose envy and egoism, culminates in sacrificing the scapegoat. With the fanatic, we confront the opposite situation in which the mimetic desire does not establish but rather destroys the society. Here everybody, and not only the scapegoat, is threatened with destruction. As such, fanaticism signifies the ground zero of sociality. This is why despotism (the ground zero of politics) and Islam (the ground zero of religion) together constitute a perfect scene for fanaticism in *Mahomet*.

But if Mahomet is merely a phantom, illusion, where does his power come from? It seems that what sustains the specular basis of power in *Mahomet* is military power, which takes us to the relationship between Mahomet and Omar.

Mahomet and Omar: the despot and the vizier

Here the link between Islam and militarism is decisive: in *Mahomet* Islam is a religion bent on conquering the entire world through military means. Thus Mahomet says that his law 'forms heroes' (Act II, Scene V). Mahomet himself is simultaneously a prophet and a despot, the commander of the military. Omar's role, in turn, can be likened to that of the vizier for he exists only for and through his master (see Grosrichard 1998: 108). In Omar's eyes, too, Mahomet is a 'god-like' conqueror (Act II, Scenes II and IV).

The essential link between Mahomet (despot) and Omar (vizier) can be projected onto a broader framework that links Islam (God) and Mahomet (as its prophet, or, 'vizier'). Mahomet, in this sense, is also subjected to a law. He must, as his subjects, obey God's laws. The despot justifies himself by blindly subjecting himself to a law higher than himself. The paradox is that the despot never can be the only sovereign, or, he can be it by not being it: he can designate himself as the highest authority (as despot) only with reference to a higher master, God (see Laustsen 2003). Through this paradox, God's law transcendentalizes the despot's while the despot's law makes God present. As the imaginary being of the despot makes it possible to imagine the being of God, God and the despot (Mahomet) come to coincide in common attributes, in being unique, singular, distinct, omnipotent, and invisible (see

Grosrichard 1998: 98). Consequently, in Mahomet's despotism, monotheism and idolatry cease to be antagonistic; rather they fold into, feed upon each other. Voltaire can therefore describe political relations in religious terms and religion in political terms.

But can this procedure not apply to Christianity as well? At this point it becomes essential for Voltaire to maintain an essential difference between Islam and Christianity, between Jesus and Mahomet: materialism. Voltaire's Mahomet's desires are thoroughly profane and self-evidently materialistic. It is interesting to recall in this context that the supreme insult against Islam in Voltaire's epoch was its 'Spinozism' (see Ibid. 109). However, this does not, in itself, explain Islam's success in becoming a widespread religion in a short time. And it is here that the emphasis on military violence comes in handy. Armed conquest, *Mahomet* leads us to suggesting, is the key to Islam's success. After all, Mahomet's 'children' are not believers but slaves. What sets Mahomet apart is his ability to use violence without blinking.

Let us open a parenthesis here. Voltaire knew well that the Christian church had extensively made use of violence throughout its history. Voltaire himself was one of the most uncompromising critics of the church. Consider, for instance, his ironic list of the 'butcheries' and 'murders committed' in the name of Jesus where Voltaire readily recognizes 'the hand of God' (Voltaire 2010: 148). Then, since the Christian church incites the same critical sense in Voltaire, since violence is also an inherent tendency in Christianity, one could safely assume that for Voltaire the ultimate distinction between Islam and Christianity cannot be drawn along the line of violence. Therefore Voltaire needs another, deeper and more convincing difference. He finds it in sexuality. Which brings us to the most significant relation depicted in *Mahomet*, that between Mahomet and Palmira.

Mahomet and Palmira: the despot and the woman

Since the debt to the despot is an infinite debt, since all existence appears to emanate from him, all flows in a despotic economy must be sustained infinitely. In this economy, therefore, the subjects who are nothing are obliged to give everything to the despot. Yet they cannot give what they do not have. In order to solve this problem, the despot/vizier relation must be extended. Thus it is reproduced throughout the whole hierarchy (Grosrichard 1998: 74–75). And each symbolic marking, the creation of each new position in the hierarchy, renews the image of the despot and increases his glory, inducing at each step 'a necessary *belief* that the despot is everywhere, when in reality he is nowhere' (Ibid. 83).

Consider the role of the eunuch, another key figure in the government of the seraglio. The eunuch, a castrated figure with no sex, is the principal official guarding and governing the harem, thus organizing the relationship between the two sexes so that the flow of all enjoyment is channeled into the service of the sultan – a task comparable to that of the saint, who performs the same task in the service of God, whose arbitrary will remains unknown (Ibid. 135). Both the eunuch and the saint are sexless men without bonds, thus ideal subjects to be enrolled into the network of religion or despotism. While they serve different masters, they make use of the same method: in return for their symbolic positions they are prepared to give their love and their lives for their masters.

What is the role of women in this context? They, too, are marked by a lack, thus they do not have any power, and their sexual services are totally subject to the despot's desires. Therefore, when the despot does not require them, they are kept in harem, overseen by a eunuch. As such, the harem is a prison. What is more crucial, however, is the women's numerical excess. As a relation between the one (despot/man) and the multitude (slaves/women), polygamy is what links the domestic and the political. Thus, in the Orient, polygamy and despotism coincide in a natural way. Sex, therefore, is more revealing than the military in explaining the difference of the Orient. For this reason Voltaire needs Palmira, or rather the relationship between Mahomet and her, to ground the difference of the Orient. For the slavery of women in the Orient constitutes a model for slavery in general:

> Metaphysically, she is an existence without essence, or a (male) essence whose actualization is hindered. It is something which exists 'in otherness', not 'in itself'. A woman, therefore, can 'be or be thought' only 'in man and through man' – as, for example, Spinoza's finite mode can be and be thought only by the attribute of the substance it expresses. And just as the difference in ontological status between substance and mode means that between substances there is a *real* distinction, while between the finite modes of the same substance there is only a *numerical* distinction, so – *mutatis mutandis* – between man and woman the distinction is real, while between women there can be only numerical distinctions: man is to woman what substance is to mode ...
>
> [...]
>
> Finally, just as Spinoza's substance can have several attributes, or express itself in an infinity of finite modes, while a mode, conversely, cannot express two or more substances, so a man can have two – indeed, an infinity of wives, but a woman can have only one husband.
>
> (Ibid. 144)

Herein we also find a perfect image of governmentality, which implies an infinite 'plurality' of what is to be governed and perceives what is to be governed as 'specific finalities' (Foucault 1991: 95). It is therefore not surprising that the Orient (and thus Islam) serves as the image of an extreme case in which total governmentality and total sovereignty fully coincide. 'Islam' is the cipher of this coincidence. Thus Islam is to Christian theology what despotism is to political philosophy. What is excluded from the bipolar machine – the coincidence of sovereignty and governmentality – returns as a paranoid fantasy in the figure of 'Islam'. Hence in Voltaire the figure of Mahomet serves 'as a foil the better to enhance the divinity of the Christian religion' (Grosrichard 1998: 107). In this, he is following a long tradition. Consider, for instance, the role of Islam in Spinoza. Superstition as a 'system', he writes, 'has been brought to great perfection by the Turks, for they consider even controversy impious, and so clog men's minds with dogmatic formulas, that they leave no room for sound reason, not even enough to doubt with' (Spinoza 1951a: 5). 'Turks' here is a stand-in for the multitude-mob, the despot's slaves, who, especially in danger, 'are wont with Prayers and womanish tears to implore help from God' and who believe 'the phantoms of imagination, dreams, and other childish absurdities, to be the very oracles of Heaven' (Ibid. 4). In this way Spinoza juxtaposes superstition, which takes the divine commands literally and reduces religion to ceremony, and 'the universal faith', the moral core of organized religion, which does not need ceremony (worship and literalness):

> Therefore, if a man were to read the Scripture narratives believing the whole of them, but were to give no heed to the doctrines they contain, and make no amendment in his life, he might employ himself just as profitably in reading the Koran or the poetic drama, or ordinary chronicles, with the attention usually given to such writings; on the other hand, if a man is absolutely ignorant of the Scriptures, and none the less has right opinions and a true plan of life, he is absolutely blessed and truly possesses in himself the spirit of Christ.
>
> (Ibid. 79)

Voltaire, then, is not exactly original in his denigration of Islam as the superstitious, fanatical other of true religion. But then again, one must not take this critique of literalness literally. Thus, Spinoza writes, when he is pushed into 'proving' that Mahomet was an 'impostor':

> Even if this were not so, am I, I should like to know, bound to show that any prophet is false? Surely the burden lies with the prophets, to prove that they are true. But if he [Spinoza's adversary] retorts, that Mahomet also taught the divine law, and gave certain signs of his mission, as the rest of the prophets did, there is surely no reason why he should deny, that Mahomet also was a true prophet. As regards the Turks and other non-Christian nations; if they worship God by the practice of justice and charity towards their neighbour, I believe that they have the spirit of Christ, and are in a state of salvation, whatever they may ignorantly hold with regard to Mahomet and oracles.
>
> (Spinoza 1671)

Spinoza allows for the possibility that Islam could teach 'the universal faith' as well as superstition. Likewise, Voltaire writes, 'What is the least harmful religion of all? That in which we see less dogma and more virtue. What is the best? It is the simplest!' (Voltaire 2010: 159). It is too difficult not to hear here an echo of Spinoza's 'universal faith' which is cleansed of all dogma and ceremony characteristic of organized religion. Voltaire's target is not really religion as such but organized religion. He is not an atheist but a critic of the perversion of religion. One could claim that Voltaire tells the truth of all organized religions through the fiction of 'Islam'. What he defends is not Christianity as such but Jesus: 'Every priest, I have no doubt, would be, if he could, a tyrant of the human race. Jesus was only a victim. See, then, how they resemble Jesus!' (Ibid. 141). Organized religion, including the Christian church, is 'absolutely opposed to the religion of Jesus and is even blasphemous' (Ibid. 114). It is significant in this respect that Voltaire also admits:

> We have imputed to Koran a great number of foolish things which it never contained. It was chiefly against the Turks, who had become Mahometans, that our monks wrote so many books, at a time when no other opposition was of much service against the conquerors of Constantinople. Our authors, much more numerous than the Janissaries, had no great difficulty in ranging our women on their side; they persuaded them that Mahomet looked upon them merely as intelligent animals; that, by the laws of the Koran, they were all slaves, having no property in this world, nor any share in the Paradise of the next. The falsehood of all this is evident; yet it has all been firmly believed. [...] We do not pretend to justify either his ignorance or his imposture; but we cannot condemn his doctrine of *one only God*. These words of his 122nd *sura*, 'God is one, eternal, neither begetting nor begotten; no one is like to him'. These words had more effect than even his sword in subjugating the East. [...] Still the Koran is a ridiculous collection of ridiculous revelations and vague and incoherent predictions, combined with laws which were very good for the country in which he lived, and all which continue to be followed. ...
>
> (1824: 67, 70).

'Cannot condemn' but 'still ... ridiculous': this is Voltaire's formula for understanding all organized religion, not only Islam. All organized religion has a tendency towards superstition while it contains an essential core. This formula helps Voltaire to keep atheism at bay for he cannot accept a godless reality, for his world is 'a beautiful machine' that would be unthinkable without an engineer/creator, without a just God:

> Although I claim to be tolerant, I am inclined to punish whoever would say today, 'Ladies and Gentlemen, there is no God. Slander, betray, deceive,

steal, murder, poison, it's all the same as long as you are the strongest and most clever'. It is clear that this man would be very pernicious to society ...

(Voltaire 2010: 21).

For 'social' coherence, then, a 'simple' religion is necessary. Without God the social would fall apart. This is why Voltaire can condense his similarity to and his difference from Spinoza, whom he sees as an atheist, in one single sentence: 'Let a philosopher be a Spinozist if he wants. But let the man of the state be a theist' (Ibid. 157).

Fanaticism, intoxication

Voltaire thinks of theism (the 'simple religion') as an antidote to fanaticism, which is, in turn, a perversion of theism. Seid articulates this idea clearly in the end of the play: 'All that mankind hold sacred, urged me on / To do the worst of actions' (Act IV, Scene V). In this sense, fanaticism constitutes Voltaire's political problematique. The problem with his critique of fanaticism, however, is his wholesale denial of the role of passion and partisanship in politics (see Toscano 2010: 111).

To be sure, fanaticism often turns to spiteful destruction. However, passions that lead to fanatical destruction can also take the form of a revolutionary, creative destruction. Hence the pharmakon-like gift of Zarathustra: fire. Or, Marx's insistence on the 'leap' that creates 'something that has never yet existed' (Marx 1977: 10). The lesson of fanaticism is thus that one can 'burn' with fire as well as 'leap' with it (Melville 1998: 450). Herein lies, too, the aporia of *kairos*: true political action always requires both strategy and intoxication, calculus and conviction, knowledge and fidelity. On the one hand, an engagement with the actual, a strategic calculus, is necessary. On the other hand, however, intoxication is equally indispensable to the subject. If you lose faith, there is no point in engaging in politics. Strategy without intoxication is as useless as intoxication without strategy. Both sides of *kairos* are vital. What matters is to keep them in relation. Whenever the link between strategy and intoxication is broken, conviction appears as fanaticism. It is in this context that Voltaire's denunciation of fanaticism is problematical.

So, if you say fanaticism is bad, you are right. If you say fanaticism is good, you are also right. If you say this is contradictory, you are also right – for fanaticism is an empty sign that is meaningful only when it is accompanied by other signs, only when it is transfigured: 'the sign itself is nothing; accompanied, it becomes inescapable' (Baudrillard 1999: 187). If fanaticism can make itself an event only by redoubling itself, the problem with fanatical conviction is not the fanatic-ness of the conviction as such but the transformations, metamorphoses the fanatic can or cannot go through.

2 Love, love of God, intellectual love of God

> In reality there is no relationship nor friendship nor even enmity between religion and real science: they live on different stars.
>
> (Nietzsche 2008: 74)

Let us start with the three levels of knowledge in Spinoza: imagination, reason, and intuition. Imagination consists in inadequate, vague ideas acquired on the basis of the perception of singular phenomena through chance encounters and of signs, without knowing the causal relations behind them (Spinoza 1993a: 54–61, 68). Since it is the 'phantoms of imagination' (Spinoza 1951a: 4) that define religion as superstition, the task of practical thought vis-à-vis superstition consists in denouncing illusions. And this task can be undertaken only by the second level of knowledge, which corresponds to reason, that is, a knowledge of 'common notions', through which what is singular is positioned in relation to other singularities through general categories. At this level things are no longer regarded as contingent but as necessary, that is, as part of a relational network (Spinoza 1993a: 71). Consequently, the joy attained on the basis of the second kind of knowledge is an active joy that corresponds to our power to act and to understand. Ultimately, with the third and the highest form of knowledge, intuitive knowledge, one attains the knowledge of eternity, of the virtual. One no longer only conceives of things as actual but as 'contained in God and to follow from the necessity of the divine nature' (Ibid. 211). Knowledge now goes beyond the actual, beyond things in their relationality in chronological time and empirical space, and seeks to perceive the essence of things as singular events outside time and space, as singularities which directly express their virtual cause, God. The active joy that arises here is what Spinoza calls the 'intellectual love of God', a joy that is 'accompanied by the idea of God as its cause' (Ibid. 212).

From imagination to reason, from reason to intuition

On this account, the difference between imagination (sign) and understanding (expression of a cause) is also the difference between prophecy and reason. A sign is always linked to prophecy and signifies a commandment that demands obedience; understanding, on the other hand, is always attached to an expression of an essence that has no need for signs (Deleuze 1992: 57). Because of this difference the move from the first kind of knowledge (imagination) to the second (reason) appears like a clean-cut break, a leap. Thus Spinoza insists that obedience, which faith calls for, has nothing, in principle, to do with knowledge because faith and reason, theology and philosophy, are irreducible to one another: theology is about piety and obedience; the sphere of reason is truth and wisdom (Spinoza 1951a: 194).

However, there is no necessary contradiction between imagination and reason either. Revelation, theology, is in reality 'in accordance with reason' (Ibid. 195). The break, in other words, is not clear-cut; there is a possibility of correspondence, a sense of continuity between the first and the second kinds of knowledge. It is imagination that provides the ground for the formation of common notions and anticipates philosophical reasoning. So, there is a 'strange harmony between reason and imagination' (Deleuze 1992: 294).

A similar point can be made regarding the transition from the second to the third kind of knowledge, from common notions to the idea of God. The idea of God is related to common notions but is not a common notion itself. Because we cannot imagine God, we cannot form a knowledge of God which is as clear as our knowledge of common notions (Spinoza 1993a: 74). But again we can reach the idea of God only through common notions. Without them we cannot form the third kind of knowledge for the idea of God is only expressed through common notions.

As such, the idea of God is the basis for what Spinoza calls 'true religion'. But the true religion must not be confused with the 'universal faith'. Even though they are both universal in orientation, 'common to all men', the universal faith (or the universal religion) only appeals to obedience on the basis of moral concepts such as sin, repentance and forgiveness, 'mixing' ideas that relate to both superstition and 'true religion' (Deleuze 1992: 395). In contrast, the love of God which pertains to the 'true religion' is an *intellectual* love grounded in an active joy that arises from reason.

While 'superstition' and the 'universal faith' are based on imagination and can only obtain consistency through signs, the 'true religion' appeals to reason. The decisive difference comes into sight through common notions and the idea of God. It is the 'knowledge of the second and third kinds, and not of the first kind, [that] teaches us to distinguish the true from the false' (Spinoza 1993a: 69). With the second kind of knowledge (common notions) we form adequate ideas and overcome the inadequate ideas that pertain to superstition and the universal faith. With the third kind of knowledge (the idea of God), we move from a religion of imagination to one of understanding. In this movement nature takes the place of signs and the intellectual love of God replaces love as obedience, that is, voluntary servitude.

> For the love of God is not a state of obedience: it is a virtue which necessarily exists in a man who knows God rightly. Obedience has regard

to the will of a ruler, not to necessity and truth. Now as we are ignorant of the nature of God's will, and on the other hand know that everything happens solely by God's power, we cannot, except through revelation, know whether God wishes in any way to be honored as a sovereign. [...] The Divine rights appear to us in the light of rights or commands, only so long as we are ignorant of their cause: as soon as their cause is known, they cease to be rights, and we embrace them no longer as rights but as eternal truths; in other words, obedience passes into love of God, which emanates from true knowledge as necessarily as light emanates from the sun.

(Spinoza 1951a: 276–77)

What is the nature of this love that emanates from reason, then? In order to reach an answer we need to understand why reason is the antidote to passive emotions and thereby to superstition. The power of the intellect is, precisely, to open up the space for freedom because reason can tear down passive emotions, from which superstition arises, by demystifying them, by showing their external causes and providing us with clear and distinct ideas as to the causal network behind their formation (Spinoza 1993a: 197–98). The intellect can see the necessity behind what appears contingent, and this increases our power over emotions. There is 'no emotion of which we cannot form some clear and distinct conception' (Ibid. 198).

There are, however, emotions that arise from reason itself, and they are more powerful than those emotions grounded in imagining absent things. The most powerful emotion, the highest joy, is achieved through the intellect. 'Intellectual love of God' is such an emotion. It is 'intellectual' for it can only be reached through reason. It is 'love' because such understanding is always accompanied by the idea of God as its cause and therefore is pleasurable. And this intellectual love is love of 'God' because the human mind is partially eternal. It 'cannot be absolutely destroyed with the human body, but something of it remains, which is eternal' (Ibid. 208). Indeed, the third kind of knowledge depends on the mind 'insofar as the mind is eternal' (Ibid. 211). We are affected by the joy arising from the intellectual love (*amor intellectualis*) to the extent that we perceive the world in the perspective of eternity (*sub specie aeternitatis*).

Such love of God is 'the greatest good which we can desire according to the dictate of reason ... and it is common to all men' (Ibid. 205). Here we also arrive at Spinoza's definition of 'blessedness', the highest virtue grounded in the intellectual love of God. But this virtue does not come as a reward for following an ethical codex or a moral law. 'Blessedness is not the reward of virtue but the virtue itself' (Ibid. 218). Since reason is the 'best part of our being', the highest good must consist in intellectual perfection. And since nothing can exist or be thought of without God, this highest good depends on the knowledge of God. And yet, for the same reason, that is, since nothing can exist or be thought of without God, everything that exists, all natural phenomena, must 'involve and express the conception of God'. Thus 'the greatest virtue of the mind is to understand or know God' (Ibid. 157). Our knowledge of natural phenomena is proportional to our knowledge of their cause, of God. 'So, then, our highest good not only depends on the knowledge of God, but wholly consists therein' (Spinoza 1951a: 59).

And God, for Spinoza, is not in conflict with, but synonymous with, Nature. What we have here, however, is not a relativistic indifference between immanence (Nature) and transcendence (God), for Spinoza identifies both Nature and God with 'power' (*potentia*) in terms of an infinite potentiality of action in contrast to 'power' (*potestas*) which indicates a relation between an anthropomorphic sovereign and passive subjects. *Potestas* refers to hierarchic relations of dominance; '*potentia* names the immanent (in this sense "divine") productivity or causality of nature' (Balibar 2012: 30). Hence, seen from within the second kind of knowledge, the idea of God as nature is opposed to the anthropomorphic God of monotheism.

But within the third kind of knowledge an anthropomorphic remainder resurfaces. To discuss this, we must return to the transition from the second to the third kind of knowledge. Since the idea of God is what expresses all causal relations behind the infinite network of nature (since it relates our imagination to common notions), it is the basis for 'true religion'. But this God, which is related to common notions, is an 'impassive God' who does not respond to our love (Deleuze 1992: 297). 'God is free from passions, nor is he affected with any emotion of pleasure or pain' (Spinoza 1993a: 204). In other words, insofar as it is expressed through common notions, the idea of God remains within the domain of the second kind of knowledge and is accompanied by the joys grounded in (the power of) understanding.

At the same time, however, since it is not itself a common notion, the idea of God drives us towards the third kind of knowledge. Thus, although the second kind of knowledge is necessary to reach the idea of God, once we arrive at the idea of God we enter the third kind of knowledge (Ibid. 299; see also Spinoza 1993a: 205–7). Now the idea of God, which in relation to common notions signifies a sovereign being without love or joy, receives a new qualification: the active joy we experience in the intellectual love of God is also the joy experienced by God himself (Deleuze 1992: 309). 'God loves himself with an infinite intellectual love' (Spinoza 1993a: 213). Intellectual love of God is nothing else than the love with which God loves himself, because God himself can be explained through the human mind considered from the perspective of eternity. Following this, one can say that 'the love of God for men, and the mind's intellectual love of God are identical' (Ibid. 214). And so we move from 'the love of God who cannot love us' to 'the love of a God who is himself joyful, who loves himself and who loves us with the same love by which we love him' (Deleuze 1992: 309). This is the sense of Spinoza's provocative claim: 'Man is a God to man' (Spinoza 1993a: 161).

Crucially, in this process Spinoza re-appropriates love, profaning what is sacralized by religion. For in the end everything which we feel towards God is an objectified version of what we feel towards human beings (Feuerbach 1989: 281). The love of God originates in the love of human beings. It is, in this sense, life itself that is divine. For this reason:

> Love to man must be no derivative love; it must be original. If human nature is the highest nature to man, then practically also the highest and first law must be the love of man to man. *Homo homini Deus est*: – this is the great practical principle.
>
> (Ibid. 271)

Christ

There is, then, no other way of loving God than loving one's neighbor, that is, humanity. But have we fallen back, in this movement, upon the universal faith? No, because in the process we have also moved from obedience to freedom, from imagination to reason. The crucial point in this movement is, according to Spinoza, Christ.

Three points are relevant in this respect. First, Spinoza's Christ is an exceptional person: 'a man who can by pure intuition comprehend ideas which are neither contained in nor deducible from the foundations of our natural knowledge, must necessarily possess a mind far superior to those of his fellow men' (Spinoza 1951a: 18). Second, whereas other prophets such as Moses presumably 'spoke with God face to face', as a person speaks with another, 'Christ communed with God mind to mind' (Ibid. 19). That is, God was revealed to Christ's mind immediately, through clear and distinct ideas, without the mediation of signs, 'without words or symbols' (Ibid. 64). And finally, Christ's message was addressed to the whole humanity, to be accommodated not only to the opinions of the Jews but to the opinions common for everybody, that is, 'to ideas universal and true' (Ibid. 64).

Spinoza perceives the religion of Christ as true religion because of its appeal to reason. Christ's teaching was not only based on signs (the Christian ideas of resurrection and the Passion belong to the first kind of knowledge) but was in accordance with common notions even though he did not need them (Deleuze 1992: 395 f6). As such, Spinoza's Christ is the singular name of the transition from imagination to reason. With him, imagination anticipates philosophical reasoning revealed by the natural light of reason common to all.

Christ 'humanizes' and 'secularizes' God, transforming the universal faith into an intellectual and moral relationship which is no longer mysterious or supra-natural (Balibar 2012: 34). In this passage from love of God to human love we also see an alternative to the traditional theology of incarnation: what matters here is no longer Christ's becoming God or God's becoming human; rather, the focal point of the 'true religion' is that it is only human relations that can 'save' them from their unhappiness (see Ibid.). The profane 'world' and the divine 'God' are not in opposition. Nature is God under another name, and our ignorance of God is 'co-extensive' with our ignorance of nature (Spinoza 1951a: 25). But, one could ask, does this mean that philosophy and theology are compatible?

Imagination and reason – antagonism, parallax, or perfection?

Insofar as there exists 'no connection' between faith and reason (Spinoza 1951a: 189), the relationship between imagination and reason seems to be a parallax like the case of 'two faces or a vase': not being able to see them both at once, one can choose to focus on philosophy, which reduces God to Nature, or on theology, which reduces Nature to God. Consequently, Spinoza's phrase 'God or Nature' links together two seemingly different propositions: God is Nature; Nature is God. In Spinoza immanence itself seems to become a transcendent principle while transcendence is understood in terms of immanence. The point here is not only that Spinoza is not an atheist; more interestingly, in the perspective of eternity (*sub specie aeternitatis*) the difference between immanence and transcendence is dissolved (Albertsen 1995: 161). Within the third kind of knowledge, the immanent transcendence of God and the transcendent immanence of Nature become indistinguishable; atheism and theism, non-religion and true religion, coincide.

However, the difference between imagination and reason is not only of kind but also of degree. There is, in addition, mediation between them. This mediation takes the form of 'perfection'. As we move from the first kind of knowledge towards the second and the third kinds, our knowledge and thus our joy increase; we are enlightened. The problem in this respect is that reason can lead us 'to love God, but cannot lead us to obey Him' for we cannot rationally conceive of God as a sovereign (Spinoza 1951a: 277). Thus reason must find a way to 'accommodate' revelation. After all, it is because the basis of faith is not reducible to reason that 'revelation was necessary' (Ibid. 195). Since obedience only requires the will of a ruler who sets commands, and not necessity or truth, and since we cannot know what God wills while knowing that everything exists and happens by God's power, 'we cannot, except through revelation, know' what God wants (Ibid. 276).

As such, accommodation is that which both unites and separates theology and philosophy. It is the only possible connection between philosophy and theology. Seen in this way, the relation between reason and faith is a disjunctive relation. Faith without reason leads to superstition for it reduces religion to illusion, but trying to demonstrate the value of revelation through reason only means bringing theology under reason's domination (Ibid.197). This is also to say that the separation of philosophy and theology from each other is as necessary as accommodation. Neither should be put in the service of the other; each 'should keep her unopposed dominion' (Ibid.198). Insofar as philosophy and theology have different methods and goals, they are two distinct domains. There is thus no necessary relation, and thus no necessary conflict, between them.

Yet, this differentiation does not bring with it full reconciliation. First, whereas theology cannot access reason, that is, utter claims about truth and nature, philosophy can investigate truths about morality and God as well as nature, which shreds the space of theology and puts it in an unequal position in relation to philosophy, pointing out that the relationship between philosophy and theology, after all, is not symmetrical (James 2012: 216). But second, two very different understandings of salvation are juxtaposed here. On the one hand, Spinoza contends that, since reason cannot perceive that obedience is the path of salvation or blessedness, theology is the sole authority regarding the question of salvation (Spinoza 1951a: 198, 276). But on the other hand, 'true salvation and blessedness' consist in the assent of the soul, in understanding (Ibid. 113; 1993a: 214). True salvation is achieved through the third kind of knowledge. And most importantly, salvation can be attained in the actual world: the path to the true contentment of the mind is admittedly very hard and is seldom found: 'it can yet be discovered' (Spinoza 1993a: 219). In a sense, therefore, Spinoza demonstrates that there is another, profaned path to salvation which philosophy alone can establish, and this other path turns the theological view of philosophy, the view that philosophy cannot contribute to true salvation, on its head (James 2012: 222).

> While the surface argument of the *Treatise* promises to liberate theologians from philosophical interference, and guarantees them an independent, though limited, domain of inquiry, its underlying implications threaten their existence. Theology and philosophy are not after all independent, and philosophy has the potential to engulf its weaker partner.
> (Ibid. 229)

In a certain sense, therefore, Spinoza's philosophy is antagonistic towards religion. In this sense one can call Spinoza 'atheist' (Deleuze and Guattari 1994: 92). Profanation necessarily obliterates theology by obliterating the distinction between theology and philosophy. If one can love one's neighbor for rational reasons, for reasons other than obeying divine commands, if, in other words, 'truth' (philosophy) and obedience (religion) can be harmonized 'under the dictates of reason', then philosophy itself can become a way of life. The apex of reason is, to recall, blessedness, a new relationship to 'God' and thus a new understanding of being with others through 'God'. Consequently, one could say, philosophy not only tends but also intends to take the place of religion by re-appropriating its terrain. In order to step into the place hitherto occupied by religion, to be able to 'replace religion', philosophy, as philosophy, seeks to 'become religion' (Feuerbach 1972: 148). No wonder, therefore, that theology has always treated Spinoza as an enemy rather than adversary, while Spinoza's followers have always treated theology and religion with suspicion.

In short, then, seen as a disjunctive relation, reason and faith are, first, different from and irreducible to one another; second, they can co-exist in 'harmony' (love of God), each in its own dominion (Spinoza 1951a: 198); third, they can conflict with one another (as is the case with superstition versus reason). And finally, each is necessary. It is significant in this framework that the polarization between reason and imagination, between freedom and (political–theological) authority, is not *only* an antagonism. After all, 'reason ... is always on the side of peace' (Ibid. 276). It is possible that reason can establish peace with religion to the extent that it teaches the same principles as natural reason, to the extent that religion is 'true religion'. At any rate, peace is possible because imagination and reason signify, despite separation, different levels of knowledge. Thus, the relation between them is potentially non-antagonistic; a relation of perfection or enlightenment.

Accommodation versus appropriation

While Spinoza preserves the place of faith in the 'true religion', he also 'profanes' religion, redefining both love and God in immanent terms, as profane relations. Since the origin of the sacred is the profane, there is always a possibility for profanation, a potential 'atheism to be extracted from a religion' (Deleuze and Guattari 1994: 92). Consider Spinoza's treatment of religious categories such as the soul, immortality, salvation, and blessedness. Against the postulates of conventional theology Spinoza asserts that the soul, like the body, has extensive parts such as affections and memory. In this sense the soul only exists while the body exists. However, the soul in Spinoza is also an 'idea' that expresses the body's essence. In this sense the soul is inevitably eternal and we do not need any revelation in order to know the ways in which it survives. 'To feel and experience that we are eternal, it is enough to enter into the third kind of knowledge, that is, to form the idea of ourselves as it is in God' (Deleuze 1992: 314). In this way, as Spinoza profanes the idea of salvation while preserving its affirmative core, 'blessedness' becomes an outcome of the intellectual love of God:

> And this love or blessedness is called in the Scripture 'glory' – not without reason. For whether this love has reference to God or the mind, it can rightly be called contentment of mind, which in turn cannot be distinguished from glory.
>
> (Spinoza 1993a: 214)

What religion calls 'glory' is in fact something natural, the 'contentment of mind' which is grounded in (intellectual) love (of God). Effectively, 'glory' can no longer be considered to be the property of a sovereign God, and becomes a common, universal virtue that is immanent. Only when it is captured by religion and institutionalized as a 'sacred' property of religion, separated from the domain of the commons, does 'glory' turn into an apparatus of regulation and domination. Seen in this prism, the intellectual love of God is an idea that seeks to untie glory from the domain of religion and refer it back to immanent life. The problem it articulates is how to think 'contentment' as an immanent category outside the religious apparatus of glory (see Agamben 2011a: 249).

In reality the human being is 'the Sabbatical animal par excellence' (Ibid. 246). Human life does not have a predetermined purpose; it is the very absence of aim that makes it possible for human beings to dedicate themselves to praxis, to work. As such, Sabbath, inoperativity, is 'a sui generis "praxis" that consists in rendering all specific powers of acting or doing inoperative' (Ibid. 251). It is this inoperativity which the governmental machine has separated from life and sacralized in the concept of 'glory' (Ibid. 249). But although it has captured inoperativity from within the domain of the profane, religion creates the illusion that inoperativity is a result of an economy that will only end at the end. Thus, it promises that, in paradise, in the eternal Sabbath, there will be no operativity, no 'work' any more. The ultimate promise of the governmental machine, in other words, is inoperativity, glory. Religion promises to give back to life what it has taken from it, but only in the end, when the economy is dissolved.

In this perspective religious appropriation/alienation designates not merely an external force (juxtaposed to the profane) but a strategic field of formation in which religion seeks to govern the profane itself. Since religion is an apparatus of capture, its power is always in relation with the profane, the world of the commons. Therefore religion can always, in principle, appropriate, or 'capture' any idea, any force from this domain. Hence the two senses of religion: excluding the profane and appropriating it. Thought of in this framework, profanation lies not necessarily in crossing a line, say, by denying religion and its truths, but in folding, in profaning it in the way the 'atheist' Spinoza distilled philosophical concepts from religious images (Deleuze and Guattari 1994: 92).

Profaning Paul

Badiou's Paul, 'a poet-thinker of the event' (Badiou 2003: 2), is a contemporary case for the philosophical re-appropriation of religious images. Badiou reads Paul as the founder of universalism. In Paul's perspective, there has been a singular event (the crucifixion), which is irreducible to social conditions of the Roman Empire or to any general law. Truth consists in naming this event and remaining faithful to it. Consequently, for Paul, truth is subjective; there is no law for it. And since truth is a subjective process rather than a revelation, fidelity to it is essential. Fidelity in Paul is contextualized in relation to 'faith', 'love', and 'hope' (Ibid. 15). The core of faith, of conviction, is a declaration (Ibid. 88). It is its declaration of a truth that constitutes the subject as a subject. But in order to turn faith into a militant endeavor, to give it a consistency and discipline, love, too, is necessary. Love is, precisely, the post-evental fidelity to the declaration, which also underwrites its own law (Ibid. 89). Finally, hope is an effect, an outcome of the ordeal of remaining faithful to the event and confronting the practical struggle which it demands (Ibid. 95).

> The pure event is reducible to this: Jesus died on the cross and resurrected. This event is 'grace' (*kharis*). Thus, it is neither a bequest, nor a tradition, nor a teaching. It is supernumerary relative to all this and presents itself as pure givenness.
>
> (Ibid. 63)

As such, evental grace is opposed to the law. In relation to the event, we are 'no longer under the rule of law, but of grace' (Ibid. 75). While the law always signifies a particularity in the sense that it addresses only those who acknowledge and obey its commands, Paul's single 'God', the 'mono' in his monotheism, is 'for all', and 'without exception' (Ibid. 76). There is an essential link between the event and universality. The universal is 'the only correlate' of a single God that assigns no difference among the subjects it addresses. Christ's resurrection can only mean the resurrection of all.

It is in this sense that Paul is the founder of universality. But still, and herein we approach the crux of the matter, Paul is the 'anti-philosopher' of universality (Ibid. 27, 108). The problem is not that the pure event he refers to, the resurrection, is a fiction, that he invokes a 'mere fable', a 'mythological assertion', in the place of truth (Ibid. 6). The problem is that in Paul the event remains enclosed within the order of the fable, which bars the emergence of a philosophical understanding of subjectivity as a real truth procedure (Ibid. 108). In our terminology, the Pauline event is inscribed within the domain of the first kind of knowledge. Following this, the difference between Paul and Badiou is the difference between theology and philosophy. 'For Paul, the truth event repudiates philosophical Truth, while for us the fictitious dimension of this event repudiates its pretention to real truth' (Ibid.). Imagination versus reason.

This is why Badiou is keen to re-appropriate the language of grace for philosophical discourse, to extract a profane conception of grace from religious mythology, to 'tear the lexicon of grace and encounter away from its religious confinement' (Ibid. 66). 'Everything hinges', in this procedure, on the notion of immortality: on the possibility of changing the course of time by following a universal truth, thereby overcoming the limitations of one's biological life (Ibid. 66). The aim of philosophy, after all, is to make it possible to live 'like immortals', fighting the idea of finitude through the affirmation of infinity (Badiou 2009b: 118).

If we can think of immortality in materialist terms, we have 'no need for an All-Powerful' (Badiou 2003: 66). If God is the 'one' which is 'for all', it is synonymous with universality (see Ibid. 76). Along the same lines, in a profaned horizon, faith becomes conviction; love, fidelity; hope, confidence. 'Salvation' can be understood in terms of the evental operation (of resurrection), a truth process (Ibid. 84). And 'evil' can be re-articulated as the reduction of truth to a simulacrum or the betrayal of the fidelity demanded by a truth procedure (see Badiou 2001: 78–80). Grace itself, the key concept Badiou seeks to re-appropriate from Paul, becomes in this context a condition in which the subject is 'seized by what happens to it' (Badiou 2003: 66). What makes the subject of the event 'immortal' is, precisely, its absolute receptivity, enthusiasm for the event: its willingness to be formed by the moment, its intoxication, which seizes it, as much as its will to seize the moment.

In this way Badiou's re-appropriation of the religious-transcendental lexicon opens up the religious imagination to reason. To use Spinoza's language, instead of turning his back to religion, Badiou 'perfects' its imaginary truths, 'accommodating' them in his own philosophical discourse. In the same movement, the promisory aspect of religion (salvation) is re-inscribed in the democratic-communist tradition.

But we must recall that the relation of appropriation/accommodation runs both ways. Just as philosophy could lead to profanation, to re-appropriation of the commons from the domain of the sacred, what is common is always prone to being appropriated or captured by religion. Such appropriation is what lies in the origin of religion: love, contentment, morality, the idea of justice, and so on, are common to all humanity but are appropriated by religion, the forgetting of which, in turn, defines religious alienation à la Feuerbach and Marx.

Appropriation and secularization

So, profanation is not the only way the sacred is re-appropriated. One can also 'secularize' the sacred. The difference between profanation and secularization is essential in this respect:

> Secularization is a form of repression. It leaves intact the forces it deals with by simply moving them from one place to another. Thus the political secularization of theological concepts (the transcendence of God as a paradigm of sovereign power) does nothing but displace the heavenly monarchy onto an earthly monarchy, leaving its power intact. Profanation, however, neutralizes what it profanes. Once profaned, that which was unavailable and separate loses its aura and is returned to use. Both are political operations: the first guarantees the exercise of power by carrying it back to a sacred model; the second deactivates the apparatuses of power and returns to common use the spaces that power had seized.
> (Agamben 2007: 77)

Schmitt's political theology is paradigmatic regarding secularization for it regards modern political concepts as secularized derivatives of theological concepts (1985: 36). Thus the 'exception' in political theory is analogous to the 'miracle' in theology (Ibid.). Likewise, the sovereign decision is comparable to God's creation *ex nihilio*. Such secularization is necessary because modernity, for Schmitt, unfolds in the direction of positivism. The modern age is 'the age of neutralizations and depoliticizations' (Schmitt 2007: 80). Today, politics is reduced to a matter of economic management, to interest negotiation, and the state has turned into what Weber's dystopian sociology envisioned: 'a huge industrial plant' (Schmitt 1985: 65).

Vis-à-vis this pragmatic and de-politicizing modernity, and its disenchanting consequences, secularized theological concepts can re-introduce the transcendent, magical core of politics: the political. Central in this re-enchantment is Schmitt's concept of sovereignty, which is based on a quasi-transcendental decision on exception (Ibid. 5). But the secularized quasi-transcendent concepts do not need to be identical to the theological concepts from which they are driven. Exception is not necessarily the same as miracle. Rather, secularization marks the concepts displaced from the religious to the political domain with an excess, with the signature of the divine, referring them back to religion (see Agamben 2011b: 4). In this sense secularization is ultimately a religious category.

To be sure, such endorsement of theology for political reasons can take place in different ways and for different purposes. In Schmitt, the state of exception serves to keep disorder (civil war, revolt, revolution) at bay. As such, political theology is a katechontic device that delays the 'apocalypse'. We could contrast Schmitt's take on the apocalypse, which legitimizes state power in general and counterrevolution specifically, with Taubes's revolutionary eschatology, which seeks a total de-legitimization of power. If the 'katechon' signifies the justification of power with reference to the divine, the 'eschaton' stands for the endorsement of the divine with a view to resisting power.

For Taubes, the starting point of eschatological apocalypticism is the concept of alienation in the Gnostic sense. In the existing world, injustice is abundant, and both man and God are alienated (2009: 26). Gnosticism claims that since the existing world is an alienated world, to which God is indifferent, and since alienation cannot be the result of a true god, there must be another power behind this world, a power of revision: the demiurge, which signifies the 'perversion of the Divine' (Jonas 1958: 327). This world, the work of the demiurge, is characterized solely by manifestations of power and dominance relations. For the demiurge has only retained from the true God the power to act, but to act blindly, without knowledge or compassion:

> The world, then, is the product, and even the embodiment, of the negative of *knowledge*. What it reveals is unenlightened and therefore malignant force, proceeding from the spirit of self-assertive power, from the will to rule and coerce. The mindlessness of this will is the spirit of the world, which bears no relation to understanding and love. The laws of the universe are the laws of this rule, and not of divine wisdom. *Power* thus becomes the chief aspect of the cosmos, and its inner essence is ignorance ...
> (Jonas 1958: 327–28)

Beyond *this* world, there is *that* other world, the world to come, which promises freedom (Taubes 2009: 27). But the difference between *this* and *that* is not a blueprint for nihilistic escapism; rather, it implies, according to Taubes, a transvaluation in the Nietzschean sense, questioning the value of (existing) values with a view to creating new values. And corresponding to the two sets of values, there are two Gods: the God of creation, of the existing world, and the God of redemption (Ibid. 29). The latter will come by annihilating the existing world. This God to come, who is '*new* to the world', is also a promise, a 'turning point': he 'will annihilate the world and then appear in his might' (Ibid. 10). Since freedom from what exists is its goal, the revolutionary event involves looking beyond *this* world. It brackets the actual order and existing beliefs, which are the foundations of the actual world. What is significant is that, in this tradition, spanning from the Gnostic theology to the Exodus to Maccabean revolt, the Zealots and Thomas Müntzer, the dialectic between *this* (natural) and *that* (supernatural) world interlocks not in the heart of the individual, as a personalized faith, but as two different but interrelated systems, two 'kingdoms'. The 'moment when "this" world touches "that" world ... is the *kairos*' (Ibid. 68).

So what we have in Taubes is a transcendent/theological philosophy which operates with concepts such as eternity, the God of redemption, and so on. But what is noteworthy is its structure, its understanding of revolution as a relation to the virtual infinity, and of *kairos* as 'the mystery of the universe' (Ibid. 68). In Schmitt, the same structure is endorsed from the point of view of power. Schmitt, the 'apocalyptician of counterrevolution' (Taubes, quoted in Ratmoko 2009: xvi), puts *kairos* in the service of power, seeking a theological legitimation of the political. Thus, while the apocalyptic world view seeks redemption in the 'end' of the world, Schmitt advocates *translatio imperii*, that is, the evolution of the Roman Empire into the Holy Roman Empire and the Third Reich. However, according to the apocalyptic tradition, this worldly power cannot become 'holy', for the holy is, precisely, the 'measure' of the God to come (Taubes 2009: 194).

In this radical sense, the idea of messianic apocalypse cannot be really assimilated by sovereignty. Therefore, one could turn Schmitt's logic against himself and claim that his decisionism is not genuinely political: while it sublimates order as an absolute value, the state of exception ultimately seeks to save the condition of normality, that is, to avoid a true exception, a radical transformation of the actual social structure (Žižek 2002a: 108). This is why the state of exception is different from chaos or anarchy and is characterized by an order, even if that order is not a juridical order (Agamben 2003: 32).

Secularization and economic theology

The birthmark of political theology is the link between monotheism and monarchy, between God and the king. Thus, as already mentioned in the previous chapter, in both divine and earthly monarchies it is commonly assumed that one absent sovereign 'reigns but does not govern' (Peterson 2011: 71). Erik Peterson emphasizes that 'monotheism as a political problem' has its origin in this link, in the amalgamation of the monotheistic Jewish God with the monarchical principle of pagan Greek philosophy. Along the same lines, political theology is possible only on the condition of overcoming Judaism (people who have a monotheistic God but have 'no king') and paganism (people who 'have only Caesar'), and this is precisely what the Trinitarian dogma enabled for Christianity (Ibid. 150). However, the Trinitarian dogma had a paradoxical effect on political theology:

> the doctrine of the divine Monarchy was bound to founder on the Trinitarian dogma, and the interpretation of the Pax Augusta on Christian eschatology. In this way, not only was monotheism as a political problem resolved and the Christian faith liberated from bondage to the Roman Empire, but a fundamental break was made with every political theology that misuses the Christian proclamation for the justification of a political situation. Only on the basis of Judaism and paganism can such a thing as a 'political theology' exist. The Christian proclamation of the triune God stands beyond Judaism and paganism, even though the mystery of the Trinity exists only in the Godhead itself, and not in Creation. So, too, the peace that the Christian seeks is won by no emperor, but is solely a gift of him who 'is higher than all understanding'.
> (Peterson 2011: 104–5)

But the impossibility of political theology does not mean for Peterson the impossibility of politics as such. Christian politics is still possible vis-à-vis Judaism and paganism (Ibid. 150). But now its central assumption must be that the fulfillment of the eschatological promise, the second coming, is delayed. At this point Peterson seeks support in Augustine's theology of deferral which resists the identification of the divine with an earthly power, denying any necessary overlap between the city of God and the earthly city (Ibid. 103–4). The specific reason for the deferral is noteworthy, namely the persistence of Judaism, the Jewish people's rejection of Jesus: 'So long as they remain obdurate, the return of the Lord and the coming of the Kingdom will also be delayed' (Ibid. 38).

And so long as the Kingdom is delayed, the Church must exist. However, the Church can only exist with an 'ambiguity': it will not be the messianic Kingdom but on the other hand 'something of the Kingdom' will cling to it (Ibid. 38). Herein, through this ambiguity, we get a glimpse of what Peterson means by 'political action', the kind of action required for a truly Christian politics while the second coming is deferred. True politics, for Peterson, is the public practice of the Church which links the earthly city to the heavenly 'city of the angels and saints' (Ibid. 107):

the Church is more than just a human religious society because the angels and the saints in heaven also belong to it. Seen from this perspective ... the Church's practice is never a merely human affair: no, the angels, like the entire cosmos, take part in it. To the Church's singing corresponds heavenly singing, and, the church's inner life is also organized like the participation in the heavenly singing. The angels demonstrate that the Church's worship is public worship offered to God, and through them the Church's worship also acquires a necessary relation to the political sphere, because the angels possess a relationship to the religio-political world in heaven.

(Peterson 2011: 142).

The angels are linked with the Church in the sense that they awaken mystical life in it, which finds its fulfillment when the choirs of angels and humans join together in glorifying God. 'Therefore', continues Peterson, 'we sing in the *Te Deum*':

We praise you O God, we confess you as Lord,
You, the eternal Father, the whole world worships,
To you Cherubim and Seraphim cry out unceasingly,
Holy, holy, holy, Lord God of Hosts,
Heaven and earth are full of the majesty of your glory.

(Ibid.)

A lot is happening here: first and foremost, while Peterson negates the possibility of political theology, he affirms the religio-political character governmentality of the church, through a strategic link between angels and the Church (see Agamben 2011a: 145). The originary political relationship which the Church practises is ceremonial in character: the public worship which is enabled by the angels' participation. Then, if politics is basically an angelological practice, Christian worship can be political only to the extent that it brings singing, a 'song of praise' that glorifies God, into worship; the song of praise, glory, is precisely the political aspect of the angels (Ibid. 147).

Crucially, angels have a dual function in that they can be either 'assisting' (contemplating) or 'administering' (executing) angels. In the first case, the blessedness of the angels consists in their ability to see and glorify God; in the second, in their ability to 'govern' world affairs (Ibid. 149). Following this distinction, the paradigm of *oikonomia* operates through a parallel between the celestial hierarchy of angels and the worldly bureaucracy. Accordingly, the divine power descends from the Trinitarian God through angels to earthly instances, which both links the spiritual and secular power together and sacralizes actual power relations (Ibid. 153). In this sense governmentality has its origin in angelology.

[T]he central mystery of politics is not sovereignty, but government; it is not God, but the angel; it is not the king, but the ministry; it is not the law, but the police – that is to say, the governmental machine that they form and support.

(Ibid. 276)

So, what happens to angel-bureaucrats after the Judgment Day? Will they remain and continue to 'govern'? The mainstream Trinitarian answer to this question is: since all angelic administration is organized to conduct humanity to its end, once the end has come, government must end. Then the main function of the angels will be contemplation, that is, they will become inoperative, only singing hymns to glorify God:

> The doctrine of Glory as the final end of man and as the figure of the divine that outlives the government of the world, is the answer that theologians give to the problem of the end of the economy. The angelic ministers survive the universal judgment only as a hymnological hierarchy, as contemplation and praise of the glory of the divine.
>
> (Agamben 2011a: 162)

And so, with Schmitt and Peterson's two different views on the katechon, we get two different takes on power: the sovereign decision on the one hand and the liturgical/governmental action on the other. In Schmitt's perspective the political is grounded in political theology and is identified with an earthly power, the Christian empire, acting as katechon; in Peterson's, liturgy is what enables the anticipation of the end, of the eschatological glory, without the intervention of secular political powers for what acts as katechon is not a political power but the Jews' rejection of Christianity (Ibid. 16).

What is common in both registers is the logic of exception/miracle. But while the sovereign exception produces *homo sacer*, the main production of the angelic-governmental miracle is glory. While the first is biopolitical in its origin, the latter generates a society of spectacle.

Excursus II
The Devils, possession, and truth-telling

Ken Russell's film *The Devils* (1971) focuses on a crisis situation in seventeenth-century Loudun that turned the whole town into a 'theater' (Certeau 1996: 199). It is a divisive film. To some, it is Ken Russell's masterpiece. In an interview included with the DVD version of the film, Russell claims that *The Devils* is his 'most, [indeed] only political film'. Many others, though, have condemned the film for being shockingly pornographic and satanic, and it was censored in the United Kingdom and the United States for many years.

The film is based on Aldous Huxley's documentary novel *The Devils of Loudun* (1952) and John Whiting's play *The Devils* (1965). It deals with political, religious, and sexual corruption around two related themes, possession and exorcism, and problematizes the relationship between love and politics. It is set in Loudun, a Protestant stronghold in Louis XIII's France, in the year 1634, when feudal law is on the verge of losing its power.

It opens with a regal spectacle. As the camera focuses on a seventeenth-century baroque play, *The Birth of Venus*, we realize that the king, Louis XIII, is himself acting in it. This scene, a play within the play, immediately introduces us to an elementary aspect of power: its theatricality. Certainly the sense of the world as theater had existed before, but in seventeenth-century Europe that sense was significantly intense. Thus action in the public sphere and role-playing were seen to be analogous activities (Schmitt 2009: 40–41). Sovereignty, too, was on stage. Thus this initial scene must be read as a reference to the significance of the spectacle for the events to come.

As the audience is cheering and exclaiming we notice Cardinal Richelieu among the crowd. He is bored, yawning. We instantly sense a tension between the king and the cardinal, the state and the church. 'A most original conception, Your Majesty, the birth of Venus', Richelieu says to Louis XIII. In reality, however, he is more interested in assisting the king in the birth of a new France, 'where church and state are one'. 'Amen', says the king to this, sarcastically. At this moment, the camera focuses on the faces of the two men, and the title of the film appears, coinciding with their faces. 'And may the Protestant be driven from the land'. Hereby the dominant ideology of the time is revealed: the unification of the state and the church – nation-building – which means the end of the autonomy of (self-governing) cities.

The second scene familiarizes us with Loudun as a plague-stricken city and introduces the protagonist: Urbain Grandier – a charismatic priest, a clever politician, and a handsome lover. Self-indulgent and vain, he is also well-regarded and well-liked among the people of Loudun. We meet him in the middle of a funeral speech he is giving for the plague's latest victim: George de Sainte Marthe, the governor of Loudun. Grandier is praising the governor for having prevailed upon all faiths to keep the peace, saving Loudun from self-destruction: 'Religious wars are over. Catholic no longer fights with Protestant. We have survived.' The speech concludes:

> People of Loudun, as often as you see our city walls, standing, still proud and erect, no matter what your faith, then surely you must feel a need to build a temple in your hearts in remembrance of he who preserved them for you.

During the following funeral procession, we enter the convent, where the nuns are trying to catch a glimpse of the handsome Grandier from a small window: 'Oh, hurry up, it's my turn now'. 'Is he as handsome as they say?' Sister Jeanne, a hunchback, reprimands them: 'Why have you left your devotions? Satan is ever-ready to seduce us with sensual delights'. But shortly after, we realize that she, too, is obsessed with Grandier.

Love, love of God, and manhunt

In the next scene, we see Grandier in bed with a young woman – Philippe, the daughter of Trincant, who is the magistrate of Loudun. When Trincant discovers his daughter's affair, he forces Grandier into a duel, one that Trincant cannot win. Ridiculed and resentful, Trincant shouts to Grandier: 'I will see you in hell!' Grandier is not perceptive enough, though, to foresee the hell being prepared for him. He soon meets another young woman, Madeleine, and gradually the two fall in love; later, he secretly marries her. Hereby the film articulates another significant set of questions: What is the relationship between love of God and love of a human? And can a man reach God through the love of a woman?

When Grandier is asked whether a priest can marry, he answers that nowhere in the New Testament is there an injunction against marriage. Paul had said that while marriage is a good thing, remaining chaste is better. But Grandier says he is 'content merely to do a good thing and leave the best to those that can face it'. Christ, he notes, never prevented his apostles from marriage. If they gave up their marriages to follow him, it was 'out of convenience, not obligation'. There can be no law of God compelling celibacy, Grandier says, and quotes the book of Genesis: 'It is not good for man to be alone'. This scene is significant not only in terms of its content, as it introduces love as a central politico-religious theme, but also in focusing our attention on the process of truth-telling rather than on truth itself. Here Grandier starts to appear as a courageous person who dares to speak out (his) truth even though it does not fit into the structure of dominant opinion. Along the same lines, he demonstrates courage relative to the religious and political authorities when, early in the film, as state authorities arrive with orders to demolish the city walls, Grandier summons the town's soldiers, successfully forcing the Baron de Laubardemont, commissioner for the demolition of the fortifications, to back down. The crowd cheers him. 'Well done, Father', 'God bless you, Father'.

At this point, the camera switches to a conversation between Richelieu and Louis XIII. The cardinal is explaining to the king that fortifications provide opportunities for Protestant uprisings: 'It is a simple matter to understand, Your Majesty. The self-government of the small, provincial towns of France must cease. The first step is to pull down all kinds of fortifications.' Louis XIII, however, does not seem to be paying attention to the cardinal. Instead, he is enjoying 'hunting', shooting real men dressed up like birds. This scene is a reference to a central theme in the film: sovereignty. For despite its theatricality, 'hunting' here is not merely an allegory; King Louis really shoots and kills, although the hunt is 'acted' out. In the fifteenth century, during the time of King Louis XI, the manhunt had become a royal sport in France. It consisted of the pursuit of a convict who was released on the grounds wearing the skin of a newly killed animal (see Chamayou 2012: 1). As such, the manhunt reveals the crux of sovereignty, the reduction of man to *homo sacer*, to bare life, which is excluded from both the sphere of the profane and the religious at once (Agamben 1998: 82). Bare life belongs to the domain of (bio)politics; that is, it can be killed but not sacrificed (Ibid. 111–15). In other words, *homo sacer* and the sovereign are two symmetrical figures. Subjects are subjected to the sovereign's will because of his capacity to kill. The sovereign's power consists in capturing subjects, abandoning them from the domain of the human, which presupposes the manhunt (Chamayou 2012: 4).

Against this background, a four-fold coincidence determines the course of the events to come. First, Grandier decides to go to the king to get reassurance from him that he will not touch Loudun's city walls, which results in Grandier's absence from Loudun. Second, it turns out that Sister Jeanne's convent needs a new confessor. She asks Grandier, but, to her disappointment, he declines the offer and instead sends another priest, Father Mignon. This disappointment, which is followed by gossip about Grandier's secret marriage, drives Sister Jeanne to insanity. She informs Father Mignon of Grandier's secret marriage and makes accusations of witchcraft against him: 'He plies me with caresses, lustful, obscene. He enters my bed at night and takes from me that which is consecrated to my divine bridegroom, Jesus Christ'. When Father Mignon asks, 'And what form does this incubus take?', she leans towards him, laughing: 'Cock!' She adds: 'Grandier'. 'What?' 'Grandier,' she repeats. 'Are you aware, my dear, of the seriousness of what you are saying?' 'Yes, help me, Father,' she replies. Third, Cardinal Richelieu knows that Grandier, who has had a progressive upbringing as a Jesuit priest, is willful and bold: 'If he were allowed to become governor of Loudun, he would defend Catholic and Protestant alike'. As long as Loudun stands, the state and the church cannot gain control of the southwestern part of France: hence the fortifications of Loudun must be destroyed. Fourth, Father Mignon tells Laubardemont about Grandier's secret marriage as well as about Sister Jeanne's claims of possession. Laubardemont is already busy trying, together with the cardinal, to devise a scheme to remove Grandier from local power; therefore he is very interested in the claim that Grandier has bewitched the convent and has had commerce with the devil. Father Mignon tells him: 'But of course I can prove nothing. This Mother Superior may be little more than a hysterical nun'. Laubardemont, however, has decided: 'It must be substantiated, of course. But if it is a genuine case of possession by devils and if Grandier himself was proved to be involved, yes, I think it bears investigation'. Then another form of hunt is introduced: 'We need a professional witch hunter. We must send for Father Barre'.

In short, then, the state and the church together seek a method to undermine Loudun's resistance and discover in this process a peculiar psychological phenomenon: possession. With Grandier conveniently away from Loudun, Laubardemont and Father Mignon decide to find evidence against him. And the witch hunter, Father Barre, arrives in Loudun to do just this.

Pastoral hunt

Let us, at this point, turn to the link between sovereignty, manhunt and religion. Chamayou (2012: 11–18) has developed an interesting but also problematic reading of the Bible. His starting point is that, in the biblical tradition, sovereignty is directly related to the manhunt. Thus, the book of Genesis tells the story of Nimrod, the founder of Babel and the first king, who also 'was a mighty hunter before the Lord' (quoted in Ibid. 11). Nimrod's authority is grounded in capturing and bringing his subjects together by force. Aristotle had conceived of manhunt as an art, 'art of acquiring slaves' (quoted in Ibid. 5). But since, for Aristotle, the slave was by definition excluded from political life, he viewed manhunt not as a political art but as an activity circumscribed by the domain of the *oikos*, by the despotic economy (Aristotle 1995: 20). In this sense, the Bible mobilizes the 'economic' power of the Aristotelian despot under the sign of political theology. Chamayou, however, insists that a very different kind of power is juxtaposed to this form of despotic domination in the Bible in the form of Abraham, as the good shepherd, who 'glories only in his obedience to the Lord and his devotion to his flock' (Ibid. 14). While the sovereign is defined by 'hunting' and capturing, the shepherd's defining character is pastoral 'love', and Christianity uses this opposition, according to Chamayou, 'to distinguish between the spiritual and the temporal modalities of governing humans':

> The Gospels say: 'As he walked by the Sea of Galilee, he saw two brothers ... casting a net into the sea; for they were fishermen. And he said unto them: "Follow me, and I will make you fishers of men". Immediately they left their nets and followed him.' Christian proselytizing finds here one of its great metaphors: fishing for men. To gather its faithful, Christianity does not hunt; it fishes.
>
> (Chamayou 2012: 18)

'Hunting', then, pertains to the earthly power of the sovereign; 'fishing' to the spiritual power of the church. But fishing can be a violent endeavor. More importantly, opposing Christian pastoralism or governmentality to sovereign power is untenable. As discussed before, sovereignty and governmentality, hunting and fishing, together form a single bipolar machine and the two kinds of power cannot be fully separated even though they do not coincide. So, it is not violence as such that separates the king and the shepherd. Sovereignty, 'nomos', is connected with the shepherd, 'nomeus' (Foucault 2002: 304). Thus Chamayou needs a third category to deal with this impasse: 'pastoral hunting'. In order to protect the flock, the shepherd must be able to prevent the wolves from attacking and be able to discipline the rams (who can harm the ewes), as well as have power over the sheep in general (Chamayou 2012: 20). In a sense, therefore, 'pastoral hunting' is a form of hunting that seeks to exclude both external and internal potential danger, both the wolf and the ram. Just as the wolf must be kept at bay, a male sheep that has become a threat must also be kept away from the flock. As Chamayou notes:

> To this imagery correspond techniques for identifying, excluding, and eliminating dangerous elements, as well as a theory of the diseased sheep and the corresponding practices of investigation, excommunication, and burning at the stake. The great task of the Inquisition consisted in identifying heretical individuals. This involved unprecedented activities of surveillance and control, a whole archival apparatus. This was again the case, at the threshold of modernity, with the great witch hunts.
>
> (Ibid. 21)

This is what happens to Grandier. He is the heretic ram that must be excommunicated and kept away from the church. As the protection of the shepherd is withdrawn, Grandier is abandoned not only by the church but by the entire political community, which allows the church's monopoly of truth to be protected. But, in this process, it also becomes impossible to distinguish between the 'hunter' and the 'shepherd'. One of the primordial religious scenes is, after all, hunting: God's angels hunting the devil. The church has thus always been obsessed with the figure of the angel throughout its process of centralization. Indeed, the exception is what 'confers on the angels a special power of government' (Agamben 2011a: 268). In the film the angelic role is carried out by Father Barre, the witch hunter. Grandier, in turn, is the one who exposes the mysterious coincidence of the hunter and the shepherd, making the distinction problematic. He achieves this as a mystic.

Possession and mysticism

It is well known that Europe at the end of the sixteenth and the beginning of the seventeenth centuries witnessed a significant upsurge in possessions, which made manifest the gap between the increasingly undermined certainties of a religious culture and the coming Enlightenment (Certeau 1996: 2). Possession can be understood as one part of a tripartite structure that consists of the sorcerer, the judges, and the possessed. Within this structure, the possessed are perceived as victims, the sorcerer as guilty. Since possession was an urban phenomenon, and often occurred in convents, exorcisms often took the form of theatrical events, although one in which the show required an execution (Ibid. 4–5). In the process, the exception became normalized, the horror was turned into a spectacle, and the spectacle itself became a sermon (Ibid. 3). Consequently, the discourse of exorcism no longer constituted merely an 'exceptional' (real or imagined) instance of governmentality but had become a dispositif, a technique of governance that imposed a particular conduct, a model of truth and normality on sociality. In most cases of possession, there has been a connection between the possessed and religious communities, therefore, in seventeenth-century France the most 'devout' religious groups and the cases of possession tended to appear in the same places (Ibid.). In other words, possession by the Holy Spirit (mysticism) and possession by the devil were 'symmetrical' phenomena. As de Certeau notes,

> Both 'possessions' present an analogous structure. In the modality of contrary solutions, they respond to a problem of meaning, but stated in terms of the formidable and constraining alternative – God or the Devil – that isolates the quest for the absolute from social mediations.
>
> (Ibid.)

As such, possession both requires and problematizes the distinction between the divine and the profane. In its framework, God and devil are bound together; there is no God without the figure of the devil, no rule without the exception, in spite of the apparently antagonistic relation between them. In this sense the dyadic structure of possession demonstrates, in spite of the absence of immediate resemblance, a radical ambivalence: on the one hand mysticism, possession by the love of God; on the other sorcery, possession by the devil. Taken together, the two forms of possession express a close but troubled alliance, a non-resolving, un-dialectical duality. In this context mysticism signifies an unmediated love of God. The mystic believes that God can be known directly in a transfiguring union of the soul with the divine (see Huxley 2005: 321). Significantly, this desire for oneness, for direct union with God, is as erotic as the 'erotomania' of the possessed nuns of Loudun (see Certeau

1996: 135). If intercourse with the devil is the classic case of possession, mysticism is, so to speak, intercourse with God. What is crucial in this respect is that the mystic claims direct possession by God and seeks to go to God directly, without mediation. Therefore mysticism has always been a problem for the church. Thus, in some cases, the church has labeled mysticism as 'heresy'. In others, it considered mysticism to be, so to speak, on the same side, on the way to the same God. But there is one crucial aspect that is as unacceptable to the church as it is indispensable to mysticism: the refusal of *oikonomia*. Since it refuses mediation, mysticism excludes economic theology. In this sense, mysticism is nothing but a religious alternative to the religious economy. This is the point at which the church rejects the mystic, claiming that he is possessed by the devil.

This is also to say that God and the devil are undecidable categories. What is interesting, therefore, is how the church refines its government in order to re-appropriate the mystic position or to exclude it altogether. In this, the mystic becomes either accepted as a true expression of God or excluded as a heretic, a dangerous subversion, and an expression of the devil. The church is a governmental apparatus because this issue must be decided all the time, not once and for all. It is, among other things, in the process of resolving this issue that the church becomes the locus of governmentality.

Let us now return to the film, to the scene in which Sister Jeanne is interrogated publicly by Father Barre, the witch hunter.

> 'Do you remember the first time your thoughts were turned to evil things?'
>
> 'Yes, Father. I had a vision. I saw a man walking across the waters of a lake. I dry his person with my hair. I had a great knowledge of love, which persisted throughout my prayers. I could not rid my mind of this man for several days.'
>
> 'Who was this man?'
>
> 'There was a mist. I couldn't see him.'

When Sister Jeanne is not able to name the man in her vision, Laubardemont impatiently intervenes: 'That was no devil. She spoke with her voice. The voice of a frustrated woman'. But Father Barre is resolute: 'Do not be so easily deceived. Her very innocence is a sham, a mask of deceit devised by the cunning of Satan. Be assured, the fiend is silently lurking in some hidden recess of her body'.

Witches in the Middle Ages were essentially deemed weak or feeble; however, their weakness was exactly what made them the prime target of devilish seduction. Weak they were but at the same time extremely powerful and dangerous. Thus witches were seen as capable of causing death, destroying crops, and introducing plagues (Denike 2003: 14). They were, and this might have been their greatest asset, even capable of transmuting into other shapes and forms, which is why one could never be sure whether one encountered an exemplar of this devilish pack or not (Ibid. 35). Their ability to disguise themselves was, in turn, what made witches a vulnerable target in social and political contexts. Even their normality could be seen as proof of their wicked abnormality. Those who seemed most innocent might, in fact, be the most dangerous. The use of torture against these women was seen as an activity of unmasking. Further, in *Malleus Maleficarum*, perhaps the most important medieval work of demonology, we are told that 'witchcraft is high Treason against God's majesty' (quoted in Ibid. 25). The person who is accused of high treason is not, of course, an ordinary criminal, but somebody who attacks the king in his capacity of being the arbiter of the law. In the case of high treason the very system of law is under attack and in such a state of emergency the use of 'illegal' means is accepted. Legal obstacles are removed allowing the inquisitors to unleash their regimes of brutality (Ibid. 29). The case is more complex though than 'just' a suspension of the law. The Inquisition was part of the church's struggle to enlarge its jurisdiction, which had been diminishing vis-à-vis the developing system of public law. Witchcraft in this context was seen as a set of exceptional crimes that allowed for the suspension of ordinary secular judicial procedures (Ibid.). The state's growing influence at the cost of the church could thus be countered. But the state itself also made use of the same trick. Jean Bodin, for instance, one of the most prominent legal theorists of his time, recommended measures that closely resembled those practised by the Inquisition, that is, 'an entirely different exceptional approach' aimed against 'the crimes of Treason against God', a crime that in its wickedness 'outweighs all others' (Bodin quoted in Ibid. 34–35). The church and the state thus used the appeal to exception to gain legal monopoly. In both cases, the witch hunt laid bare the material kernel of law, its extra-legal fundament. Among the extra-legal means were punitive proceedings, the use of 'judicial' torture, and permission for local courts to function independently of central political and judicial control (Denike 2003: 33). The lower court judges constituted witchcraft as a *crimen exceptum* allowing for a suspension of procedural rules. There was no possibility of appealing to higher courts or of having evidence further scrutinized (Ibid.). The witches were, so to speak, included and excluded from the law at the same time. Reminiscent of *homo sacer*, they were included within the realm of law through the suspension of legal procedures, that is, through exclusion or abandonment.

Thus in the same scene discussed above, Father Barre turns to Sister Jeanne and says: 'It must be extreme measures. The fiend must be forced from you'. Next we see Sister Jeanne tortured to get from her a 'confession'. But she is not alone; Laubardemont and Father Barre also force the other nuns into 'confessing' Grandier's guilt. By the time Grandier returns to Loudun, the nuns are naked, screeching in religious frenzy, whipping themselves, kissing, speaking with the voice of the devil, and so on. He is shocked. Covering a naked nun, he shouts to Father Mignon, Laubardemont and Father Barre:

> You have turned the house of the Lord into a circus! And its servants into clowns. You have seduced the people in order to destroy them! You have perverted the innocent!

This indignation coincides with another detail: while he is away, Grandier has realized that 'Richelieu rules the king'. Just as Loudun will need courage, so will Grandier when he finds out that Sister Jeanne has accused him of being a devil. He resolutely denies this: 'No! Call me vain and proud, the greatest sinner ever to walk on God's earth. But Satan's boy I could never be! I haven't the humility'. However, he is seized and charged with heresy. The plot develops according to the book: the nuns are made to sign confessions of possession, fake evidence is gathered, and he is publicly mocked in a show trial.

Since the church is supposed to embody the truth (e.g. on the essence of evil), it cannot, by implication, make mistakes. Hence the result of the possession trials was always known in advance, which made them appear farcical. As comedies of terror, the trials sought to conceal a fundamental fact: the internal perversion of the church. The confessions of possession thus concealed the true guilt: the betrayal of the church by the church itself. Thus Grandier defended himself by attacking the church.

> The devil is a liar and the father of lies. If the devil's evidence is to be accepted, the virtuous people are in the greatest of danger. For it is against these that Satan rages most violently. I have never set eyes on Sister Jeanne of the Angels until the day of my arrest. But the devil has spoken. And to doubt his word is sacrilege. You have totally perverted Christ's own teaching. This new doctrine, Laubardemont's new doctrine, Barre's new doctrine, especially invented for this occasion, is the work of men who are not concerned with fact or with law or with theology but a political experiment to show how the will of one man can be pushed into destroying not only one man or one city but one nation!

The only reply to Grandier's accusation comes from the judge: 'This is not a political trial. Remove the prisoner'. Grandier is found guilty of commerce with the devil to possess and seduce, of obscenity, blasphemy, sacrilege ... His punishment will be to be burned alive.

Truth and truth-telling

After the trial, Grandier is shaved and further tortured: 'Oh, Christ ... Oh, God, I thought I found you. And now you have forsaken me'. However, there is still no confession of guilt. Just before the execution in the marketplace, an interesting dialogue takes place between Laubardemont and Grandier (who is now in pain and crying):

> 'Tell me, do you love the Church?'
> 'Not today.'

'Do you want to see it grow more powerful? More benevolent, until it embraces every human soul on this earth? Then help us to achieve this great purpose. Go to the marketplace a penitent man. Confess. And by confessing, proclaim to those thousands that you have returned to the Church's arms. By going to the stake unrepentant, you do God a disservice. You give to unbelievers. Such an act can mine the very foundations of the Church. You are no longer important.'

'I was never … important.'

'Then make a last supreme gesture for the Catholic faith.'

'Go away, Laubardemont. You are becoming tedious.'

Laubardemont *knows* that Grandier is innocent. But in the economy of the possession trials, even claiming innocence confirms a fundamental guilt, that of prioritizing one's own interests rather than those of the church. A true believer would thus sacrifice himself for the church, even when he is, personally, guiltless. In this sense Grandier's claim of innocence demonstrates a lack of fidelity to the church, which is his true guilt.

Unable to obtain a confession, Laubardemont tells Grandier: 'Do you know that the king has gone back on his word because of your crimes? The walls will come down, the city will be destroyed. We have won'. And so Grandier is taken to the marketplace. There he is confronted with Sister Jeanne to ask her forgiveness, but Grandier again refuses to confess; saying that he can only ask God for forgiveness, he turns to Sister Jeanne: 'Look at this thing that I am and learn the meaning of love!' Sister Jeanne replies, shouting: 'Devil! Devil!'

Finally, we see Grandier on the stake. Joyful music is playing, and the atmosphere is carnivalesque. The executioner promises Grandier he will strangle him before the fire is lit. Meanwhile Father Mignon keeps insisting: 'Confess, confess … beg forgiveness'. Grandier refuses again to participate in his own public humiliation by confessing, by compromising his truth. Instead, he turns to the audience of the spectacle: 'Forgive me for defending your city so badly'. At this crucial point the camera refocuses on Grandier as a truth-teller: 'I am about to meet God who is my witness and I have spoken the truth'. Father Barre is agitated; he fires the stake before Grandier is strangled. Grandier starts to burn alive, with the crowd chanting 'Burn, burn, burn … ' The camera switches to Trincant, watching the event together with his daughter and illegitimate grandchild: 'Watch bastard. See how your mother's honour was avenged'. Grandier, his face half-burned, shouts to the crowd his final words:

> Don't look at me! Look at your city! If your city is destroyed, your freedom is destroyed also! If you would remain free men, fight! Fight them or become their slaves!

The crowd is laughing. Meanwhile the fortifications of the city are being demolished.

Just before the end of the film, we see Laubardemont paying a visit to Sister Jeanne. Here we also get to know the fate of Father Mignon, who has become insane: 'He keeps babbling that we've destroyed an innocent man. And with no signed confession to prove otherwise, everyone has the same opinion. Pity, that'. But the good news for Sister Jeanne is that 'with Grandier gone, you are no longer possessed'.

'What shall I do?'
'Pray for salvation. Do penance. Stay here quietly, of course. What else? Well, there'll be a few tourists occasionally to brighten things up. But that won't last long. Soon the town will die, you will be left in peace, and oblivion. Oh, I almost forgot. Souvenir.

He shows a penis-shaped bone of Grandier's to Sister Jeanne. And then, in the final scene, we see Madeleine in the ruins of the city walls, walking out of the city. Towards us?

Possession and political spirituality

According to historical accounts, the real Sister Jeanne became a famous mystic after this drama of exorcism was played out in Loudun. In the remaining twenty-five years of her life, she traveled around France, telling the story of her past possession and displaying her hand as a sign, 'sculpted by the devil', to the nobility and laymen (Greenblatt 1996: ix). In Loudun, she became a popular attraction as part of the town's tourist-pilgrimage industry. And she wrote a lot, including her confessions. Although at one point in the film version, Sister Jeanne expresses some remorse, telling Father Mignon and Father Barre that she has 'wronged an innocent man' (Father Barre replies: 'My poor deluded child. It is not you who speaks but the devil in you'), in real life, in her written confessions, which belong to her 'mystic' (post-possession) period, she makes no mention of remorse and continues her 'systematic lying' about Grandier, identifying herself with the 'bookish fiction' of Grandier's sorcery (see Huxley 2005: 325). As such, however, her significance lies in her being able to unite a famous 'possessed' person and a famous 'mystic' visionary in her personality, illuminating how the relation to the beyond 'vacillates between the immediacy of a diabolical seizure and the immediacy of a divine illumination'(Certeau 1996: 6).

Regarding the film, however, it is more interesting to focus on the relationship between Grandier (mysticism) and Sister Jeanne (possession) as the locus of the governmental machine. In this respect, Richelieu signifies the direct politicization of religion and its instrumentalization for political purposes such as centralization, state building, and the war against Protestantism. It is also in this process that possession becomes a spectacle where the friend-enemy antagonism is displayed, and the dangers of disobedience, of alliance with the devil, are verified in continual rituals (see Ahearne 1995: 79). This is the reason why Father Tranquille, the most uncompromising exorcist, commenting on Grandier's case in 1634 writes that in the case of possession 'the demons can only be driven out by the power of the scepter', and that 'the crosier would not suffice to break this dragon's head' (quoted in Certeau 1996: 27).

The bipolar machine of sovereignty and governmentality depicted in the film is in perpetual combat with an old enemy, the devil. The essential role of the devil in this respect is opposition, to be a stumbling block (Forsyth 1987: 4). However, the devil is 'a being who can only be contingent: as the adversary, he must always be a function of another, not an independent entity' (Ibid.). Following this, naming the devil, differentiating the devil as an enemy, is a decision or act internal to the system that undertakes the differentiation. Therefore the figure of the devil is bound to be a fiction, an image. By the same token, it is the devil that gives monotheistic theology its mythological dimension: no devil, no God (see Ibid. 7). This is the reason why, translating 'devil' into 'enemy', Carl Schmitt insists that the friend-enemy distinction is constitutive of all antagonistic politics. No enemy, no society.

Where do Grandier, his mysticism, and his political spirituality stand in this scheme? In this scheme, the political is about secularizing the essentials of theology. Such secularization is necessary because modernity unfolds in the direction of positivism (Schmitt 2007: 80). But as mentioned before (in *Introduction*), insofar as it operates in terms of profanation, modern politics is not reducible to political theology. Political spirituality can exist without religion. Every time there is an event, there are people possessed by a form of political spirituality. Political spirituality is not mysticism alone although mysticism is a form of political spirituality. Political spirituality is not religious in its essence; rather, it is a process of truth-telling. *Parrhesia* is what Grandier is practising in the film: he develops a specific relationship to truth through frankness, by expressing his opinion and saying directly what is on his mind. But he is not only frank; his opinion is also his truth. Thus he risks his life, for in every 'parrhesiastic game in which your own life is exposed, you are taking up a specific relationship to yourself: you risk death to tell the truth instead of reposing in the security of a life where truth goes unspoken' (Ibid. 17). Grandier prefers truth-telling to false life, risking his life through fidelity to the truth. He perceives critique – truth-telling – as duty.

For the truth is opaque. Paradoxically, this opaqueness is grounded in the governmental machine and its veridical apparatuses (the possession trials, exorcisms, interrogations ...) that claim to be unearthing the truth. In the very gesture of showing the truth they prevent it from being seen. The practice of transparency is what, precisely, obscures the truth. The spectacle dazzles in the very act of illuminating. Hence one of the most significant scenes in the film comes when a couple of dissenters shout to Mignon and Barre during Sister Jeanne's possession interrogation: 'Stop with this spectacle. You are blind'. This blindness is not prior to the spectacle but its effect. It is the same blindness

Grandier's truth-telling targets, expressing the desire to reduce the obscurity of truth, a desire for enlightenment.

But what does the spectacle hide? In a public exorcism the king visits Loudun in disguise, accompanied by a 'holy relic' that, he claims, can remove the 'devils' possessing the nuns. Father Barre starts to 'exorcise' the nuns with it, and the nuns appear cured. Then the king reveals that the case containing the relic is empty:

> 'Do you see, Father?'
> 'What sort of a trick have you played on us?'
> 'Oh, Reverend, sir, what sort of a trick are *you* playing on us?'

There is only a void, emptiness, an inoperativity at the center of power. Hence the empty relic can be taken as a perfect symbol of the spectacle. The originary gesture of the spectacle is to hide this emptiness at its heart of power. Thus it must blind as well as be illuminating. Perhaps therefore, in spite of the logical proof that the relic case is empty, that possessions and exorcisms are merely spectacle, the stories of possession and exorcism in the film persist, eventually turning into an orgiastic mass during which the nuns sexually offend and desecrate a statue of Christ.

But, then, who is the real devil in this scheme: Grandier or the church? From the perspective of truth-telling, evil can only be the perversion of, or lack of fidelity to, a truth – the reduction of *kairos* to strategic-economic thinking. This is Grandier's accusation against the church establishment. The church, in turn, declares that Grandier's practice is heretical, because the church recognizes the threat of the truth in his discourse.

3 From political theology to politics

> Philosophers conceive of the passions which harass us as vices into which men fall by their own fault, and, therefore, generally deride, bewail, or blame them. ... For they conceive of men, not as they are, but as they themselves would like them to be.
>
> (Spinoza 1951b: 287)

How, then, can we move from political theology to politics? Can the 'true religion' be translated into true politics? What kind of politics is imaginable on the basis of reason? If religion is fundamentally grounded in passion (imagination), how can it then relate to politics?

Just as imagination can perfect itself by ascending to the intellectual love of God, political theology can transform itself into democracy, 'the most natural form of government' (Spinoza 1951a: 263; see also Brown 1991: 109). But the transition from passion to reason, from nature to the city as a political association, is not a pure break. There is always a remainder of nature, an irrational residue at the very center of the city. In Spinoza's genesis of the city this unassimilated rest is constituted by passions. Even though the city is basically a reasonable form of human togetherness, passions such as love, hatred, envy, ambition, pity, and so on, are significant elements of conduct in it. And we do not get far by simply mocking or denying their existence, the fact that 'man is always necessarily liable to passions' (Spinoza 1993a: 145). So, political subjectivity cannot be constituted independently from passion. The 'harassment' of passions is an omnipresent political possibility. Because there are passions, there are antagonisms, and because there are antagonisms, there are passions in the city. Thus, even though reason is a potentially unifying factor, passions can always lead to dissention. And reason is, in itself, impotent to bond unreasonable subjects (see Spinoza 1951b: 289, 294–95).

But does this fact, that there is a passive genesis, passions, as well as reason in the origin of the city, mean that the city is opposed to passions? To start with, affect and reason point towards two different but interrelated origins of the city. The distinction between affect and reason is also a distinction between two cities: the 'despotic city' founded on superstition, and the 'free city' founded on reason. In the first, the domain of the law is colonized by superstition, and free opinion is treated as crime. Superstition deceives the citizens and masks their fears with reference to transcendent authorities 'so that men may fight as bravely for slavery as for their safety, and count it not a shame but highest honour to risk their blood and their lives for the vainglory of a tyrant' (Spinoza 1951a: 5). The free city, on the other hand, is one in which everyone may worship as their conscience dictates and 'where freedom is esteemed before all things dear and precious' (Ibid. 6).

Reason and the city

On the basis of what, then, can despotism be avoided and a free city established? Spinoza's answer is nature: the 'natural rights' of the individual which are co-extensive with citizens' desire and power. One's 'natural right' is everything in one's power, everything a body can do; in the state of nature one's power, its exercise, and right are one and the same thing. For the same reason in the state of nature 'no one is bound to live as another pleases' (Ibid. 10). In this sense, natural right refers to an initial desire to increase one's *conatus*. Here, reason is not privileged; both the reasonable and the unreasonable (that is, the person who is governed by passions) act with the prime motive of persevering in their being, their *conatus*. Following this, the state of nature is not a reasonable but a pre-social condition. At this point the natural right is determined 'not by sound reason, but by desire and power' (Ibid. 201).

Reason becomes a motive force only afterwards, only in the city. Nobody is born reasonable, or religious; for in the state of nature 'no one knows by nature that he owes any obedience to God' (Spinoza 1951a: 210; see also Deleuze 1992: 259). Thus Spinoza insists, alluding to Paul, that there can be no sin previous to the law (Spinoza 1951a: 201). Wrongdoing can only take place in society, but as a 'weakness of mind', not as sin. Since one is free to the extent that one's actions are guided by reason, 'we cannot without great impropriety call a rational life obedience, and give the name of wrong-doing to that which is, in fact, a weakness of the mind' (Spinoza 1951b: 298). Likewise, a Hobbes-style covenant is neither possible nor can it be effective in the state of nature. For in nature there is one single law, which must be counted as an 'eternal truth', that 'no one ever neglects anything which he judges to be good, except with the hope of gaining a greater good, or from the fear of a greater evil; nor does anyone endure an evil except for the sake of avoiding a greater evil, or gaining a greater good' (Spinoza 1951a: 203). Thus in the state of nature 'no one honestly can promise' anything, that is, enter into a social contract by transferring one's natural rights, in a binding manner (Ibid).

What is primary in the state of nature is not one's 'duties' but natural rights, that is, one's power. Since in nature each individual seeks to increase its *conatus*, to persevere in its existence, without regard to anyone else (like fish naturally conditioned to swim and to eat smaller fish), everyone has a right to do what they can (Spinoza 1951a: 200). Hence in the state of nature 'men are naturally enemies' (Spinoza 1951b: 296). Everyone decides on what is good or bad alone, without the interference of others. 'Thus defined, the state of nature itself shows us what makes it intolerable. ... In the state of nature I live at the mercy of encounters' (Deleuze 1992: 260).

The solution is the city: by organizing the encounters, it enables a body to increase its *conatus* through associations with other bodies that agree with itself. Therefore 'there is ... nothing more useful to man than man'; nothing, after all, is more desirable for mankind than to 'seek at the same time what is useful to them in common' (Spinoza 1993a: 153). There is an intimate relationship between reason and the city as a form of association, in which the citizens can freely enjoy security and rights, and do so without losing their natural rights. Crucially, however, this does not mean that the city is a reasonable association as such; it is not. What primarily forces the formation of the city is not reason but passions: the fear generated by the state of nature and, concomitantly, the renunciation of natural rights (Deleuze 1992: 265–66). Through a social contract, rights can be delegated to the city, which, in turn, guarantees individuals' safety (Spinoza 1951a: 10, 202).

> A body politic of this kind is called a Democracy, which may be defined as a society which wields all its power as a whole. The sovereign power is not restrained by any laws, but everyone is bound to obey it in all things; such is the state of things implied when men either tacitly or expressly handed over to it all their power of self-defense, or in other words, all their right. For if they had wished to retain any right for themselves, they ought to have taken precautions for its defense and preservation; as they have not done so, and indeed could not have done so without dividing and consequently ruining the state, they placed themselves absolutely at the mercy of the sovereign power; and, therefore, having acted ... as reason and necessity demanded, they are obliged to fulfill the commands of the sovereign power, however absurd these may be, else they will be public enemies, and will act against reason, which urges the preservation of the state as a primary duty. For reason bids us choose the least of two evils.
>
> (Ibid. 205)

However, it is not necessarily a third party, a sovereign Leviathan as in Hobbes, who gains by the contract, but potentially everybody, the multitude. So, even though its origin is not reason, its pre-rational character does not stop the city from paving the way for reason; 'the City's own nature thus determines it to aim as far as possible for reason's ideal, to strive to make the sum of its laws conform to reason' (Deleuze 1992: 266–67). After all, the motivation behind the renunciation of natural rights is the individual's own interest, safety.

But does this renunciation turn the subjects into slaves? For Spinoza the slave is the person who is driven by his passions without being able to see what is good for him and to act accordingly: 'he alone is free who lives with free consent under the entire guidance of reason' (Spinoza 1951a: 206). Certainly, obedience to society takes away one's freedom in a certain sense, but it does not make one a slave insofar as this obedience is to a democratic society in which the sovereign power is established on the basis of the will of all under the guidance of reason. Whereas the slave obeys a master's orders and this obedience is only in the master's interest, the free subject 'obeys the orders of the sovereign power, given for the common interest, wherein he is included' (Ibid. 206).

> In [democracy] no one transfers his natural right so absolutely that he has no further voice in affairs, he only hands it over to the majority of a society, whereof he is a unit. Thus all men remain as they were in the state of nature, equals.
>
> (Ibid. 207)

This is the reason why there is no necessary opposition between the city and reason. Spinoza's 'reason' only demands, as nature does, that everyone should seek to increase their *conatus*. As such, 'reason' is not an artificial order but refers to natural relations among citizens. Reason is nature. It does not contradict but raises natural rights 'to a power without which such rights would remain unreal and abstract' (Deleuze 1992: 264). Thus there is no necessary opposition between reason and affects either; reason, the good city, is not an obstacle to passions. Renouncing one's natural rights does not mean renouncing perseverance in one's being. What the citizen renounces by committing himself to a collective, common affection is his personal affection. Thus, even though freedom to act is surrendered to the city, 'affections of reason', that is, freedom of thinking and free speech cannot and should not be surrendered. Free speech remains an indispensable natural right, the compromise of which is precisely what introduces violence into the city (Ibid. 268). Peace and piety require co-operation and association among subjects, and without freedom to express one's passions and thoughts, this is rendered difficult. The lack of this freedom is a breeding ground for superstition (see James 2012: 315–18).

Let us, at this point, return to imagination, to the first kind of knowledge. As mentioned before, Spinoza insists that the state of nature is prior to religion. The state of nature should therefore be conceived of without religion and law, and consequently without notions such as sin or wrong. Likewise, the distinctions between good and evil, free and unfree, and so on, do not apply to the state of nature; they are social/religious in origin. And since obedience is originally a theological principle, obedience to the social contract cannot be justified philosophically, in terms of reason (Spinoza 1951a: 195). This is also why initially 'revelation was necessary' (Ibid.). Society is constituted not on the basis of rational fear (as in Hobbes, for instance) but on the prophetic proselytization of the idea of God; the social contract was initially a theocratic covenant (see Brown 1991: 110). For this reason, since there is a religious aspect to the social contract, Spinoza describes the theocratic Hebrew Republic as an early form of democracy, a system in which people both absolutely retained their sovereignty and, at the same time, 'were not bound by anything save the revelations of God' (Spinoza 1951a: 220):

> God alone, therefore, held dominion over the Hebrews, whose state was in virtue of the covenant called God's kingdom, and God was said to be their king; consequently the enemies of the Jews were said to be the enemies of God, and the citizens who tried to seize the dominion were guilty of treason against God; and, lastly, the laws of the state were called the laws and commandments of God. Thus in the Hebrew state the civil and religious authority, each consisting solely of obedience to God, were one and the same. The dogmas of religion were not precepts, but laws and ordinances; piety was regarded as the same as loyalty, impiety as the same as disaffection. Everyone who fell away from religion ceased to be a citizen, and was, on that ground alone, accounted an enemy: those who died for the sake of religion, were held to have died for their country; in fact, between civil and religious law and right there was no distinction whatever. For this reason the government could be called a theocracy, inasmuch as the citizens were not bound by anything save the revelations of God.
>
> (Ibid. 219)

In this sense all politics, in its origin, is essentially theological. Just as imagination is the first (and necessary) level of knowledge, the Hebrew-style theocracy based on revelation is, from the point of view of political organization, a necessary stage for the perfection of democracy. Just as philosophy transcends prophetic imagination by perfecting it, democracy transcends theocracy by transforming the 'inner light' (the personal asset of the prophet) into the 'natural light' of reason (common to all) and obedience into freedom. In a certain sense, therefore, democracy is 'the most perfect form of theocracy' (Brown 1991: 111). Democracy is perfection.

From contract to consent

In *A Theologico-Political Treatise,* Spinoza states that the aim of government is not to obtain obedience by fear; the true aim of government is freedom just as it is freedom that constitutes the state in the first place (1951a: 258–59). In *Political Treatise* Spinoza takes this idea to its logical extremes, to the point of substituting the idea of social contract with that of consensus (Negri 2004: 16). The foundation of the state is no longer social contract but free association. Politics itself is constituted through free association: if people come together they will have more power than they would have had unconnectedly, and the more they unite forces the more right they will acquire collectively (Spinoza 1951b: 296).

Whoever is entrusted by common consent the state power is the sovereign. If this power belongs to the general multitude, the form of government will be democracy, which is, again, contrasted with aristocracy, the rule of some, and to monarchy, the rule of one (Ibid. 297). In democracy there is no presupposition of a transcendent, divine authority or state. Its power can neither be justified nor criticized with reference to an instance external to power, divine or earthly. Now, rights are 'derived from a continuous process of legitimation' that passes through the multitude (Negri 2004: 17). In this way two significant illusions, which are inherited from political theology and which engender despotism, are excluded: the idea of the transcendental transfer of natural rights and the idea of unlimited sovereignty. The citizen is a 'subject' in democracy, but only in terms of an originary freedom which is channeled and rearranged into a reasonable state (see Ibid. 17).

And crucially, if the conception of the state does not require any transcendence, revelation, which *was* hitherto necessary, becomes redundant. Therefore it would be neither possible nor advisable, according to Spinoza, to 'imitate' the theocratic commonwealth of the Hebrews:

> If a people wished to transfer their rights to God it would be necessary to make an express covenant with Him, and for this would be needed not only the consent of those transferring their rights, but also the consent of God. God, however, has revealed through his Apostles that the covenant of God is no longer written in ink, or on tables of stone, but with the Spirit of God in the fleshy tables of the heart.
> (Spinoza 1951a: 237)

In a democracy everyone can become their 'own prophets' and transcend the 'idolatrous worship of God's earthly vicegerent', discovering the true God written in the heart rather than in the books (Brown 1991: 111). In this sense Spinoza's immanent democracy, built upon the affections of reason, negates superstition, which emerges on the basis of passive emotions, especially fear. In fact, superstition can evolve into an 'enemy' of the city insofar as the enemy is defined as the one who, 'because he is attached to this or that religion, judges the laws of a dominion [city] worse than any possible evil' (Spinoza 1951b: 304). But sovereignty must be absolute. Thus the enemy 'may lawfully be coerced by force' (Ibid.). But how can the freedom of thought and the freedom of speech be articulated with such absolute sovereignty? Does the city become 'totalitarian' by holding sovereignty absolute against the superstitious 'enemy'? Or, does 'peace' equal the absence of conflict?

Certainly, the idea of 'peace' can be perverted by a repressive state in which free speech and agonistic debate are impossible. Thus, Spinoza's endeavor to deal with superstition must not be turned into an unambiguous rule in line with the preservation of the state; we must also ask whether the state itself conforms to the demands of reason for an illegitimate state legitimates revolution (see Balibar 1998: 27). 'Contracts or laws, whereby the multitude transfers its right to one council or man, should without doubt be broken, when it is expedient for the general welfare to do so' (Spinoza 1951b: 311). Since the transfer of power is only 'partial' (Spinoza 1951a: 204, 207, 214), it keeps intact the possibility of an opening – of revolutions, which are 'by definition illegal and illegitimate – until they have succeeded' (Balibar 1998: 35). In such cases the sovereign rights will have been 'transferred already' (Spinoza 1951a: 209).

Conflict in the city

While equating the 'human' with 'God', Spinoza does not reduce the 'neighbor' to a friend defined by his similarity to us. The 'similarity' among neighbors is not given but achieved: in Spinoza it is not so much that neighbors are God to one another but rather they 'together make God, or produce the divine as such' (Balibar 2012: 36). And this process may include conflict, even antagonism (see Spinoza 1993a: 143). How, then, must the difficult relationship between peace, the ultimate aim of the city, and conflict, a continuous potentiality in the city, be understood? What does this mean in terms of linking passion and reason, belief and unbelief?

An illuminating concept is this regard is agonism. Since the ancient Greek *polis*, agonism is regarded as a decisive element of a politics that can accommodate conflict among beliefs. In contemporary versions (see for instance Connolly 2005 and Mouffe 2005), the concept suggests that the violence of passions in the city is an ubiquitous possibility that 'can never be eradicated' (Mouffe 2005: 12). De-politicizing such violence, for instance in cultural or religious terms, is not a solution either. When their political core is not recognized by the system, passions often become radicalized and transform into antagonism. De-politicization of passion leads to its ultra-politicization, which, in turn, tends to threaten the social order. Democratic politics, in contrast, aims at 'defusing' or 'sublimating' antagonism, that is, translating it into agonism, so that conflict does not destroy the political association (Ibid. 19–21). 'Agonism' thus designates an us/them relation in which the two sides of the relation are not illegitimate 'enemies' but legitimate 'adversaries' who share a common ground, even though they can acknowledge that 'there is no rational solution to their conflict' (Ibid. 20).

But the question is whether one can operate with a clean-cut distinction between rationality and affect, between reason and passion. This is, for instance, what Mouffe seems to do, suggesting that the city is opposed to passions. Accordingly, in her Weberian perspective, values are considered to be irrational per definition and in a society characterized by a pluralism of values there will always be 'unavoidable value conflicts' (Mouffe 2000: 103). When all values are perceived to be irrational, when reason moves out of politics, value becomes a matter of decision in the Schmittian sense. Yet, even though at an ontological level it is impossible, at an epistemological level (for instance in agonistic dialogue) antagonism can disappear on a rational basis.

Due to a 'spiritualization of enmity', the adversaries 'can become bonded together ... through an enhanced experience of the contestability problematic each pursues most fervently' (Connolly 1993: 382). It is, at least theoretically, possible that value conflicts are not essentially unavoidable; one cannot rule out the epistemological possibility of what is ontologically (politically) impossible. In this context Connolly proposes 'agonistic respect' as a principal political virtue, as a relation of negotiation between interdependent partisans who hold different beliefs (2005: 81, 123). Agonistic respect is tolerance in conflict or conflict in tolerance.

Agonistic respect cannot be taken for granted because it is not rooted in a habitus, in language, or in any other fundament; it must be created and protected. It is, in other words, a question of grounding the city, politics, itself. Connolly exemplifies agonistic respect with a reflection on his own Spinozist background, by deliberately showing, so to speak, his own weaknesses to his adversaries. In this, he turns to Leo Strauss' critique of Spinoza, which addresses the relationship between reason and religious belief, concluding that Spinoza cannot provide an ultimate refutation of religious faith:

> The genuine refutation of orthodoxy would require the proof that the world and human life are perfectly intelligible without the assumption of a mysterious God ... Spinoza's *Ethics* attempts to be that system but it does not succeed; the clear and distinct account of everything which it presents remains fundamentally hypothetical. As a consequence its cognitive status is not different from that of the orthodox account. Certain it is that Spinoza cannot legitimately deny the possibility of revelation. But to grant that revelation is possible means to grant that the philosophical account and the philosophical way of life are not necessarily, not evidently, the true account and the right way of life; philosophy, the quest for evident and necessary knowledge, rests itself on univalent decision, on an act of will, just as faith. Hence the antagonism between Spinoza and Judaism, between belief and unbelief, is ultimately not theoretical but moral.
>
> (Strauss quoted in Connolly 2005: 45)

Endorsing much of the above formulation, Connolly claims that the dispute between religious belief and reason is not really between 'belief and unbelief'. Rather, the dispute must be re-articulated as 'the difference between a positive belief in transcendence of the world and a positive belief in the immanence of the world' (Ibid. 46). The first holds the view that the world is created, the second believes that the world is a world of becoming, a world without an aim or purpose. Yet, he goes on to argue, this debate cannot be resolved:

> My view, to put it briefly, is that the most noble response is to seek to transmute cultural antagonisms between transcendence and immanence into debates marked by agonistic respect between the partisans, with each

set acknowledging that its highest and most entrenched faith is legitimately contestable by the others.

(Ibid. 47)

This understanding of agonism is prone to problems. For instance, even though such 'critical responsiveness' (Ibid. 126) might be an estimable gesture, it is no guarantee that one's opponents will do the same. Why, after all, should one assume in political situations characterized by antagonism that one's opponents/enemies will refrain from using their force, from doing what they can do? Such an assumption is itself a moralizing tendency for it essentially reduces power to something that can be separated from what it can do (e.g. the nihilistic assumption that a bird of prey can stop preying on lambs). Crucially in this respect, that 'the antagonism ... between belief and unbelief is ultimately not theoretical but moral' (Ibid. 47) does not mean that all values are moral values or that values and beliefs cannot be ranked. To decide on values is, precisely, an act of will and the question of will is always active or passive, not value or non-value, or, belief or unbelief. The question here is, in other words, whether agonistic politics should replace or supplement the antagonism between reason and faith, philosophy and theology.

A related problem is idealism. Connolly operates with an ideal image of self-criticism and the possibility of self-reflexivity. But we know from Spinoza that most people do not behave according to the dictates of reason. Therefore the question is how much self-reflexivity one can expect in antagonistic circumstances. Also, even if faith is contestable, what makes a belief belief is precisely its refusal of such contestedness. In this respect Connolly's agonistic pluralism boils down to normative political imagining, to a hidden idealism. This idealism is modeled on Gallie's discussion of 'essentially contested concepts' (see Albertsen 2006; Gallie 1964: 157–91; and Connolly 2002). Like Gallie, Connolly assumes that if all participants in a conceptual debate hold the view that what is under debate is essentially contested, this will in itself contribute to the quality and the communicative rationality of the debate, even if no agreement is reached (see Albertsen 2006 for an extended discussion). However, the problem with treating conflicts based on antagonism as though they were conflicts about essentially contested concepts involves a generalization of Galllie's discussion from epistemology to ontology, from a conceptual level to the level of political philosophy. In Gallie, essential contestedness refers to situations in which the parties in dialogue fundamentally agree that what is discussed (an essentially contested concept) is important. Connolly transfers this implicit condition (of conceptual discussion) to a normative condition of general political dialogue. In this movement, critical responsiveness tends to assume a non-perspectival common platform. The problem is that in Gallie essential contestedness is related to concepts, not to the political. In contrast, in the political field, essential contestedness draws on different resources (ontology, with no minimal consensus) than the conceptual (epistemology, with the possibility of minimal consensus). With such aestheticization of agonism, ontology collapses into epistemology while an idealized concept gets a transcendent status, giving confidence to a curious sentimentality that promotes affects/emotions rather than the will, respect rather than antagonism, concept rather than life. Consequently, political agonism tends to become an ersatz transfiguration. But despite the fact that it is profoundly related to affects, politics cannot be created through affects; the political is not an emotion. It demands the interpretation of the world rather than fetishizing agonism.

Along the same lines, religion becomes a blind spot for agonistic politics. Indeed, although Connolly (1999) had argued in the past that in liberal democracies there is an inbuilt contradiction between religion and politics, in *Pluralism*, religion moves from the domain of agonism to that of respect. Becoming elevated above the demands for justification or truthfulness, faith attains an absolute, non-perspectival epistemological authority. And paradoxically, while others' religion becomes a blind spot for one's discourse, one's own belief is subjected to 'critical responsiveness' (see Connolly 2005: 22–23). Yet agonism is not reducible to respect for others' beliefs. In this context, despite being heavily influenced by Spinoza and Nietzsche, Connolly remains a harmony-seeking thinker and his theory a slightly more antagonizing version of the Habermasian theory that blurs the line between agonism and liberal tolerance.

However, when 'respect' dominates agonism, politics necessarily becomes indexed to an artificial conflict between post-political 'tolerance', which demands 'respect' for otherness, and a fundamentalist 'dogmatism', which habitually accuses its opponents of 'blasphemy' (see Žižek 2008a: 110). The paradox here is that demanding respect for his otherness means for the fundamentalist acknowledging in advance the framework of the post-political discourse of tolerance, while avoiding blasphemy for a non-religious person is impossible in practice. Consequently, the two 'worlds' can only be united in the form of a disjunctive synthesis that discloses a 'secret solidarity' between the two poles: 'the nightmarish prospect of a society regulated by a perverse pact between religious fundamentalists and the politically correct preachers of tolerance and respect for the other's beliefs, no matter how ... superstitious this other is' (Ibid.). Thus the only radical response to the twinning of tolerance and blasphemy is to renounce their common root, to return to an atheism à la Spinoza and Nietzsche.

> Isn't it time to restore the dignity of atheism, perhaps our only chance of peace? As a rule, where religiously inspired violence is concerned, we put the blame on violence itself: it is the violent or 'terrorist' political agent who 'misuses' a noble religion, so the goal becomes to retrieve the authentic core of a religion from its political instrumentalization. What, however, if one should take the risk of inverting this relationship? What if what appears as a moderating force, compelling us to control our violence, is its secret instigator? What if, then, instead of renouncing violence, one were to renounce religion, including its secular reverberations

such as Stalinist communism with its reliance on the historical big Other, and to pursue violence on its own, assuming full responsibility for it, without any cover-up in some figure of the big Other?

(Ibid. 113–14)

Only a truly profaned politics that can look religion in the eye can transgress the deadlock of respect–blasphemy and avoid patronizing the other by respecting his illusions more than himself, without, at the same time, collapsing into the passivity of relativism devoid of any principle of selection or ranking. In this regard agonistic respect always potentially risks bordering on liberal tolerance. What we need is a political agonism that aims at keeping agonism and affects together not in an ideal communicative framework but in a radically political framework that, when necessary, can be as antagonistic as agonistic.

Religion versus politics

Should religion determine politics or the other way around? Or should the powers of the state and the church be separated? Spinoza's answer to the first question is in favor of politics, while he replies to the latter with an insistent no, for sovereignty must be absolute; the sovereign 'possesses supreme right and power over all things' (Spinoza 1951a: 37). If religion is allowed to become an alternative authority in the city, the possibility for passions to destabilize the city increases, association and co-operation are jeopardized, and the emerging sectarian divisions threaten peace and security, the fundamental goals of the city. Most importantly, the relationship between religion and the state contains an asymmetry: a religious way of life is only possible in a political association, in a city. In the state of nature it is impossible to be religious. By the same token, the dissolution of the city also endangers piety itself. Therefore one cannot obey God if one does not obey the authority of the city, the sovereign – 'God only rules among men through the instrumentality of earthly potentates' (Ibid. 246).

Spinoza's absolute democracy makes use of religion at the level of the universal faith but here religion does not determine politics. This perspective excludes what Laustsen aptly calls 'religious politics', which either takes the form of a frontal negation of secularism (for instance when the so-called 'fundamentalism' affirms theocracy and elevates the religious dogma above the level of politics) or, if secularization is taken for granted, reduces the political to the implementation of religious dogma (see Laustsen 2011: 148). Democracy is not reducible to religious governance.

Likewise, the link between the universal faith and the true religion is not reducible to a 'civil religion' in the sense of an abstract religion which seeks to transcend the existing, established religions with a view to grounding a political community, often in a nationalistic–patriotic framework, while other 'normal' religions are referred to the private sphere. In the American case, for instance, it is argued that civil religion is a 'differentiated' religion that exists alongside other religions (Bellah 1974: 21). When American presidents refer to religion or God in their speeches, they do 'not refer to any religion in particular' but only 'to the concept of God, a word which almost all Americans can accept but which means so many things to so many different people that it is almost an empty sign' (Ibid. 23). For the American civil religion, the constitution occupies a place similar to that of the scripture, Americans are supposed to be the elected people, significant presidents appear holy (George Washington as the American Moses, Lincoln as a martyr), there exist national holidays (Thanksgiving and Memorial Day), and so on, to the point that there emerges a pendant to every aspect of 'normal' religion within civil religion (Laustsen 2011: 149). Interestingly, apparent similarities exist between Spinoza's 'universal faith' and 'civil religion' (both are abstract, both are grounded in the public space, both seek to unite rather than divide ...). But there are significant differences as well. Above all, 'civil religion' is often closely related to a national culture and thus tends to be partial and particularistic, often legitimizing, in our case, American expansionist policies abroad (such as the Vietnam War), while suppressing conflicts within (such as racial conflicts) with reference to 'national' interests (Ibid. 150). In contrast, the universal faith is common to all, irreducible to a national culture, has no 'elected' addressees, and enables agonistic relations rather than suppressing conflicts between different political imaginations. Most importantly, it does not seek to legitimate the political with reference to the religious, or reason with reference to imagination.

In this regard the political theology of absolute democracy is clearly differentiated from other political theologies, most notably Schmitt's. In both Spinoza and Schmitt the focus dramatically shifts from the religious to the political. But while Schmitt is predominantly interested in 'secularizing' the sacred (the transfer of religious concepts to the political domain), Spinoza's main interest is in 'profaning' it. Thus the 'miracle' is excluded from Spinoza's democracy. Most substantially, while both Schmitt and Spinoza are against the separation of powers (sovereignty must be absolute), in Schmitt the 'absolute' leads to direct securitization and thereby de-politicization. But Spinoza's 'absolute' democracy seeks politicization. Likewise, in both Schmitt and Spinoza there is a metaphysical aspect both in life and in politics for which protection from neutralization is sought. But while in Schmitt metaphysics refers to Christianity and the Nazi ideology, in Spinoza it is philosophical. The mythical and ceremonial aspects of Nazism, which are reminiscent of both an instrumentalist use of civil religion (see Ibid. 153) and a Peterson-style economic theology, have no space in Spinoza's political theology.

So, the state must decide on religion. Yet it is essential to recall two points here. In this context what Spinoza means by 'religion' is basically the 'universal faith' and its minimal commands (love of God and love of neighbor). Thus, that the state decides on religion does not mean that it elevates one of the existing–competing religions to the level of official religion or invents a new religion as an alternative to them. The state does not legislate or 'make' the divine law; it only interprets it, without forcing people to worship in a particular way (see James 2012: 299). It is because both reason and revelation agree that love of God and neighborly love are essential for both political and religious association that the state can dictate a religious way of life. But it cannot reduce the 'universal faith', which is the common aspect of all faiths, to a particular religion and demand that its subjects practice that particular religion. It is also significant in this respect whether the state is democratic or not. The more democratic it is, the more it would reflect a common position, thus the more legitimate the state's take on religion will be. While religion or a religious way of life is reduced in Spinoza to obeying the laws of the city, the assumption is that the more democratic the city is the less repressive this reduction will be. Further, but not less significantly, for Spinoza even the worst tyranny is preferable to falling back upon the state of nature in which the city is dissolved (see Ibid. 258–59). That is, even if the state were not democratic, the law would still be essential to the perseverance of the social bond. Paradoxically, only within a democracy can the law de-activate itself.

To understand this paradox, we first need to understand another paradox, namely, that putting limits to religion by delimiting it to the 'universal faith' is precisely what opens up a space for religious freedom: insofar as the 'universal faith' functions as a common ground, everyone can interpret, accommodate and practice this common faith according to their own particular opinions. Such a shared platform makes it possible for both equality and divergence among different religions and sects to exist, and, at the same time, stimulates agonistic encounters among them. In this sense, disagreement will always exist among the different understandings of God – for at this point we are still within the domain of imagination where the understanding of God depends on everybody's partial perspectives affected by their passions. In any case, in the city 'brains are as diverse as palates' (Spinoza 1951a: 257). This pluralism is constitutive of the city. And each time an official religion, overlooking this essential plurality, dictates its own dogma and practice, it effectively weakens this pluralism and reduces real religious freedom. Every time a ruler dictates his own religious opinion, he undermines the democratic basis for potential agonistic interactions among different religious interpretations and turns them into antagonistic forces.

The real danger is not plurality but the tendency for superstition within the multitude which is more susceptible to emotions than reason and that 'always strains after rarities and exceptions' (Ibid. 213). The multitude:

> rushes headlong into every enterprise, and is easily corrupted either by avarice or luxury: everyone thinks himself omniscient and wishes to fashion all things to his liking, judging a thing to be just or unjust, lawful or unlawful, according as he thinks it will bring him profit or loss:

vanity leads him to despise his equals, and refuse their guidance: envy of superior fame or fortune (for such gifts are never equally distributed) leads him to desire and rejoice in his neighbor's downfall.

(Ibid. 216)

What is difficult is to establish a democratic society in which the multitude prefer public right to private advantage and move beyond superstition. In this respect the universal faith provides the multitude with a basis for maintaining the fiction of God (obedience to the divine law or the universal faith operates within the domain of imagination) while avoiding superstition and, eventually, opening up a space for the emergence of the 'true religion' in which love of God can lead to intellectual love of God.

As such, what Spinoza suggests is a relation of accommodation or the realization of a (disjunctive) synthesis between imagination and reason, the universal faith and the true religion, a 'synthesis' in the sense that insofar as the universal faith belongs to the first kind of knowledge, it is also a necessary step towards reason and as such prepares the ground for reason. However, the relation is potentially disjunctive for the obvious reason that even though reason and imagination can be reconciled they are irreducible to each other.

Remarkably, Spinoza's absolute democracy completely sidesteps institutionalized religion. Its outcome is threefold: first, in the process of 'perfection', the transcendent aspect of the law is progressively de-activated or profaned. Second, this profanation is synonymous with the proliferation of the 'true religion'. Third, this is also a process of democratization in the sense that the heteronomous aspect of religion is gradually superseded by the increasing autonomy of the moral actors, while avoiding, at the same time, ethical neutralization, or, adiaphorization. And finally, the process is one of pluralization, promoting agonistic respect and thus peace and security.

Now we are in a position to understand why democracy is the 'most natural form of government' for Spinoza (1951a: 263). Democracy is 'what approaches nearest' to an 'absolute' form of government, against which other governments are measured (Spinoza 1951b: 347). In other words, democracy is the truth of other regimes, 'the internal tendency at work in all forms of government; it channels the displacement of the relationship between the power of the multitude and the state in a direction that tends to make them coincide' (Kouvelakis 2003: 304). Or, in Marx's formulation that embraces Spinoza's, 'democracy is the resolved mystery of all constitutions' (Marx 1970: 29–30).

At this point, however, we must recall that the relationship between imagination and reason, or religion and democratic politics, is not based exclusively on perfection. There is also an antagonistic aspect to it because, although democracy is the truth of other forms of governments, the relationship is not symmetrical. Thus Marx compares monarchy and democracy in the following way:

Democracy is the truth of monarchy, monarchy is not the truth of democracy. Monarchy is necessarily democracy in contradiction with itself, whereas the monarchial moment is no contradiction within democracy. Monarchy cannot, while democracy can be understood in terms of itself. In democracy none of the moments obtains a significance other than what befits it. Each is really only a moment of the whole Demos. In monarchy one part determines the character of the whole; the entire constitution must be modified according to the immutable head. Democracy is the generic constitution; monarchy is a species, and indeed a poor one.

(Ibid. 29)

Insofar as democracy is taken as a generic concept, the relationship between democracy and other forms of governments is not reconcilable for the difference at issue is a difference in kind. In this regard agonism gives way to antagonism. The real meaning of democracy appears in its antagonistic relation to other forms of governments as well as in the agonistic processes of 'perfection' through which other regimes can approach or diverge from democracy as a measure of politics as such. In this precise sense there is an antagonistic aspect that pertains to democracy itself, an aspect that takes the form of an explosion of the egalitarian impulse, which often escapes the established rules of representative democracy such as voting.

This is also to say that, while other forms of government can be 'perfected' towards democracy, democracy itself can only be corrupted or perverted towards other forms of governments.

Democratic perversion

Indeed, democracy has always been subject to corruption, both from inside and from outside. The democratic form is a form that corrupts itself for democracy is a question of what Derrida calls 'autoimmunity': it is a system that can attack itself because it consists of not only a promise but also a threat, or rather, a 'threat *in* the promise itself' (Derrida 2005: 82). It is remarkable in this context that the common denominator of concepts such as 'post-politics' (Žižek 1999), 'post-democracy' (Rancière 1999), or 'democratic materialism' (Badiou 2009c), which seek to critically describe contemporary democracy, is a gesture towards articulating a vision of perversion of politics in general and of democracy specifically. They all designate a political way of emptying out the political content of democracy. After all, the history of modernity is the history of how its founding concepts are appropriated and revised, thereby suppressed, by capitalism and the state.

Not surprisingly, therefore, today's democracy takes itself for granted, depicting itself as the 'end of history'. But the more a society becomes its own justification, the more it brands as blasphemy every suspicion 'against the notion that what is, is right – just because it exists' (Adorno 1967: 101). This accord with what exists, which adopts the actual as its norm, paradoxically restores the mythic power in the form of a new taboo, and in this framework disagreement only provokes *ressentiment*: 'the war against' everything that does not fit into 'our' democracy. Yet, one can only 'become' democratic. Democracy has a virtual dimension that must not be confused with or reduced to the actually existing constitutional states. As such, democracy is a paradoxical concept, a virtual 'problem' in the Deleuzean sense, a problem that can be actualized in different conceptions or solutions. Democracy is always 'to come' and therefore the idea of democracy must be distinguished from its actual forms (Derrida 1994: 73, 99), not because it points to a promise that belongs to the future but because 'it will always remain aporetic in its structure' (Derrida 2005: 86). Therefore a democratic society can only be imagined as a unity of multiplicities in which multiple conceptions and solutions signify actual diversification. Only on this basis can it be possible to hold a common *concept* of the democratic society while everybody can agree to disagree about its different *conceptions*. What makes such a society interesting is the surface, the mediation, between its virtual and actual components, which is precisely what disappears in 'perversion'.

However, this mediation does not need to be a religious one, for one does not need religion to have values. This is also why the idea of profanation has inspired many thinkers in their discussion of democracy. Consider Nietzsche's critique of liberal democracy. For Nietzsche, too, democracy is a paradoxical concept in that it can always degenerate into a perfect environment for *ressentiment* covered as a moral (rather than political) demand for justice. This internal perversion can occur because modern democracy has overtaken, although by secularizing it, the notion of the 'individual' from Christianity: the immortal soul as an abstract, unconditional, and indivisible category (Nietzsche 1972: 107). Just as the private space of the Christian soul provided an escape route from the social and the political, from the world as it is, modern liberal democracy 'turns this escape into a political foundation' by representing the body politic as an entire sum of private spaces (Warren 1988: 215). Thus liberal democracy is marked by a fear of totalitarianism, of the colonization of private spaces by the state. Paradoxically, however, what makes totalitarianism possible is the very process of individualization. As Foucault puts it, in modernity the Christian soul reappears as an object of 'salvation oriented' scientific rationality that aims at disciplining and normalizing populations, that is, at creating 'docile bodies' reminiscent of Nietzsche's last man (see Foucault 1977: 135–69; 1982: 214–15). In other words, it is passive nihilism, the survival of the Nietzschean 'last man' that makes the colonization of the self by the state possible and probable. This is why, for Foucault as for Nietzsche, the political task in modern society is 'not to discover what we are, but to refuse what we are' (1982: 216). To refuse the kind of individuality imposed on us by the state.

Nietzsche distinguishes three elements in the origin of Christianity: the oppressed, the mediocre and the discontented. The first enabled Christianity to fight against the nobility, the second against the exceptional and the privileged, and the third against the instincts of happiness and health. Gradually, however, the second element has stepped into the foreground in the sense that Christianity has persuaded the warrior classes to its side together with the powerful, which had an interest in the conquest of the 'mob' (Nietzsche 1967: 126). Finally, the self-consciousness of the mediocre, the herd instinct, grew to the extent that, in liberal democracies, it 'arrogates even political power to itself' (Ibid.). In this sense, modern democracy is 'Christianity made natural' (Ibid.). It is for this internal reason, because of its nihilistic heritage, that democracy can always degenerate, resulting in the 'mediocritizing of man – a useful, industrious, highly serviceable and able herd-animal man ... a type prepared for slavery in the subtlest sense' (Nietzsche 1972: 154; see also 1967: 80, 256).

As such, Nietzsche's critique of slave morality is still as relevant as ever, provided that the 'slave' here is not confused with someone dominated. The 'dominators' can also be the bearers of slave morality to the extent that they are influenced by passive, reactive forces. Even 'totalitarian regimes are in this sense regimes of slaves, not merely because of the people that they subjugate, but above all because of the type of "masters" they set up' (Deleuze 1983: x). In line with this, and in contrast to another common misunderstanding, Nietzsche is not against the possibility of the weak's struggle for more power in order to create a better, more just world: the weak can, and should, engage in a struggle for power but this struggle must be a power struggle, not a moral one (see Hass 1982: 150). What defines *ressentiment* is precisely the translation of the political issues into moral ones. Insofar as 'freedom' is defined as freedom from external constraints rather than their overcoming, the democratic ideal comes to legitimize passivity and slave morality: a degenerated democracy as the form of the city's decay (Ibid. 108, 161). The freedom, which democracy brings with it, paradoxically opens up the space for nihilism:

> *My conception of freedom.* – The value of a thing sometimes lies not in what one attains with it, but in what one pays for it – what it *costs* us. I give an example. Liberal institutions immediately cease to be liberal as soon as they are attained: subsequently there is nothing more thoroughly harmful to freedom than liberal institutions. One knows, indeed, *what* they bring about: they undermine the will to power, they are the leveling of mountain and valley exalted to a moral principle, they make small, cowardly and smug – it is the herd animal which triumphs with them every time. Liberalism: in plain words, *reduction to the herd animal*. ... As long as they are still being fought for, these same institutions produce effects; they then in fact promote freedom mightily. Viewed more closely, it is war which produces these effects, war *for* liberal institutions which as war permits the illiberal instincts to endure. And war is a training in freedom.
>
> (Nietzsche 1969: 92)

What matters, in other words, is 'becoming democratic' and then again 'war' has an indispensable role to play in this. However, once the goals are 'attained', they turn into harmful monuments of leveling. Thus Nietzsche does not, in any way, find it desirable 'that the kingdom of righteousness and peace should be established on earth' because it 'would be the kingdom of the profoundest mediocrity' (1960: 343). A democracy that declares itself to have arrived, a democracy that cannot question itself any more, can only be a nihilistic form of government. The ultimate paradox of democracy is that it is a democracy that wants to overcome itself.

Excursus III
The emancipated city: notes on the Gezi revolts

Contemporary politics is haunted by a paradox: while most political problems are thematized as particular issues, what causes them is often universalistic in nature. Capital, for instance, is a universal measure of value while it mediates particular, time-space bound relations. It is this dialectical power of money that enables the Right to insist on the role of the market in social regulation, on its ability to link the particular and the universal. Hence any Leftist politics must invent a link between the particular and the universal which can challenge the market's universalism–particularism. The political question, in other words, is grounded in the movement from the particular to the universal (Albertsen 2002: 49; Harvey 1996: 332, 360–62).

The 2013 revolts in Turkey provide an interesting case in this respect. The event started as a particular, issue-based demonstration: a small group of environmentalists protesting against an urban renovation project in Taksim Square in Istanbul, where the government decided to build a shopping mall and a mosque on the site of a public park. Demonstrators gathered in the park as the authorities started to cut the trees. It was seemingly an 'inessential' moment, one among many. But on May 29, when the police started to use violence against the demonstrators, this habit of the police triggered a political fire which the government could not put out for months. In a country polarized by economic inequalities, cultural conflicts, and Islamic governance, the particular claims of the demonstrators metamorphosed into universalistic demands for equality, freedom, and solidarity. The major opposition parties and professional organizations started, after a period of hesitation, to give their support to the demonstrators. In no time, the demonstrations grew, and Taksim became a political magnet, attracting thousands of demonstrators. Police violence continued, and Recep Tayyip Erdoğan, the Prime Minister, expressed his firm determination: they would not allow 'a few çapulcus' (a few marauders) to stop the projects (Erdoğan 2013c). This remark became another 'insignificant' moment that gave impetus to significant events. More and more people started to react to police violence and to the Prime Minister's remarks. What started as relatively small-scale opposition to an urban renewal project turned into refusal of government policies that aim at creating a neo-liberal paradise in Istanbul. And finally, the refusal became the refusal of Islamic governance, of the government itself. This movement from the particular to the universal found its expression in the most wide-spread slogan of the revolt: 'Every place is Taksim'.

The establishment media ignored the first large-scale demonstrations on 1–2 June. While one of the greatest crowds Istanbul has ever seen was marching from the Asian part of the city towards Taksim, for instance, CNN Turk, a major TV channel in the country, was showing a crowd of penguins in the North Pole. (The day after, some demonstrators dressed up as penguins were carrying a placard: 'Record this CNN Turk! We, too, are here today!' Another placard was less humorous: 'Corrupted media!') But all Turkish TV channels were giving prime time to the Prime Minister who was stubbornly defending the project in Taksim as well as other governmental policies such as the alcohol ban in public spaces. 'They say we are realizing the commands of religion. Is it bad to do what religion says if religion commands something that is good for society, for humanity?' (Erdoğan 2013a). This remark, which blurs the difference between the state and religion, is indeed essential to understand both the social psychology of the Turkish revolt and its difference from the Egyptian revolts of 2011.

A tale of three republics

The revolt was a reaction to Islamic governance. Significantly, however, the governing party, AKP, itself was born as a reaction to the republican idea, which was a reaction to the Ottoman theocracy. Originally, Turkish republicanism emerged at the beginning of the twentieth century as the war of independence against Western imperialism on the one hand and Ottoman rule on the other. This republicanism articulated itself as a demand for freedom and equality as well as a strong desire for secularization. However, its secularism was triangulated with two other elements: the project of capitalist modernization on the one hand and the ideology of nationalism on the other. In terms of economy, the republic leaned against liberalism, its main project being the creation of a national bourgeoisie. But in the following decades the economy increasingly fell into the orbit of imperialism and globalization. In political terms, however, the republic retained its nationalism in the same period. Indeed it was exacerbated by the personality cult established around Mustafa Kemal and the increasing militarization of the political culture. In this sense, the twentieth-century Turkish Republic can be read as a history of (internal and external, nationalist and imperialist) perversion of the republican ideals.

What is usually called the 'second republic' is the period of Islamic governance of AKP, a so-called 'moderate' Islamic party. Crucially in this regard, AKP did not meddle with the economy: it pushed the economy more towards neo-liberalism, experimenting with the varieties of Islamic neo-liberalism and neo-liberal Islamism. Likewise, it preserved the political language of nationalism, but with an Ottoman/Islamic twist. Its project was to dismantle the republican heritage on the third front: religion. Thus, while it changed little regarding the economic (liberal) and political (nationalist) aspects of the first republic, it systematically attacked its secularism. In this sense what is 'new' in the second republic is the tendency to replace the governance of religion by religious governance.

Let us, at this point, open a parenthesis regarding the early days of the Turkish Republic, which were marked by a historical disjunction between the republican and theocratic idea(l)s. Ottoman rule had consisted in a combination of monarchy and the caliphate, and the caliphate, as well as the monarchy, had acted as a counterrevolutionary force during the independence war which resulted in the birth of the republic in 1923. A fatwa, for instance, which the caliphate issued in 1920, defines those participating in the independence war and their leader, Mustafa Kemal, as 'outlaws' who attempt at 'deceiving the Sultan's subjects' and disobey both the 'holy sharia and the orders of the Sultan'. Therefore, the fatwa concludes, it is 'legitimate and obligatory to kill them' (see http://www.filozof.net on this fatwa, known as 'Şeyhülislam Dürrizade Fetvası' in Turkish history). That is, the independence war took place not with the support of but in spite of the caliphate, which saw in the freedom fighters only *homini sacri*. Soon after the war, therefore, the republic dismantled the institution of the caliphate. But the republic did not reject religion as such. Religion was seen as a necessary institution but it was confined to the private sphere, which, in turn, enabled the differentiation of religion and the caliphate. In this sense, the first republic sought to preserve religion as something akin to Spinoza's 'universal faith' (see *Chapter 2*) and tried to oppose the religious 'economy', that is, the ceremonial aspects of organized religion. Its Islam was a religion in which there is not much room for priesthood or clergy. 'The republic cannot risk its existence and freedom because of scholastic fallacies. For us, the caliphate cannot bear any meaning beyond being a historical memory' (Atatürk 2004: 390). All religious affairs were brought under the control of the state, under a new ministry of religious affairs. Mustafa Kemal argued that this was not done only to free politics from religion; in this way faith was to be freed from politics as well: 'for centuries Islam has been used as a political instrument; Islam must be liberated from this role ... ' (Atatürk 2004: 392). The condition for this to happen was freedom of thought and belief.

Thereby we can formulate the difference between the first and the second republics in the following way: for the first republic, religion is distinct from politics; for the second, the 'commands of religion' justify, if not decide, politics. The urban renewal project that triggered the revolt has an ideological–symbolic meaning in this context. The revolt, as mentioned before, was clearly against religious governance. But its significance is not reducible to an opposition between the two republicanisms. There is a third, more politicized republicanism expressed in the demonstrations:

> It is crucial that we don't see the Turkish protests merely as a secular civil society rising up against an authoritarian Islamist regime supported by a

silent Muslim majority. What complicates the picture is the protests' anti-capitalist thrust: protesters intuitively sense that free-market fundamentalism and fundamentalist Islam are not mutually exclusive.

(Žižek 2013)

The third republicanism was against both *Islamic* neo-liberalism and *neo-liberal* Islam. To discuss this we must focus on the political dimension of the revolts.

The politics of Gezi

It is well known that the Gezi demonstrations have united an extremely diverse set of people who are against the government's polarizing politics: the youth, the elderly, students, bureaucrats, feminists, housewives, Muslim Leftists, the Kurds, the Alevi Muslims, the Kemalists, Leftist liberals, social democrats, socialists, communists, Fenerbahçe supporters, Beşiktaş supporters ... Against this background Nilüfer Göle, a Turkish sociologist, insists that:

> it is wrong to read this movement from a political perspective. The movement can renew the democratic imagination, its texture, only insofar as it remains autonomous, independent of political parties, as long as it retains its innocence. ... If, on the other hand, it positions itself as a political movement, it will sail away from democracy.
>
> (Göle 2013; my translation)

A liberal, Göle wants the particular to remain particular. For her the demonstrators' attempt at toppling the government signifies the 'transgression' of democracy and 'ignoring elections' (Ibid.). But what if the demonstrations are political precisely because they seek to redefine the framework of politics rather than being content with post-political interest negotiation within a given framework?

Consider the case of the 'woman in red'. The critique of police violence found its iconic image in the photograph of an activist, a woman in a red dress, surrounded by police officers. In the photograph she appears standing, colorful and totally immobile, while the police officers, in gray-toned colors, are spraying tear gas towards her. This woman was referred to in the media as 'Kırmızılı Kadın' (KK, 'woman in red'). Later it turned out that her name is Ceyda Sungur, a researcher in the Department of Town Planning, Istanbul Technical University. This is perhaps no coincidence. After all, the most significant spaces in a city from the perspective of town planning are public spaces, the *agora*, and in contemporary society the *agora* is under attack: both *oikos* (privatization) and *ecclesia* (state control) threaten to colonize public spaces today (see Bauman 1999: 87). The first tendency is rooted in economic theology (*oikonomia*); the latter in political theology (see *Chapter 1*). No wonder that the most powerful dystopias of our society emphasize either the first (*Brave New World*) or the other (*1984*) tendency. As against both tendencies, which are abundant and co-existing in contemporary Istanbul, the Gezi demonstrations express a desire to protect the *agora*. They are a reminder that the colonization and/or privatization of the *agora* always signify the disappearance of true democracy. Thus the revolts found their expression in and through the *agora*, Gezi Park and Taksim Square.

But in a second, more metaphorical sense, KK's involvement in the demonstrations as a town planner has a 'Kafkaesk' aspect. Recall Kafka's *Castle* which addresses the problematique of subjectivity in relation to the law. The protagonist, K., makes repeated attempts to be accepted into the 'castle' and to settle in the village, but with no luck; he stubbornly tries to understand the content of the law, but systematically fails in finding meaning in that which can have no meaning. Ultimately, he cannot access the castle, for the castle is his own invention, the product of his own desire. The law is a fiction, a spectacle. But Kafka's choice of K.'s profession, a land surveyor (*Kardo* in Latin), is interesting. As Agamben (2011b: 35) points out, this is a strategic choice from Kafka's side because K. is precisely a figure who problematizes the 'boundaries' of the castle –the boundaries between the village and the castle, between people and the bureaucrats, and ultimately between humans and the divine: 'What the land surveyor is concerned with is the border that divides and conjoins the two, and this is what he wants to abolish or, rather, render inoperative' (Ibid. 36).

K.'s 'war' is not necessarily a war against the divine, but against what people say about the divine; not a conflict with God but with 'the angels, the messengers, and the bureaucrats who appear to be [his] representatives' on earth (Ibid. 35). Similarly, KK's primary concern was the constitution of the limits of the city. Her conflict was not (primarily) with God (both around the environmentalist group she represented and in the demonstrations in general, religious groups had been present) but with the angels/bureaucrats: the 'moderate' Islamic government of Turkey, which had been busy redrawing the boundaries between God and humans, between the law and its subjects, between the *ecclesia* and *oikos*. Thus, contra many commentators who emphasized that the whole revolt originated in an 'innocent' environmentalist protest (see for instance Kongar and Küçükkaya 2013: 59) one must insist on the diabolically refined and radically political gesture inherent in her desire: to render the given boundaries inoperative.

Another inspiring figure of the revolts was the 'immobile man'. After Gezi Park was evacuated by police force, one man, Erdem Gündüz, started to stand still in the square. Then others mimicked him. Soon the act was copied in different settings. The impact of the 'immobile man' was disproportional. The Prime Minister himself felt obliged to post a Twitter comment on it: 'we say: there is no stopping, continue moving; they say: the immobile man' (Erdoğan 2013b; my translation). Tellingly in this respect, in the initial phase of the demonstrations the government had insisted that the plan was not to cut the trees but merely to 'move' them elsewhere (see Kongar and Küçükkaya 2013: 15). The image of 'immobile man' must therefore be juxtaposed to that of mobile trees. Mobility versus immobility: to discuss this dimension of the revolt, let us turn to two theorists of mobility, Deleuze and Guattari.

As is well known, in their ontology everything constitutes a mobile network, an 'assemblage', a process of interaction and connection between heterogeneous elements. What is significant, however, is that assemblages face two tendencies at once: organization and disorganization. Insofar as they constitute the relations that result in stratification, assemblages are part of the strata, that is, of actual, extensive reality. But on the other side assemblages face 'something else, the body without organs', which causes disorganization and disarticulation to the strata (1987: 40). The 'body without organs' is, like Spinoza's monist 'substance', an all-encompassing flux, a mutable chaos, from which everything emerges and to which everything eternally returns. As such, it is a concept that refers to 'absolute immobility', to absolute disorganization of 'organs'/assemblages. In other words, what is at play in this mobile ontology is the dialectic of organization and disorganization, connection and disconnection, stratification and de-stratification. This is why 'de-territorialization', for Deleuze and Guattari, is not reducible to physical linear movement but refers, above all, to disorganization, to a deviation from the strata, through a link to the body without organs. Therefore, at the heart of the production of the assemblages, which create the strata, we find a tendency of anti-production; at the center of a mobile ontology, we meet immobility: assemblages 'work only when they break down, and continually by breaking down' (1983: 8).

Crucially, however, such immobility is not merely a supplement to mobility (e.g. the airport as the immobile support of mobility), or even a consequence of mobility (e.g. sitting motionless during a flight). Rather, the point is that every mobile assemblage exhibits a paradoxical relation to the body without organs, to 'an immobile motor' (Ibid. 141). Concomitantly, 'becoming a body without organs' is the highest ethical, political and social ideal for Deleuze and Guattari. It is not the empirical mobility of social assemblages as such but their breaking down, relating to the domain of the virtual, their reaching the level of an 'absolute immobility', that creates the new. The new, or what they call the 'line of flight', is always linked to the body without organs; it always emerges as a subtraction from, as a dis*organ*ization of the strata. This is also what 'revolution' means to Deleuze: linking society to its body without organs, to its 'immobile motor', by means of which 'the faculty of sociability is raised to its transcendent exercise' (1994: 208).

This idea also brings to mind Benjamin's (1999) earlier reflections on history as a pile of pseudo-events, the indistinct flow of chronological, 'empty' time as a catastrophe. Hence his modernity is a mobile hell, the ideal of which is bare repetition, the eternal recurrence of the same non-events which produce no difference. In turn, 'revolution' to Benjamin is the 'emergency break' of history, which makes it possible to arrest the indistinct flow, to break free from the historicist conformism (1999: 252–54), an event in which 'time stands still and has come to a stop' (Benjamin 1999: 254). Thus, if history repeats itself as farce, if in pseudo-history the tragic reappears as comedy, this is not necessarily a reason for melancholic detachment but rather an occasion for a joyful separation – history has this course 'so that humanity should part with its past *cheerfully*' (Marx 1957: 46; see also Agamben 1999: 154). 'Happiness' is a cheerful separation from pseudo-history, from bare repetition. In this sense, the ever-new political problematique the 'immobile man' has re-articulated is the link between subtraction and emancipation, his repetition of Bartleby's slogan/statement – 'I would prefer not to'. The Prime Minister, in contrast, insisted that 'there is no stopping'. His statement borders on the discourse of the police:

> 'Move along! There is nothing to see here!' The police says that there is nothing to see on a road, that there is nothing to do but move along. It asserts that the space of circulating is nothing other than the space of circulation. Politics, in contrast, consists in transforming this space of 'moving-along' into a space for the appearance of a subject: i.e., the people, the workers, the citizens: It consists in refiguring the space, of what there is to do there, what is to be seen or named therein.
> (Rancière 2010: 37)

Another remarkable contribution to the demonstrations was the video published by the Ukrainian feminist group Femen (see http://www.haber3.com/femen-gezi-parki-icin-soyundu-haberi-2002022h.htm). A militant group, Femen's members are specialized in turning the naked female body, the spectacular object of patriarchal repression, into political statements against power. In Istanbul, too, they experimented with naked bodies. Their slogan was 'resist Islamization!'

Another, though not equally mediatized, symbolic figure using the naked body as a slogan was the so-called 'naked man', who, during the demonstrations on 15 June, walked towards the police completely naked, shouting slogans against Islam. In spite of being shared through the social media, this act did not appear on TV and was not mimicked by others (http://www.youtube.com/watch?v=3CeByxygysQ). However, his short-circuiting of the relationship between nakedness and religious governance demands a comment for it is a fundamental political act. As is well known, in religious imagination, Adam and Eve were covered in human clothing only after the fall – before the fall they were wearing 'a dress of mercy, of tight-fitting glory' (Agamben 2008). Because of sinning, they have lost this 'glory' and were forced to cover themselves with fig leaves. This 'dress of sin', the reminder of lost glory, is thus also a promise of glory to be re-gained through redemption. Along the same lines, theology can only perceive nakedness as something negative, as a temporary absence of glory. 'Nakedness exists, if at all, only in Hell' (Agamben 2008; see also 2011b: 57). Then, if religion sacralizes the bodily nakedness by removing it to a separate sphere, with Femen and the 'naked man' we are forced to sense the reverse gesture of profanation, the transformation of the body from a sacred object (whose use is proscribed and regulated by religion and economy) into 'pure means' (means without a determinate purpose) that can only be expressed as a potentiality for whatever use (Agamben 2000: 59; 2005: 61–64). In this reverse movement nakedness is related not to hell but to an event. Not that nakedness was an event as such. Rather, the naked man's nakedness forces us to try to think a possibility:

> We must try to think a possible nakedness of man – something that theology, and then reification and pornography, have made unthinkable. What we must find again is the nakedness of Adam, before God covered him in a dress of glory. This, however, should neither be understood as a natural condition, nor as a promise of something to come. This nakedness is, rather, something that we, here and now, must liberate, piece by piece, from the theological fabric that is wrapped around it.
> (Agamben 2008)

What religion captures is this potentiality that pertains to human nudity. The naked man, in contrast, showed a profaned nudity that is detached from the notion of sin and from the political–economic theological apparatus that grounds itself on the assumption of *homo sacer*'s naked life.

Çapulcu as subject

Through the desire for 'immobility', for withdrawal from the existing framework of politics, a collective subject emerged: the masses of 'çapulcu'. As mentioned before, the term was first used by the Prime Minister as an insult. Later, as the demonstrators identified with it, the term came to signify fidelity to the Gezi demonstrations, an operation through which the rebels related to the revolt-event and moved into a re-defined, new present. Thus, apart from who 'çapulcu' might be as an empirical figure, the name signifies a historical becoming, which redefines the past, and a subjective will, expressing the decision to become part of a political event, synthesizing the relationship between the political, the historical and the subjective.

Seen in this prism, the 'çapulcu' movement is not apolitical but politics par excellence; a gesture of politicization, which requires the metaphoric universalization of particular demands, the restructuring of the whole social space (see Žižek 1999: 204–8). After all, universality exists only insofar as it is incarnated in some particularity. The demonstrators could imagine a new world only by focusing on a particular problem, the future of the urban park. In this sense the event opened up a new political space, gaining its impetus from an ideological refusal of political sovereignty and its economic–governmental apparatuses. As such the Gezi demonstrations signify, vis-à-vis religious governance, a general flight from religio-social determinations.

The event was singular because it relied on the free association of people who did not restate some particular, familiar demands. Along the same lines, the temporality of the event was *kairos*, the moment at which everything seems possible. The Gezi revolt offered a straightforward moment of choice: the event or the state. The demonstrators seized the moment and were seized by it. Particular positions joined forces, transforming themselves into a common name, 'çapulcu', and exposing themselves to a virtual world of possibilities. Taksim Square, too, had undergone a metamorphosis: it was no longer merely an empirical space but had become a virtual political center: 'Everywhere is Taksim'.

> Once a certain threshold of determination, obstinacy, and courage has been passed, a people can indeed concentrate its existence in one square, one avenue, a few factories, a university.
>
> (Badiou 2011)

The miracle of the event, after all, is to transcend empirical space, to condense a place into a virtual 'center', a space of spacing, or, to use a metaphor dear to Nietzsche, into a 'labyrinth of the future' (1967: 3).

Many commentators have pointed out that the demonstrations were expressions of anxieties fueled by neo-liberal globalization and Islamic governance. But Taksim Square was also the place where the demonstrators have overcome their anxieties vis-à-vis power and found the courage to disobey the authorities, showing an allegiance to a truth, risking their socio-symbolic positions as well as their lives. They undertook a passionate, even mad act, which also, as a disruptive force, enabled them to redefine themselves as citizens. To use Lacan's phrase, the demonstrators 'went through fantasy', dismantled the illusion that sustains the spectacle of power and keeps them in their proper places. This decoupling from the socio-symbolic also initiated a particular form of violence that 'immobilized' the social order and problematized its legitimacy.

What we have is a repetitive chain: the first republican revolt (against the Ottoman rule and the sultanate), followed by a counter-revolt (Erdoğan's second republic), which is then followed by another revolt (the 'çapulcu' as a new figure of republicanism). But insofar as it only expresses itself as a reaction, the figure of 'çapulcu' would remain part of an unproductive relationship without leading to any notion of a 'new'. Thus, the crucial question which the future will try to answer is whether the çapulcus' courage has played a part in recomposing a new situation as well as punctuating the existing situation. So far there is no doubt that Gezi has changed a lot in Turkish politics. Most notably, it has re-opened up a space for profaned politics and has caused scissions within 'moderate Islam'.

But whatever its consequences, the event must not be reduced to those consequences (see Deleuze 1995: 171). One way to repress the event is always to reduce it to its historical consequences, allowing its virtual aspect to disappear into actual facts. Most of the demonstrators, after all, objectively knew that they would not have a strong chance against the government in the long run, which is why their overall strategy was un-bonding and im-mobility.

For one thing, the majority of Turkish people did not join the çapulcus, which constituted only a tiny proportion of the population. Further, the çapulcus were a disorganized group which was not united by a shared ideology. Yet they were not opportunistic in orientation; they did not postpone the event with reference to 'objective facts', knowing well that such a position of the objective observer is the key obstacle to the event (see Žižek 2002b: 9). The event, after all, is a 'leap' of faith, and its spectral truth is 'perceptible only to those who accomplish this leap, not to neutral observers' (Žižek 2002c: 187). One cannot feel the 'magic' of the event without already being part of it. This is perhaps the ultimate meaning of saying 'I am çapulcu'.

Insofar as the basic premise of an event is that 'people are missing' (Deleuze 1989: 216), that people are 'to come', politics is an activity that produces such 'people' rather than representing existing people. In this Deleuzean sense the figure of çapulcu functioned as 'minority': a figure which escapes, deviates from the majority by subtracting itself from it, because non-integration, disorganization, is its precondition (Deleuze 1995: 173–74). As such the name çapulcu necessarily refers to the virtual potentiality (*potentia*) of the multitude, which cannot be contained within actualized dispositifs or strategies of power (*potestas*).

The obscure subject

But how did the revolt look from the 'other' side, from the side of the reactionary subject? Let us, to see this, dwell on an essay by Bengül Güngörmez in a government-friendly, Islamist newspaper, *Yeni Şafak* (Güngörmez 2013). In a nutshell she says that, for all their anger against the Islamic government, the demonstrators are themselves in the grip of religion in paradoxical ways. Indeed, 'for the Turkish Left and the laicist nationalists', Taksim is a 'politically sacred' site. More generally, the idea of 'revolution' itself has roots in religion; it is the 'continuation of religion by other means'. Paradoxically, therefore, the demonstrators are really mimicking a religious ritual all the while they think they are fighting against religious governance. Here, rather predictably, she leans against Schmitt's thesis: 'All significant concepts' of modern politics are 'secularized theological concepts' (1985: 36). Modern politics is based on 'stealing' the role of religion and 'instrumentalizing' its promise of salvation for this-worldly purposes. And since this process basically took place within Christian circles, 'the revolutionary hope is basically the Christian hope'. The Gezi revolt, in other words, is really an apocalyptic–Messianic religious movement with a secular mask. 'Why Taksim but not another place? Why did people not revolt en masse when trees were cut in other places?' It happened in Taksim, because Taksim Square is a 'sacred temple', the 'Jerusalem' of the 'modern messiahs', a place where the Leftists and the nationalists practice their 'well known rituals'. Then the author's rhetorical questions follow: 'who is saving whom from whom?' 'Do the people really want to be saved from Tayyip Erdoğan?' Finally, the author claims that she is not against protesting as such; she is merely against the Gezi protests' 'method', 'a degenerated religious ritual', which forecloses any 'dialogue' with its adversaries. Such non-dialogical 'ritual' is neither just nor democratic.

> Suppose that the conservative front organizes thousands of people in the mosques and gathers them in Taksim Square, shouting their slogans and demanding a mosque to be built here. Are they to be considered 'just'? Is the one who can gather thousands in a square, who shouts a lot, swears, and thus becomes more 'visible' in the public sphere to be considered 'right'?
>
> (Güngörmez 2013; my translation)

The article is rich in its ideological mystifications but here I can make four points that are relevant to our present context. First, the author implies that the Gezi revolt, as a modern phenomenon, is inauthentic or almost fake because all modern political concepts are 'stolen' from religion, specifically 'Christianity'. Gezi demonstrators are thus confronted with a new accusation: they are thieves appropriating Christian ideals. But from where, in the first place, did those concepts come to Christianity? Why has Nietzsche, for instance, called Christianity 'Platonism for "the people"'? (1972: 14). The author is blind to a well-known fact: Greek philosophy, especially Plato and Aristotle, has had a decisive impact on monotheistic theology. In general, religion itself is a machine of appropriation/sacralization – yes, of 'stealing' concepts and practices from profane sources. One could therefore effectively reverse the accusation: all theological ideas are political ideas in the first place. 'Political theology' is effectively a set of political theories of sovereignty and governmentality in the guise of religion (see *Introduction* and *Chapter 2*). Further, it is farcical to reduce modern politics to religion (see *Chapter 3*). Certainly, people sometimes 'anxiously conjure up the spirits of the past to their service and borrow from them names, battle cries and costumes' in order to present the new in a 'borrowed language' (Marx 1977: 10). But sometimes they create 'something that has never yet existed' (Ibid. 10). This is what happened in Taksim and this is what the author is deliberately obscuring by reducing the demonstrations to 'farce'. If anything, Taksim is a space of profanation par excellence – a space in which the spectacle of theological-political power is laid bare, and people discovered once more that the emperor is naked.

Second, the author is accusing the demonstrators of busying themselves with a 'spectacle' rather than engaging in 'dialogue' with their adversaries. But let us not forget: one of the most tragi-comic moments of Turkish politics occurred when, in 2012, the government caused a sensation by attempting to privatize public theatres because they are 'doing art for the sake of art' and their actors are 'pseudo-intellectuals, snobbish and elitist'. 'Get privatized, get autonomous. The State is pulling itself out of the theatre scene' (*Hürriyet*,

4 May 2012). Following this, public debate took the form of an opposition: AKP versus theatres. But what went unnoticed in this debate was the theatricality of the AKP-style politics itself, AKP's visible determination to use all the sources of the 'society of the spectacle' (populism, scandal, sensation, person cults, image management, commodity fetishism, and so on). Hence one suspects that AKP's opposition to theatres had one purpose: to hide its own theatricality. What would be left if theatricality is taken out of contemporary politics? We had a glimpse of this thanks to the Gezi revolts. Debord would have loved to watch it.

Third, the author airs an essentially petty-bourgeois sentiment in her search for 'dialogue'. But even the deaf have heard and the blind have seen that the Gezi demonstrations were triggered precisely because the government bypassed the *agora*, that is, it did not appreciate the value of dialogue. But there is another issue here. This relates to the fact that, once it all turned into a revolt, the demonstrators openly refused 'dialogue'. Any revolt or revolution is naturally the enemy of every bond, including 'dialogue'. Revolt necessarily scorns and avoids dialogue for it wants to create new ways of thinking and acting. The critical nexus of the Gezi demonstrations consisted in questioning the social order from the point of view of what it excludes, subtracting itself from prevailing consensus. Precisely therefore, from the perspective of the existing social order, it looks like an excess forcing the limits of given opinions. In this sense the demonstrators did not want dialogue; 'truth' counted more.

Which brings us to the fourth point: 'suppose that the conservative ... ' arrange a big scale demonstration. Recall Foucault's wonderful discussion of *parrhesia*, truth-telling, which he inextricably links with risk taking: when demonstrators address themselves to a sovereign, and tell him that his rule is disturbing and unbearable, they speak the language of truth, believe they are speaking the truth, and most importantly, they take a *risk*. 'It is because the *parrhesiastes* must take a risk in speaking the truth that the king or tyrant generally cannot use *parrhesia*; for *he* risks nothing' (Foucault 2001: 16). So, if such a crowd of demonstrators were gathered by the establishment, which risk were they going to take? What truth were they going to tell?

A hybrid subject: anti-capitalist Muslims

Before the Gezi events Turkey was internationally perceived as an exemplary example of 'moderate Islam'. Its governance of Islam, however, is increasingly problematized today not only by secular groups but also by groups such as 'anti-capitalist Muslims' that accuse AKP-style 'moderate Islam' of revising and de-politicizing Islamic politics through a 'protestant' reformism that justifies capitalism. Seen in this 'radical' perspective, 'moderate' Islamic governance looks like a diluted 'comedy' of real religion.

In this context it might be useful to focus on how 'anti-capitalist Muslims' view the dominant Islam in Turkey. Ergun's book (2011) can be illuminating here. He argues that Islamism in Turkey has always been on the side of power, always silent on class conflict, claiming a third position 'outside both capitalism and socialism' (Ibid. 65). However, this position is impossible, for throughout history there have only been two ways: 'good or evil' (Ibid. 66). In this Manichean prism 'classical Islamism' appears an 'emptied out monotheism with no aim, no promise of salvation, justice, equality or freedom' (Ibid.). Its image of God is a despotic and totalitarian God whose power is grounded not in love but in fear; a God that 'protects private property and wards off class struggle' (Ibid. 106). This 'pragmatic' Islam has a revisionist and reductionist approach to the Koran for it only sees ceremonies and rituals in it, overlooking its spirit (Ibid. 59). This Islam, which especially during the last two decades has been articulated with capitalism, really functions like 'opium'. True religion, on the other hand, exists to emancipate mankind from its chains. There is revolt, not obedience, in its nature. After all, 'all prophets are people who revolted against the dominant powers of their time, who denied the authority of those who enslave people through wealth and power' (Ibid. 61). Interpreted in this way, Islam is against the concentration of wealth (Ibid. 59). More importantly, 'Koran dictates that the ownership of the skies, the earth and everything in-between only belongs to Allah' (Ibid. 89).

This attempt at the appropriation of the idea of communism by Islamism invites a series of questions though. In the first place, if Islam in Turkey has never delivered a radical critique of what exists, if it has always 'institutionalized' itself on the basis of existing power relations (Ibid. 67), why should we expect a realistic change now? And what precisely makes 'anti-capitalist Muslims' anti-capitalist? What is capitalism in their view, if not merely consumerism? What is communism, if not the expropriation of all property by Allah in a way similar to 'state capitalism'? As long as these questions are not answered, the anti-capitalism of anti-capitalist Islamism would look like McDonald's anti-obesity campaigns. One is tempted to recall, in this context, Marx and Engels' critique of 'Christian Socialism':

> Nothing is easier than to give Christian asceticism a Socialist tinge. Has not Christianity declaimed against private property, against marriage, against the State? Has it not preached in the place of these, charity and poverty, celibacy and the mortification of the flesh, monastic life and Mother Church? Christian Socialism is but the holy water with which the priest consecrates the heart-burnings of the aristocrat ...
> (Marx and Engels 2002: 246–47)

Perhaps anti-capitalist Islamism is but the holy water with which its militants consecrate the heart-burnings of the 'beautiful souls' who cannot see their own role in the picture they criticize.

This 'Islam' is parasitic upon much external input: thus it often appropriates the ideas of radical thinkers (such as Nietzsche, Marx, Proudhon, Nazım, Kropotkin ...) within an Islamic discourse, emptying out their communist, anti-religious content. Tellingly, Ergun admits that in Turkey: 'Islamism, up to this date, has almost never occupied itself with something decent: Nazım Hikmet [a Leftist poet] wrote the poetry of the oppressed; Yılmaz Güney [a Leftist film director] directed their films; Ahmet Kaya [a Leftist pop musician] made their music; Ruhi Su [a Leftist folk musician] made their folk songs … It is possible to multiply the examples' (Ergun 2011: 171). Then why should 'Islam' appropriate and speak in the name of those Leftist artists today?

Further, 'radical' Islamism often seems to be trapped in what it criticizes: that is, in comedy, the symptom of unsuccessful repetition/revolution (Marx), or a sign of 'transcendental stupidity' (Deleuze). 'Radical' Islamism itself speaks the language of comedy in the sense that, for all its abstract references to equality, anti-capitalism and antagonistic politics, it cannot articulate an emancipatory politics that can move beyond the utopia of returning to a golden age, the time of Mahomet. In this sense the Gezi revolts demand the critique of the radicalism of 'radical' Islam as well as the pragmatism of 'moderate' Islam, and calls for the re-reading of their religious critique in the horizon of the critique of religion.

De te fabula narratur!

When a phenomenon appears to occupy a central position in thought, it is often a sure sign that that phenomenon is about to vanish, illuminating, like a dead star, in the very process of disappearing. This happened to the concept of 'revolution' long ago. Thus it does not appear in the public sphere or in popular culture. It is equally absent in the philosophical and social scientific discourses, except, that is, in the works of a few Leftist philosophers such as Badiou, Negri and Žižek. Do their efforts signify the last, cramp-like movements of a dying concept? This is, at any rate, the view of mainstream philosophy and social science.

The paradox in this context is not only that we live, as ever, in a world saturated with enormous conflicts and misery, that there is all the more reason to criticize existing and emerging forms of oppression and injustice. After all, if we look at the contemporary world through the prism of classical theories of revolution, what we see is a more or less permanent 'revolutionary situation' characterized by the co-existence of extreme poverty and extreme wealth. What needs to be explained in such a world is stability rather than destabilizing tendencies.

But that which has disappeared often returns. Hence we are constantly witnessing phenomena considered to be far away, 'historical', or even dead, knocking on our doors, catching us unprepared and perplexed. Ideas do not disappear. Thus, again and again, the world wakes up to new revolts. They always come unexpectedly, especially in the West. Baffled, the establishment often mystifies the spirit of the revolts, translating their reason into its own language: people's fight for 'democracy' under 'totalitarian' regimes. As if revolt is only something that can happen in the 'totalitarian' Muslim Orient. Perversely, therefore, revolution 'there', in the Orient, legitimates the absence of revolution 'here', in the West. Here, after all, we have 'democracy' and things are not nearly so bad. It is this culture of content that had made Marx consult Horace's satire:

> If, however, the German reader pharisaically shrugs his shoulders at the condition of the English industrial and agricultural workers, or optimistically comforts himself with the thought that in Germany things are not nearly so bad, I must plainly tell him: *De te fabula narratur!*
> (Marx 1976: 90)

'The tale is told of you'. The universal lesson of the recent events in Turkey, open to each and all, is that the event is possible.

4 Capitalism as religion, religion as capitalism

> Rogue, rogue, rogue!
> ...
> O thou sweet king-killer, and dear divorce
> 'Twixt natural son and sire! thou bright defiler
> Of Hymen's purest bed! thou valiant Mars!
> Thou ever young, fresh, lov'd and delicate wooer,
> Whose blush doth thaw the consecrated snow
> That lies on Dian's lap! thou visible god,
> That solder'st close impossibilities,
> And mak'st them kiss! that speak'st with every tongue,
> To every purpose!
> (Shakespeare 1970: 678)

Insofar as contemporary politics is a politics of consensus, which has its origin in the apparatus of glory, it is worth recalling that what is glorified in a neo-liberal world is first and foremost capitalism itself. Thus today people can imagine the end of the world but not that of capitalism (see Žižek 2009: 78). But why has capitalism become so powerful? One possible, and convincing, answer addresses the essential link between capitalism and religion. In our society, capitalism has become a religion and religion has become capitalism. This implies that today we should look for religion not in theological categories but in capitalism. To discuss this, we start, again, from *oikonomia*.

Economy and the chērematistikē

In *Politics* Aristotle makes an effort to differentiate between economy and the chērematistikē. This differentiation is between the 'natural' form of acquisition, which consists in attaining 'true wealth', property or goods that are necessary for the life of the household or the state, on the one hand, and the 'unnatural' form of acquisition, which consists in selfish profit gain, on the other (Aristotle 1995: 23, 326). What we have in the first case is the simple circulation of commodities whereby the household manages the availability of the supply of use-values, by selling and buying commodities. As Marx articulates it, the logic here operates in the form of C-M-C: Commodity is sold for Money in order to buy another Commodity (1976: 252). In the second, 'unnatural' case, however, one is solely concerned with money. Here the main objective is no longer to accumulate necessary use-values but to accumulate wealth in the form of money-capital. Aristotle makes two essential points here: first, referring to Midas, he says that money is a 'nonentity' that is 'useless' and 'worthless' in itself (1995: 26). This is also why wealth accumulated only in terms of money is 'unnatural'. And second, he adds that whereas the art of household management has a natural limit, in this second logic 'there is no limit to wealth' (Ibid. 24). That is, with the invention of money, the art of acquisition which was originally focused on necessity and use-values gradually 'grew into chrematistics, into the art of making money' (Marx 1976: 253). Now money becomes both the beginning and the end of the process of exchange: M-C-M. 'The movement of capital is therefore limitless' (Ibid. 252).

But the problem is that, despite the differentiation, there *is* an overlap between the two forms, between 'economy' and the 'Chrematistic' principle. As Aristotle himself admits, the two modes are 'not identical yet ... not far removed' (Aristotle 1995: 24). It is as if what is 'unnatural', the accumulation of money-capital ad infinitum, is always already at the heart of 'natural' *oikonomia*, and has a potential to become its ultimate aim. The contradiction between the two modes, in other words, remains unsettled. As such, Aristotle's discussion serves as *locus classicus* both for a generic concept of capital and for its moral–ethical critique (Albertsen 2012: 12).

Weber's discussion of the 'spirit' of capitalism is well known in this context. Since capitalism is a world without value, an inherently nihilistic system, it is constantly in need of moral justification, which can only come to it from outside. This external source is the Protestant ethic, which originally provided capitalism with a religious basis, with a 'spirit', although, according to Weber, the pact between capitalism and Protestantism has later weakened to the point that 'victorious capitalism ... needs its support no longer' (Weber 2003: 181–82). Secularization brings with it disenchantment.

However, theology persists as an active force in modern economy for capitalism and Christianity are structurally linked together. What links them together is articulated in social theory through the notion of guilt or debt. Seen in this prism, capitalism has not only found support in religion but it is itself a religion (Benjamin 1996). Capitalism is a cult religion which does not expiate but produces guilt:

> A vast sense of guilt that is unable to find relief seizes on the cult, not to atone for this guilt but to make it universal, to hammer it into the conscious mind, so as once and for all to include God in the system of guilt and thereby awaken in Him an interest in atonement.
>
> (Ibid. 288–89)

Just as the monotheistic economy presupposes a guilty god, 'capitalism as religion' presupposes a god in debt. It is through the mechanism of debt (credit) that value begets surplus-value, a process that resembles 'a god's genesis out of something that *is not*', a god's self-generation out of nothing (Hamacher 2002: 92). Thus, in Marx, the law of value functions as an abstract law that governs the relations of equivalence among commodities, as a transcendent moment within the immanent relations of equivalence. 'Money is therefore the god among commodities' (Marx 1993: 221). The paradox here consists in the movement through which the abstract value becomes totally value-free, or, 'valueless': abstract capital that seeks out further accumulation of capital whenever, wherever, by whatever means. Ultimately, therefore, the concept of value can say nothing on value. In this sense, the capitalist concept of value is nihilistic and the world of capitalism is essentially a world without value. Money, as a general equivalent of value, has a 'capacity to reduce the highest as well as the lowest values equally to one value form and thereby to place them on the same level, regardless of their diverse kinds and amounts' (Simmel 1978: 255). With the money economy, the differences between values tend to disappear; all quality is reduced to quantity. Indeed, this nihilistic leveling runs even deeper than an indifference to the possibility of different evaluations. Ultimately, money makes difficult the 'existence of values as such' (Ibid.).

God-capital

However, this cynicism, which is related to exchange relations based on money, must not be mistaken as the absence of a religious dimension in capitalism. It is coupled with the cult, with 'a strange piety', which enables the illusion that all production in a capitalist society emanates from 'God-capital' (Deleuze and Guattari 1983: 225). Capitalism posits an infinite debt to capital, which is the fetish object, the 'body without organs', of the capitalist society from which everything appears to emanate and to which everything returns. Just as in political theology the political is created *ex nihilio*, through a miracle-like formal decision on friend and enemy that cannot be explained rationally (Schmitt 1985: 36), capital is that which appears to perform miracles in economic theology. Thus already Spinoza emphasizes that money can appear as 'cause', that is, as God: money provides a short-cut to everything and therefore the multitude 'can scarcely imagine any kind of pleasure unless it is accompanied with the idea of money as the cause' (Spinoza 1993a: 192).

The specificity of capitalism as religion derives from the role credit plays in it. Notably, credit (debt) is an uneven relation: even though the relationship between the creditor and the debtor is a 'contractual' relationship, there is always an asymmetry of power involved in it (Nietzsche 1996: 45). Money, then, is not merely a means of exchange but a significant component of the measuring practices that constitute power. In other words, exchange is not an apolitical activity but is embedded in power relations. In market exchange money functions merely as a measure of value. But in the form of capital it also functions as a measure of the value of values. Hence the power of abstract capital – value producing more value – is not reducible to its market function, to exchange. Money is first and foremost 'a power for prescribing, ordering, that is, a set of possibilities for choices and decisions with regard to the future, which anticipate what the production, power relations and forms of subjection will be' (Lazzarato 2011: 84). The real significance of money, in other words, derives from its power to destroy existing values and to create new ones, from its power to decide on the value of values rather than merely measuring commodities with respect to existing values. This power is a creative power because it involves time. It appropriates not only existing values but future potentialities (Ibid. 47). Capital is always something 'to come', the promise of a future return in the form of profit. Therefore the capitalist religion has its own eschatology, its own way of anticipating an imagined future (see Goodchild 2005: 143). In this framework capital (credit, debt to the future) appears as *kairos*, that which mediates ontology and praxis.

Thought of in this way, we arrive at two series: on the one hand capital as God/abstract capital, a virtual force independent of its actual forms, and on the other actual capital as the Son, incarnated in different times and spaces; on the one hand capital as a generic potentiality, on the other the chronological time and space of capitalism, the different phases and formations of capitalism.

> That is why 'the economic' is never given properly speaking, but rather designates a differential virtuality to be interpreted, always covered over by its forms of actualisation; a theme or 'problematic' always covered over by its cases of solution. In short, the economic is the social dialectic itself – in other words, the totality of the problems posed to a given society, or the synthetic and problematising field of that society. In all rigour, there are only economic social problems, even though the solutions may be juridical, political or ideological, and the problems may be expressed in these fields of resolvability.
>
> (Deleuze 1994: 186)

God-capital is at the same time virtual (abstract) and embedded in actual relations. Thus, to deal with capital only as an empirical category is to ignore its virtuality. If, on the other hand, it is treated as a virtual 'problem', the mediation between the virtual and the actual becomes decisive. This mediation is what is enabled by the third element in the trinity: subjectivation. Debt is an apparatus of capture that targets the whole society; it 'functions as a mechanism for the production and "government" of collective and individual subjectivities' (Lazzarato 2011: 20). This is why the role of debt in the genealogy of morality is crucial. For all religious morality involves the creation of a moral subject who is able to give promises and remain responsible for them, that is '*made* calculable' (Nietzsche 1996: 40, 43). In this sense, insofar as it is linked to credit (*credos*), one can say that capitalism (not only levels but also) creates beliefs and desires, forms a moral subjectivity.

As such, the creation of subjectivity, morality, reveals itself as the truth of economy rather than a deviation from it. By the same token, the involvement of morality in credit relations neither makes it more human nor counters the alienation that pertains to commodity fetishism. This is why Marx insists that even though the credit system is built on apparent 'trust' between people, one should not be deceived by this: For

> this *return* of man to himself and therefore to other men is only an *appearance*; the self-estrangement, the dehumanisation, is all the more *infamous* and *extreme* because its element is no longer commodity, metal, paper, but man's *moral* existence, man's *social* existence, the *inmost depths* of his heart, and because under the appearance of man's *trust* in man it is the height of *distrust* and complete estrangement.
> (Marx 1844)

What constitutes the 'essence of credit' is the fact that the whole 'life' of the debtor and all his activity serves the creditor as a guarantee for the repayment of the debt. That is, 'all the social virtues [of the debtor], the content of his vital activity, his existence itself' signifies for the creditor the return of his capital with interest (Ibid.). For this reason, the death of the debtor means the death of the creditor's capital as well as the anticipation of interest. The creditor possesses both moral and legal guarantees for the debtor. For the same reason:

> *Credit is* the *economic* judgment on the *morality* of a man. In credit, the *man* himself, instead of metal or paper, has become the *mediator* of exchange, not however as a man, but as the *mode of existence of capital* and interest. The medium of exchange, therefore, has certainly returned out of its material form and been put back in man, but only because the man himself has been put outside himself and has himself assumed a material form. Within the credit relationship, it is not the case that money is transcended in man, but that man himself is turned into *money*, or money is *incorporated* in him. *Human individuality*, human *morality* itself, has become both an object of commerce and the material in which money exists. Instead of money, or paper, it is my own personal existence, my flesh and blood, my social virtue and importance, which constitute the material, corporeal form of the *spirit of money*. Credit no longer resolves the value of money into money but into human flesh and the human heart.
> (Marx 1844)

As such, as a 'moral judgment', credit is a 'subjective' measure of value (Lazzarato 2011: 59). It demands that the debtor takes upon himself responsibilities and risks. Thus debt becomes a factor of sociality. As society produces debt, debt produces society. In this sense debt is not only an 'exceptional' catastrophe (as in the case of a 'financial crisis' for instance) but also a *dispositif*, a technique of governance which imposes a particular conduct, a model of truth and normality on sociality by redefining power relations and by unmaking previous realities.

While debt offers the promise of a future return to the creditor (to abstract capital), from the point of view of the debtors (virtually everybody), debt functions as a de-politicizing mechanism because it 'neutralizes time, time as the creation of new possibilities, that is to say, the raw material of political, social, or aesthetic change' (Ibid. 48–49). The post-political effect of debt is to stifle becomings, to close off virtual potentialities, by turning societies into hostages to a pre-empted future, to 'societies of control' in which the logic of businesses tends to dominate other logics (Deleuze 1995: 181). This process involves morality, the creation of a 'soul': 'We are taught businesses have souls, which is surely the most terrifying news in the world' (Ibid.). Hence the subject of control societies: 'a man in debt' (Ibid.).

In control societies we confront two interlinked processes. On the one hand, we have capital, which demands everything, re-modeling of the whole society according to the principles of marketing. Thus the logic of capital works as the structuring principle of the entire society. And on the other hand we have subjects expected to continuously re-format their souls and to glorify the cult. One must adapt to radical transformations, modify one's life strategy in tune with the flexible demands of the market, and be always prepared to try new options. The capitalist religion needs a society in which constant systemic disembedding demands a meta-stable subjectivity in continuous transformation. Everybody must be mobilized, again and again, according to the ever-changing demands of God/capital.

In such a society, whose 'soul' is businesses, abstract money becomes a source of systemic violence, which cannot be located within social reality. What Žižek has called 'capital as Real' is worth evoking in this context (1999: 276). To recall, in psychoanalytic theory, the essence of social life is the symbolization and thus withdrawal of the Real. Religion, for instance, establishes the social bond ('religio') by keeping the Real at bay through a network of sacred and profane things and people (see Benslama 2004: 66–67). This network functions as a fiction that hides the absence of the Real. It is also this mediation that creates the idea of God as a symbolic authority which demands obedience. But if this mechanism is ruptured, we potentially no longer have the Real as the beyond of the Law; 'God' now comes too close as the Real, as a violent, vengeful superego figure (Žižek 2000: 132). Likewise, when abstract capital lacks such mediation, encounters with it, with its indifference to social reality, become much more traumatic (Žižek 1999: 287). As such, capital as the Real is a prime source of insecurity and uncertainty in today's society.

> The sudden upheavals and downfalls in collective fortunes today acquire an eerie likeness to natural catastrophes, though even this comparison looks increasingly like an understatement: as it happens, we have these

days better means to anticipate the imminent earthquake or approaching hurricane than to predict the next stock-exchange crash.

(Bauman 1999: 170)

Regarding this dimension of abstract capital, the danger is not really forgetting that there are real people and social relations behind the logic of capital. Such an explanation misses the point that the 'abstraction' at work here is not only a misperception of a social reality but is Real. Consequently, the real danger is overlooking the Real, a kind of social fetishism (Žižek 2000: 15). Capital's indifference to social reality is the source of a complex, systemic violence that cannot be attributed to concrete individuals and their intentions. 'The spectral presence of Capital is the figure of the big Other which not only remains operative when all the traditional embodiments of the symbolic big Other disintegrate, but even directly causes this disintegration' (Žižek 1999: 354). This fetishism is characteristic of the capitalist religion.

Religion, Feuerbach had said, takes over the best qualities of humans and allocates them to God, affirming in God what is negated in man (1989: 27). Hence the paradox of religious alienation, which was mentioned in *Chapter 1*: the more God is glorified, the more human life is depreciated and devalued. Marx repeats the same logic in *1844 Manuscripts*, where he depicts capital as the source of economic alienation: the more wealth the workers produce in capitalism the poorer they become (Marx 2007: 119). Since in capitalist exchange not only what is exchanged but the activity of exchange itself is alienated, capital tends to become an entity 'outside man and above man':

> Owing to this *alien mediator* – instead of man himself being the mediator for man – man regards his will, his activity, and his relation to other men as a power independent of him and them. His slavery, therefore, reaches its peak. It is clear that this *mediator* now becomes a *real God*, for the mediator is the *real power* over what it mediates to me. Its cult becomes an end in itself. Objects separated from this mediator have lost their value. Hence the objects only have value insofar as they *represent* the mediator, whereas originally it seemed that the mediator had value only insofar as *it* represented *them*. This reversal of the original relationship is inevitable. This *mediator is* therefore the lost, estranged *essence* of private property, private property which has become *alienated*, external to itself, just as it is the *alienated* species-activity of man, the *externalised mediation* between man's production and man's production. All the qualities which arise in the course of this activity are, therefore, transferred to this mediator. Hence man becomes the poorer as man, i.e., separated from this mediator, the *richer* this mediator becomes.
>
> (Marx 1844)

But where does this process originate? Marx says that 'primitive accumulation plays approximately the same role in political economy as original sin does in theology' (Marx 1976: 363). In this fictional phase (reminiscent of the 'state of nature' in political theology), we are told, while the diligent and intelligent accumulated wealth, the 'lazy rascals' were condemned to poverty, a situation in which they have 'nothing to sell except their own skins' (Ibid.). As such, the starting point of capital is divorcing the producer from the means of production, his expropriation from the soil.

Just as religion captures what is profane and sacralizes it through glorification, capitalism captures the commons and commodifies them for display in the spectacle. Thus, tellingly, Debord describes the spectacle as 'the material construction of the religious illusion' (1983: 20). Yet, while for Debord capitalism is the engine of the spectacle, with Agamben (2011a) one can claim that the originary link is not only between capitalism and the spectacle but rather, and more generally, between political theology and *oikonomia*. The relationship between abstract capital and the market (exchange) is analogous to that between sovereignty and governmentality, while the spectacle (glory) is that which links the two disjunctive poles together.

Not surprisingly, therefore, the glorification of capital parallels the glorification of God. Just as religion demands the infinite increase (subjective glorification as infinite guilt) of what cannot be increased (objective glory of God), capitalism demands infinite accumulation (subjective glorification of capital) of what is beyond human agency (objective glory of abstract capital, of capital as the Real). Paradoxically, in both cases, 'glorification is ... what produces glory' (Agamben 2011a: 216, 227). And in both cases the paradox is a cover for the fact that the center of the machine is empty. In both cases, what is at stake is human life, which is inoperative, that is, without a utilitarian purpose (Ibid. 245–46). What religion does is to capture this inoperativity and inscribe it in a religious sphere, to sacralize it, only to partially return it in the form of the 'Sabbath' when all 'work', all economy, ceases to exist and everything falls back upon inoperativity, which eschatology waits for. What capitalism does is to capture the multitude's inoperativity, its creative freedom, and inscribe it in a utilitarian sphere, only to partially return it as permitted freedom, as 'holiday', which is the main promise of work in capitalism. A post-political promise, in which work (hell) is replaced by play (paradise).

The divine ass

The idea of God, in short, is compatible with the capitalist/utilitarian religion. Disenchantment or the capitalist 'rejection' of religion does not amount to a consistent atheism. Rather, one is tempted to say that the capitalist religion merely replaces monotheistic religions with an earthly, profane deity, a cult. God did not die but rather has metamorphosed into money (Agamben 2014). A beautiful depiction of this process is found in the end of *Thus Spoke Zarathustra*, in a scene which alludes to a part in *Exodus* where Moses returns from a mountain retreat to find that his people have forgotten the commandments and fallen back upon idolatry. We meet some of Zarathustra's guests who all think they have 'unlearned' from Zarathustra the religious sentiment, the despair that prompts humans to imagine a transcendent heaven. Thus, they are in the carnival mood. Yet, Nietzsche makes it clear that a materialist, hedonist world is prone to new, this-worldly illusions, even new gods and idols. At one point in the carnival, therefore, the noise abruptly stops and, precisely when they think they have overcome it, the crowd falls back upon a religious mood. 'They have all become *pious* again, they are *praying*, they are *mad*!' (Nietzsche 1961: 321). But what they worship is a this-worldly God: an ass. They explain that the ass carries their burden, he is patient and never says No, indeed he never speaks, and so on. 'Better to worship God in this shape than in no shape at all' (Ibid. 322). In *Zarathustra*, it is the 'ugliest man', the passive nihilist, who has murdered God and delivers the tribute to the new God, to the ass, that has 'created the world after his own image, that is, as stupid as possible' (Ibid.). In the capitalist religion, that is, providence finds its key symbol in the profane: the ass is embodied in utilitarianism, in 'work' that is elevated to the level of a focal liturgical element, and the desire for change, for transfiguration, has disappeared into the cry of the ass.

Insofar as religion is separation, that is, removing an object from the domain of the profane into that of the sacred, capitalism 'generalizes in every domain the structure of separation that defines religion' (Agamben 2007: 80). Paradoxically, however, in capitalism absolute profanation and absolute sacralization become indistinguishable; the ass and God coincide.

> This means that it has become impossible to profane (or at least that it requires special procedures). If to profane means to return to common use that which has been removed to the sphere of the sacred, the capitalist religion in its extreme phase aims at creating something absolutely unprofanable.
>
> (Ibid. 82)

How to profane something that is already profane? Under the sign of this paradox, ours is a society that plays one side of the bipolar machine against the other, pushing to an extreme the administrative logic of economic theology, to a point of eliminating the transcendent God/Kingdom. In this sense:

> Modernity, removing God from the world, has not only failed to leave theology behind, but in some ways has done nothing other than to lead the project of the providential *oikonomia* to completion.
>
> (Agamben 2011a: 287)

It is crucial in this context that the spectacle not only generates consensus but also functions as the katechon, as what forecloses the event. Consider Fukuyama's neo-evangelistic 'good news' that the 'end of history' has arrived (1992: xii-xiii). On the one hand, this thesis sacralizes a particular, actual expression of temporal power, the market, turning it into the telos of history (Bradley and Fletcher 2010: 2). Thus, according to Fukuyama, all regimes in the world, including dictatorships, now evolve towards liberal democracy (1992: 212). But on the other hand, this divinized liberal democracy is distinguished from its empirical manifestations, arguing that it is a 'trans-historical', that is, an infinite, virtual idea that cannot be reduced to its actual, finite manifestations or delegitimized by use of empirical evidence (see Fukuyama 1992: 139).

> *With the one hand*, it accredits a logic of the empirical event which it needs whenever it is a question of certifying the finally final defeat of ... everything that bars access to the Promised Land of economic and political liberalisms; but *with the other hand*, in the name of the trans-historic ... ideal, it discredits this same logic of the so-called empirical event ... to avoid chalking up to the account of this ideal and its concept precisely whatever contradicts them in such a cruel fashion: in a word, all the *evil*, all that is *not going well* in the capitalist States and in liberalism ...
> (Derrida 1994: 86)

As such, the Fukuyama-style eschatology-light does not really exclude the dialectic between the actual and the transcendent. Rather, it flattens it so that the 'idea' loses its power of destroying and transvaluating what exists, becoming instead the potentiality of an already sacralized liberal democracy. In a sense, Fukuyama is doing here to the 'trans-historical' idea of democracy what Nietzsche's last man does to the idea of God by turning it into a divine ass. Thus, while he sacralizes the liberal democratic market, he also levels the transcendent ('heaven') and the actual (the 'earth') in such a way that any idea of true transcendence, of something other than liberal democracy, becomes redundant. This is a chiliasm without event. And herein we arrive at the central paradox of the contemporary society:

> On the one hand, it abolishes the eschatology and infinitely prolongs the history and the government of the world; on the other, it finds that the finite character of its paradigm returns ceaselessly ...
> (Agamben 2011a: 163)

Auto-immunity

Just as the conception of sovereignty is grounded in political theology, liberal democratic governmentality is rooted in economic theology. But what is the mechanism through which *oikonomia* relates to the 'return of religion' today? Insofar as it is an experience of the sacred, of the holy, religion is about purification and immunization, about keeping the sacred 'intact, safe, unscathed' (Derrida 2002: 61). Thus in modernity there appears to be an antagonism between the 'miracle' (religious faith) and the 'machine' (technoscience). The capitalist technoscience threatens religion with abstraction and disassociation, with uprooting, de-localization, formalization, objectification, telecommunication, and so on (Ibid. 43). In order to protect itself, to immunize itself, religion seeks to reject capitalist technoscience. The paradox, however, is that while reacting antagonistically to technoscience, religion also, at the same time, re-affirmatively outbids itself. It appropriates science while it rejects it, and thus faith and science, miracle and machine, 'overlap, mingle, contaminate each another without ever merging' (Ibid. 63). Religion's zeal for immunity leads to the loss of immunity. Like redundant 'anti-bodies' that turn against the organism in which they live, religion embodies an auto-immune pathology in relation to technoscience.

The global 'return' of religion today takes place against the background of this auto-immunity. The globalization of religion can be understood in terms of a 'strange alliance of Christianity, as the experience of death of God, and tele-technoscientific capitalism' (Ibid. 52). Derrida calls this auto-immune process which is simultaneously hegemonic and in the process of exhausting itself 'globalatinization' (Ibid.). Globalatinization is an 'essentially Christian' process whose dominant language is Latin in the sense that 'whoever speaks religiously or about religion' today remains under its influence (Ibid. 66). Insofar as speaking religion is speaking Roman, even 'Anglo-American remains Latin' today (Ibid.). Even Judaism and Islam, in a certain sense, speak Latin: the non-Christian religions are today in a desperate struggle to 'defend themselves against Christianity' while, at the same time, they 'Christianize themselves':

> To present oneself on the international stage, to claim the right to practice one's 'religion,' to construct mosques where there were churches and synagogues is to inscribe oneself in a political space dominated by Christianity, and therefore to engage in the obscure and equivocal struggle in which the putatively 'universal' value of the concept of religion, even of religious tolerance, has in advance been appropriated into the space of a Christian semantics.
>
> Derrida 2001: 74)

But why is globalatinization in the process of exhausting itself? The return of religion in global politics today brings with it a 'trivialization' through which religion destroys its own conditions of existence (Vries 2005: 367, 370).

> When religion shows itself on television, wherever it manifests and deploys itself in the 'world,' in the 'public space,' it at the same time increases its power and its power to self-destroy; it increases both the one and the other, the one *as* the other, to the same degree.
>
> (Derrida 2001: 67)

Is this banalization the end of religion? No, because the 'sacred' is not the only source of religion. Derrida distinguishes between two sources of religion. On the one hand, as already mentioned, religion is grounded in an experience of the sacred, of the holy, which it seeks to immunize against all that which is perceived as 'evil' (Derrida 2002: 42). But this attempt, which is also a promise of salvation, is not the whole story. Religion has another, more significant source, which is grounded in the promise itself but cannot be reduced to the object of promise (salvation, redemption ...). Derrida calls this source 'messianicity without messianism', a messianicity which does not depend on any messianism, any Abrahamic religion, and does not follow any revelation. The difference between messianicity and messianism is tantamount to the difference between the virtuality of an event and the actual(ized) event, between the potentiality of revelation – 'revealability' – and the actual revelation (Ibid. 59). As such, as a virtual or abstract faith, messianicity is not reducible to religious faith.

This is why Derrida can argue that within the communist and democratic traditions there is a messianism which is not reducible to religion through any deconstruction. What is irreducible in 'messianism without religion' is an experience of the 'emancipatory promise' (Derrida 1994: 74), a promise, whose effectivity keeps within itself an 'eschatological relation to the to-come of an event *and* of a singularity, of an alterity that cannot be anticipated' (Ibid. 81). In contrast to religion, therefore, the content of this promise is not determined. The 'alterity' of that which returns in non-religious messianism 'cannot be anticipated'. The absolute difference of the event forecloses the return of the absolute as a religious figure. What is 'to come', the future, remains unpredictable, new. The Last Judgment will not occur. Instead, the messianic return demands a 'messianic opening to what is coming, that is, to the event that cannot be awaited *as such*, or recognized in advance' (Ibid.). Non-religious messianism is a 'call', a 'promise' of the new, which always comes in the shape of emancipation, justice, and peace; a promise independent of the three monotheistic religions, even when they oppose one another, for it holds to the anti-nihilist belief that 'faith without religion' is possible (Derrida 2004).

There are two significant consequences of this logic. First, it becomes possible to distinguish religion and faith; faith is not reducible to religion just as religion is not necessarily faithful. What is significant is that both sources, together, render

> possible, but not necessary, something like a religion, which is to say, an instituted apparatus consisting of dogmas or of articles of faith that are both determinate and inseparable from a given historical *socius* (Church, clergy, socially legitimated authority, people, shared idiom, community of the faithful committed to the same faith and sanctioning the same history). But the gap between the opening of this *possibility (as a universal*

structure) and the *determinate necessity* of this or that religion will always remain irreducible.

[...]

Thus, one can always criticize, reject or combat this or that form of sacredness or of belief, even of religious authority, in the name of the most originary possibility.

(Derrida 2002: 93)

And second, since messianic faith is a necessary but external condition for religion, it follows that its religious appropriation (sacralization) is not an unavoidable process. Once again, profanation becomes possible. Another way of saying the same is that religion cannot fully appropriate or exhaust the messianic. The messianic is a virtual possibility, which, for all its repression and trivialization, cannot be eradicated. A real possibility, which persists, always reappears. Thus, in order to consider the space of messianicity, of the event, Derrida (1995) returns to a Platonic text, *Timaeus*, more specifically to the concept of *khora*. *Khora* signifies 'something' that is real without existing as an actual thing that can be objectively known or recognized. Having no referent, as an amorphous, unformed 'something', *khora* is itself un-representable (Derrida 1995: 95–97). As such, however, it is that which 'receives', or, 'gives place' to every representation, to all determinations, without possessing any of those determinations as its own properties (Ibid. 99). *Khora* is the place which gives place to everything but is itself not existent as an actual place. In this sense the place of the messianic, its topos, is *khora*, or, in our terminology, the virtual. This virtuality can always be appropriated by religion, but it cannot exhaust itself in religion. The religious machine can only emerge from this groundless ground. Without the second source, 'there would be neither act of faith, nor promise, nor future ... ' (Derrida 2002: 57). Indeed, insofar as religion is reduced to its 'sacred' components, it falls back upon the domain of common sense, becomes a 'fetish'. The messianic, in turn, is a break with the fetish, and signifies the opening up of the actual to the virtual.

What the religious machine, or organized religion, seeks is to codify this *khora*tic-virtual source as a rule-set. It attempts to formulate a foundationalist, supra-individual or social codex for how individuals must organize their conduct with one another. Thus the religious machine always implies that we can be moral only if, only when we are religious. It invites us to presuppose that, expelled from the Garden of Eden, human beings can only manage their lives if they have a codex to follow: 'morality as obedience to the Law and the recipe for a trouble-free life of conformity' (Bauman 1998: 13). In this scheme, the individual moral actor must be loyal to the social-religious bond, and, if necessary, must be forced into being moral, the assumption being that the moral actor would prefer obedience to moral uncertainty.

What this scheme represses is precisely the 'other' source of religion which cannot be formulated as a codex. But this other source of religion is not secondary to the first. This is the reason why Levinas called ethics 'first philosophy' (1985: 77). This thesis, that ethics comes before ontology, and thus before 'the religious' in the sense of the sacred, must of course be understood not empirically but philosophically. Without religion in this sense, organized religion would be impossible.

The new spirit

In *The New Spirit of Capitalism*, Boltanksi and Chiapello (2007: 169) discuss that today we have entered a new phase of capitalism that justifies itself with reference to creativity, difference, and mobility (Ibid. 16–20, 356). The 'new spirit' values association around 'projects' as a general form of activity (Ibid. 107). Hence the activity of the mediator in establishing and extending networks has become 'a value in itself', irrespective of the specific goal or substantial character of the mediated entities (Ibid.). 'In a connexionist world, a natural preoccupation of human beings is the desire to *connect* with others, *to make contact*, so as not to remain *isolated*' (Ibid. 111). Consequently, a networked world is a complex world of interdependencies in which, like in Spinoza's ontology, everything is connected to everything else.

But is the new spirit of capitalism Spinozist? What is decisive here is an essential open-endedness that pertains to networks, for competencies such as mobility, adaptability, and connectionism can always, potentially, be used in an instrumentalist way. This, however, is not justified in the new spirit of capitalism according to Boltanski and Chiapello: one should be networking in search of the 'common good', that is, in order to engage with others, inspire confidence, be tolerant, respect differences, and pass information to others, so that everyone in a network can gain from networking (Ibid. 115). In this sense the new capitalism has an ethical scheme of evaluation. Accordingly, to 'belong' in networks means that everything may be connected to everything else. In networks 'nothing can be reduced to anything else, nothing can be deduced from anything else, everything may be allied to everything else' (Latour 1988: 163). 'Belonging', thought of in this way, is an 'irreductionist' process that cannot be thought of in functionalistic, systemic terms. As such, instrumental reason seems to be antithetical to the logic of networking. Ideally, a 'network' is not only relations between people and things in terms of property but all kinds of associations.

However, there is a potential problem. This problem relates to the difference between what Boltanski and Chiapello call the 'network-extender' and the 'networker'. Whereas the first acknowledges debts contracted with others participating in the same network, the latter engages in opportunistic behavior, making a selfish use of the networks (2007: 356, 378). Association and connectivity therefore can have two very different meanings within networks. Moreover, the 'networker' tends to reduce others in the network to a commodity. Insofar as the pursuit of profit remains the fundamental horizon of networks, that is, insofar as the distinction between 'disinterested' sharing in the interest of the 'common good' and the strategic utilization of network relations is blurred, the intermediary starts to behave as if he has 'a property right over the person of the one whom he puts in contact with a third party, who anticipates an advantage from this liaison' (Ibid. 456). Such commodification fully coincides with exploitation in its strongest, bio-political sense, which involves an 'offence against the very dignity of human beings' (Ibid. 364, 365). Indeed, the post-Fordist logic of networking penetrates 'profoundly into people's interior being', transgressing the moral (and partly legal) imperative not to commodify human beings (Ibid. 464–65).

So, the risk of network capitalism is falling back upon bio-politics. This tendency is accentuated by a paradox internal to the new spirit of capitalism, a paradox which becomes visible if we consider a perverted, revised Spinoza as the grammatician of the new, post-Fordist spirit of capitalism, because most of his themes (anti-teleology, anti-dialectic, multitude, the plane of immanence occupied by bodies and souls, power as potentiality, the destruction of the subject, and so on) converge with the characteristics of this new capitalism (Illuminati 2003: 317; Albertsen 2005: 80). Further, in network society, Spinoza's pragmatic ethics tend to become a norm, a normative injunction. In this sense one could even claim that 'post-Fordism is the communism of capital' (Virno 2004: 111). The paradoxical logic here consists in including and excluding immanence in the same movement, transforming Spinozist connectionism into a transcendent rule in the service of capital (see Albertsen 1995: 136). It is this reversal that blurs the meaning of association and belonging, turning them into parts of a repressive dispositif. Capital reads (appropriates) Spinoza in its own way.

Excursus IV
The map, the territory, and the impossibility of painting a priest

> Anyway, we're at a point where success in market terms justifies and validates anything, replacing all the theories.
>
> (Houellebecq 2011: 135)

If Michel Houellebecq's latest novel, *The Map and the Territory*, is a 'novel of ideas' (Kipnis 2012), the pivotal idea that serves as its meta-plot is the total subsumption of the society under capital. Houellebecq's is a late modern world in which capital tends to replace, like a map, the actual experience of life, the territory; a world in which everything is modeled on the logic of businesses; capitalism has taken the place of religion. As the novel gradually takes this idea to its logical extremes we find ourselves within a dystopia even darker than *The Possibility of an Island*, which was praised as 'the first great, and thus far unrivalled dystopia for the liquid, deregulated, consumption-obsessed, individualized era' (Bauman 2012: 21). All Houellebecq novels focus on contemporary problems, including the misery caused by commodification processes and the consequent breakdown of social bonds. Religion, too, is a significant topic in this context. However, *The Map and the Territory* distils the relationship between religion and capitalism anew, and this relationship, together with the political questions it invites, will be the leitmotiv for my considerations here.

The protagonist of *The Map and the Territory* is a commercially successful photographer and painter, Jed Martin. Like all other Houellebecq characters he is a weary loner who 'never totally signed up' to his own existence (2011: 290). He is not used to seeking others' friendship (Ibid. 26). Thus he spends all his time working. A hard-working artist, his greatest ambition is to represent reality as accurately as possible, 'to give an objective description of the world – a goal whose illusory nature he rarely sensed' (Ibid. 28). Initially he specializes in photographing manufactured objects. Then he starts to take pictures of Michelin maps, which plays a decisive role in his artistic career. His photographs sell for high prices to Chinese, Russian, and Indian rich. But he achieves global fame when he starts to paint 'Professions' – a series portraying some typical professions, through which Martin studies the contemporary society, trying to give an image of its functioning on the basis of the notion of work. Indeed, Jed's artwork is 'a *homage to human labour*' (Ibid. 27).

> What defines a man? What's the question you first ask a man, when you want to find out about him? In some societies, you ask him first if he's married, if he has children; in our society, we ask first what his profession is. It's his place in the productive process, and not his status as reproducer, that above all defines Western man.
>
> (Ibid. 101)

Work is the celebration of capitalist religion (see Benjamin 1996: 288). It is perhaps due to the centrality of this idea that the book opens by describing Jed working on a painting that belongs to the 'Professions' series: *Damien Hirst and Jeff Koons Dividing Up the Art Market*.

Necromancy and pornography

> Jeff Koons had just got up from his chair, enthusiastically throwing his arms out in front of him. Sitting opposite him, on a white leather sofa partly draped with silks and slightly hunched up, Damien Hirst seemed to be about to express an objection; his face was flushed, morose. Both of them were wearing black suits – Koons's had fine pinstripes – white shirts and black ties. Between them, on the coffee table, was a basket of candied fruits that neither paid any attention to. Hirst was drinking a Budweiser Light.
>
> (Houellebecq 2011: 1)

The painting describes the two best-selling artists in a luxurious hotel, perhaps in Qatar, or Dubai, discussing wealth and the art market. Hirst is painted skilfully, in a straightforward manner, as a brutal, cynical, rebel-but-rich artist 'pursuing an *anguished work on death*'. But we realize that Jed has problems with painting Koons: 'It was as difficult as painting a Mormon pornographer' (Ibid. 2). Finally, he decides that he is 'making a truly shit painting' and destroys it (Ibid. 13). In spite of its destruction, however, this painting functions as a vanishing mediator, for through it Houellebecq defines the spirit of our times: concern with death (Hirst) and pornography (Koons).

First a few words on pornography. In the hedonistic society Houellebecq describes, bonding outside the market is impossible, and love can no longer exist. Its disappearance is grounded in 'the materialist idea that we are alone, we live alone and we die alone. That's not very compatible with love' (Houellebecq in Hunnewell 2011). It is therefore no coincidence that Houellebecq 'endlessly varies the motif of the failure of the Event of love' in contemporary society (Žižek 2008b). 'Love ... Love is *rare*. Didn't you know that?' (Houellebecq 2011: 84). And if love is an exception, the rule is economy. What matters most is one's market value in the economy of love. Thus Houellebecq writes, with an allusion to the *Communist Manifesto*:

> Just like unrestrained economic liberalism, and for similar reasons, sexual liberalism produces phenomena of *absolute pauperisation*. Some men

make love every day; others five or six times in their life, or never. Some make love with dozens of women; others with none. It's what's known as 'the law of the market'. In an economic system where unfair dismissal is prohibited, every person more or less manages to find their place. In a sexual system where adultery is prohibited, every person more or less manages to find their bed mate. In a totally liberal economic system, certain people accumulate considerable fortunes; others stagnate in unemployment in misery. In a totally liberal sexual system, certain people have a varied and exciting erotic life; others are reduced to masturbation and solitude. Economic liberalism is an extension of the domain of the struggle, its extension to all ages and all classes of society. Sexual liberalism is likewise an extension of the domain of the struggle, its extension to all ages and all classes of society.

(Houellebecq 1998: 99)

Pornography, in such a society, is the only way out for sexually pauperized people who demand 'sexual social democracy' (Houellebecq 2001: 260, 265). Why pornography, why social democracy? Let us consult a beautiful fragment by Agamben, 'The Idea of Communism' (Agamben 1995). Here Agamben states that pornography is basically parasitic on 'the utopia of a classless society' (Ibid. 73). But the happiness it depicts is always 'episodic': it always describes 'a story, a moment seized on' against the background of a normality which is, in the same movement, affirmed (Ibid. 74; see also Prozorov 2011: 77). Paradoxically, therefore, in pornography the utopian promise of classless society is coupled with an 'insistence on class markings' which affirm, rather than negating, normality (Agamben 1995: 73). Hence Agamben compares pornography to social democracy: both suspend the very promise they represent. The 'promise' at work here is profanation.

> It is this profanatory potential that the apparatus of pornography seeks to neutralize. What it captures is the human capacity to let erotic behaviours idle, to profane them, by detaching them from their immediate ends. But while these behaviours thus open themselves to a different possible use, which concerns not so much the pleasure of the partner as a new collective use of sexuality, pornography intervenes at this point to block and divert the profanatory intention. The solitary and desperate consumption of the pornographic image thus replaces the promise of a new use.
>
> (Agamben 2007: 91)

In pornography the promise of profanation (of delivering the human body from the uses ascribed to it) is coupled with the production of a pornographic body. This is the reason why most Houellebecq characters' search for happiness through the consumption of pornography leads them back to frustration and loneliness.

However, pornography is only one aspect of contemporary life depicted in the novel. When Jed goes to Zurich to visit a euthanasia clinic where his father died, he discovers that the clinic and a brothel are situated almost next to one another. Suffering and death are sold together with pleasure and sex on the same 'banal or sad street' (Houellebecq 2011: 252). Real life, in other words, is itself like a 'shit' painting. Yet Jed also notices here that the clinic is more busily attended than the brothel: 'the market values of suffering and death had become superior to that of pleasure and sex', which also explains why Damien Hirst had recently replaced Jeff Koons at the top of the global art market (Ibid.). For this reason Hirst has a more special place in *The Map and the Territory*, the first part of which gives a description of neo-liberal social decay in France. The real reason behind Jed's financial success following his exhibition 'The Map is More Interesting than the Territory' is, in fact, fetishization or mortification of the territory. Because:

> for the first time in France since Jean-Jacques Rousseau, the countryside had become *trendy* again. French society seemed to suddenly become aware of this through its major dailies and magazines, in the few weeks which followed Jed's *vernissage*. And the Michelin map, an utterly unnoticed utilitarian object, became in the space of those very weeks the privileged vehicle for initiation into what Libération was to shamelessly call the 'magic of the *terroir*'.
>
> (Ibid. 54)

In this 'territory' obsessed with mortified identity, traditional inhabitants have been replaced by incomers from urban areas who are motivated by business interests and had 'a precise knowledge of the laws of the market' (Ibid. 282). Thanks to this process, post-industrial France displays economic 'robustness' but gradually becomes a 'tourist country' (Ibid. 283):

> From Duisburg to Dortmund, from Bochum and Gelsenkirchen, most of the old steel factories had been transformed into places for exhibitions, shows, and concerts, at the same time as the local authorities tried to set up an industrial tourism, based on the re-creation of the working-class way of life at the beginning of the twentieth century. In fact, the whole region, with its blast furnaces, slag heaps, abandoned railway tracks where freight wagons rusted, its lines of identical and neat and tidy terraced houses, sometimes brightened up by allotments, was like a conservatory of the first industrial age in Europe.
>
> (Ibid. 291)

Factories turning into museums; this idea brings us back to capitalism. Capitalism per definition sets into motion a process of consecration, through which objects are separated from their use and function as the embodiment of a fetish object in the spectacle. Consequently the social world gradually turns into a museum and as spirituality (art, philosophy, religion ...) are 'docilely withdrawn' into museums, even whole cities become 'World Heritage sites' (Agamben 2007: 84). As such the museum signifies the impossibility of use, the increasing difficulty of experience in modern culture.

> The Museum occupies exactly the space and function once reserved for the Temple as the place of sacrifice. To the faithful in the temple ... correspond today the tourists who restlessly travel in a world that has been abstracted into a Museum.
>
> (Ibid. 84)

Whereas the pilgrims' sacrifice revolved around an exceptional object removed into the sacred sphere, in the tourists' world, in which everything is commodified, exception becomes the rule. Thus, unlike the faithful who through pilgrimage can mediate the relationship between this world, in which they are strangers, and the divine, 'true' world, the tourist's is an anxious experience with 'no homeland because they dwell in the pure form of separation' (Ibid. 84). Consequently the more tourists travel the more they experience the impossibility of experiencing, the more they become spectators to objects that have become property/commodity the more they are confronted with their incapability of profaning them (Ibid. 83). In this sense, the becoming museum of the 'territory' signifies the impossibility of profanation, the uncanny confrontation with the 'unprofanable'.

The church and the mystic

While working on the 'Professions' series, Jed Martin envisions doing a portrait of priests as well. 'But he had failed, and hadn't even managed to comprehend the subject' (Houellebecq 2011: 61). But why does he fail? Why is he unable to paint a priest? One obvious reason is that all of Jed's profession-paintings express a 'sensible goodwill, where submission to professional imperatives guaranteed in return ... a mixture of financial satisfaction and the gratification of self-esteem' (Ibid.). And since priests today mostly survive 'in miserable material conditions' (Ibid.), one wouldn't expect them to be part of the 'Professions' series. Yet, on further reflection, this explanation is not really convincing, not only because the church historically has had close links with wealth and power but also because Jed realizes that he is looking for religion in the wrong place, in theological categories, that is, in the church and in the priest. This brings us to the second part of the novel, and to another painting, Jed's 'masterpiece', where we effectively meet a priest.

The title of Jed's masterpiece is 'Bill Gates and Steve Jobs Discussing the Future of Information Technology'. In this painting Jed's attention turns from manufactured products to their producers. Again, Jed's style is minimal and exact, reflecting his usual detachment and coldness. In the painting Bill Gates is sitting comfortably in a wicker chair, smiling and spreading his arms out wide while talking to and playing chess with Steve Jobs. Dressed casually, he is 'relaxed, manifestly happy'. The painting shows 'a Bill Gates on holiday' (Ibid. 123).

Let us open a parenthesis related to 'holiday' here. It is well known that in Microsoft the employees were 'paid for playing with computers' (Salecl 1998: 171). But this often meant the erosion of the difference between 'work' (rule) and 'play' (exception). As the exception became the rule the employees tended to work all the time. This brings to mind one of Benjamin's main points in the fragment 'Capitalism as Religion':

> Capitalism is the celebration of a cult *sans rêveet sans merci* [without dream or mercy]. There are no 'weekdays.' There is no day that is not a feast day, in the terrible sense that all its sacred pomp is unfolded before us; each day commands the utter fealty of each worshipper.
> (Benjamin 1996: 288)

But is it not the case that Bill Gates is often perceived as a symbol of cynicism for he is 'free of the obsession to hold on to things ... he has the ability to let go' (Sennett 1998: 62)? In this context *The Map and the Territory* refers to Gates' autobiography 'where he confesses quite plainly that it is not necessarily advantageous for a business to offer the most innovative products' (Houellebecq 2011: 124). It might be more profitable to mass produce what others have invented; 'to observe what the competitors are doing ... to let them bring out their products, confront the difficulties inherent in any innovation, and, in a way, surmount the initial problems; then, in a second phase, flood the market by offering low-price copies of the competing products' (Ibid. 124). In other words, Bill Gates is cynical – but this apparent cynicism is not 'the true nature of Gates'. His true nature is:

> his faith in capitalism, in the mysterious 'invisible hand'; his absolute, unshakeable conviction that whatever the vicissitudes and apparent counterexamples, the market, at the end of the day, is always right, and that the good of the market is always identical to the general good. It is then that the fundamental truth about Bill Gates appears, as a creature of faith, and it is this faith, this candour of the sincere capitalist, that Jed Martin was able to render by portraying him, arms open wide, warm and friendly, his glasses gleaming in the last rays of the sun setting on the Pacific Ocean.
> (Ibid. 124)

As a 'creature of faith', with a dogmatic belief in the market economy, Bill Gates is the true priest in contemporary society.

In contrast to Bill Gates, in the painting Steve Jobs appears like an embodiment of Protestant ethics of austerity; 'nothing Californian' in his gestures except an 'expression of disarray', he looks ill, 'reminiscent of one of those travelling evangelists who, on finding himself preaching for perhaps the tenth time to a small and indifferent audience, is suddenly filled with doubt' (Ibid.). The same difference is ascertained by the chessboard between the two men, where the game seems to be interrupted 'in a stage unfavourable to the blacks – namely to Jobs' (Ibid.). Paradoxically, however, at a closer look the viewer notices in Jobs' eyes a 'flame common not only to preachers and prophets but also to the inventors so often described by Jules Verne' (Ibid.). Similarly, re-considering the position of the pieces, one

> realised that [his game] was not necessarily a losing one; and that Jobs could, by sacrificing his queen, conclude in three moves with an audacious bishop–knight checkmate. Similarly, you had the sense that he could, through the brilliant intuition of a new product, suddenly impose new norms on the market.
>
> (Ibid.)

If Bill Gates is the priest, Steve Jobs is the mystic/prophetic supplement to the organized religion (capitalism) and its church (the market). Together, the priest and the mystic represent a parallax view of the same religion, sometimes complementing, sometimes hunting each other. 'Jed Martin could have entitled his painting *A Brief History of Capitalism*; for that, indeed, is what it was' (Ibid. 125).

This is a beautiful way of saying that today capitalism has become a religion and religion has become capitalism, that one should no longer look for religion in theological categories but in capitalism. Are we then 'in a period of transition' in which old gods have grown old and died 'and others are not yet born' (Durkheim, 2001: 321). Or are we, in a more straightforward manner, within a Nietzschean horizon of dying gods and the twilight of idols? At any rate, the enlightened rejection of religion does not amount to a coherent atheism.

Houellebecq's previous book, *The Possibility of an Island*, is also relevant in this respect. Here the protagonist Daniel flirts with the Elohimite sect, a cult religion that promises its members material immortality through cloning. Houellebecq emphasizes in an interview that this sect is modeled on a real sect, the Raël, which is 'a mix of total optimism about scientific progress and nonmoralism about sex' (in Hunnewell 2011). Along the same lines, what is remarkable about the Elohimite sect is its under-toning of spirituality in favor of this world. Even its prophet appears 'bouncing, freshly showered, dressed in jeans and a "Lick my balls" T-shirt, and carrying a shoulder bag' (Houellebecq 2005: 88). As a whole, the religion of the Elohimite seems to be reduced to economy, not only in the sense that its spiritual dimension is minimalized, but also because of the 'excessive' emphasis it puts on rituals and material organization (see Ibid. 266). Indeed, 'it seems as if the Elohimite religion is Christianity made accessible for a 21st-century world' (Lloyd 2009: 94). Only, as Derrida would add, 'globalatinization' – the globalization of Christianity through an alliance with technoscientific capitalism – brings with it a trivialization, an emptying out of faith and its reduction to ritual (see 'Auto-immunity' above). This is why the only possible form of religion in

Houellebecq's late modernity seems to be the ceremonial religion, the opposite of what Spinoza calls 'universal faith'. If universal faith is faith without ritual, the Elohimite religion is ritual without faith.

The real and the fictive

One of the most interesting twists in *The Map and the Territory* occurs when Jed secures the involvement of a 'great writer' to pen the guide for his exhibition of the Professions-series. The name of the writer turns out to be Michel Houellebecq, 'a famous writer, world-famous even', whom even Jed's old father has read (Houellebecq, 2011: 9). So Jed plans a visit to Houellebecq's residence in Ireland where he lives alone. 'It was public knowledge that Houellebecq was a loner with strong misanthropic tendencies: it was rare for him even to say a word to his dog' (Ibid. 81). Then we meet a drunk, depressive Houellebecq, scratching at his athlete's foot and jabbering, rather comically, about his 'love' of industrial products:

> 'In my life as a consumer,' he said, 'I've known three perfect products: Paraboot walking boots, the Canon Libris laptop-printer combination, and the Camel Legend parka. I loved those products, with a passion; I would've spent my life in their presence, buying regularly, with natural wastage, identical products. A perfect and faithful relationship had been established, making me a happy consumer. I wasn't completely happy in all aspects of life, but at least I had that: I could, at regular intervals, buy a pair of my favourite boots. It's not much but it's something, especially when you've quite a poor private life. Ah yes, that joy, that simple joy, has been denied me. My favourite products, after a few years, have disappeared from the shelves, their manufacture has stopped purely and simply – and in the case of my poor Camel Legend parka, no doubt the most beautiful parka ever made, it will have lived for only one season ... ' He slowly began to cry, big tears streaming down his face, and served himself another glass of wine. 'It's brutal, you know, it's terribly brutal. While the most insignificant animal species take thousands, sometimes millions of years to disappear, manufactured products are wiped off the surface of the globe in a few days; they're never given a second chance, they can only suffer, powerless, the irresponsible and fascistic diktat of product line managers who of course know better than anyone else what the customer wants, who claim to capture an expectation of novelty in the consumer, and who in reality just turns his life into one exhausting and desperate quest, an endless wandering between eternally modified product lines.'
>
> (Ibid. 110)

Having established the mythical status of commodity, Houellebecq's self-parody continues: 'We too are products', and as such 'will become obsolete' (Ibid. 111). What is to be done, then? Such questions are not raised in the novel.

Instead, Houellebecq is savagely murdered in the third, final part. This imagined murder is interesting if we relate Jed and the fictive Houellebecq to one another.

Jed is content with reality; he merely wants to 'represent' it: 'I want to give an account of the world ... I want simply to *give an account of the world*' (Ibid. 286). But this is a futile aim for – as Borges says, even if it were possible 'to struck a map of the Empire whose size was that of the Empire' (Borges 1998: 325), then it would have been necessary to produce a map for the map itself. In other words, 'the most scrupulous representation of reality – the one-to-one map – is also the most useless' (Kipnis 2012). Jed's work receives acclaim only because it coincides with the romanticization of the countryside which characterizes the *terroir* movement (see Ibid.).

The fictional Houellebecq, in turn, seems to be a combination of Hirst and Koons; a 'thinly veiled character of Houellebecq himself' (Bettridge 2012: 7). Unsurprisingly, he is contemptuous of and disgusted by the world that surrounds him. But the most important clue about him comes through another painting in Jed's Professions-series:

> In *Michel Houellebecq, Writer*, as most art historians stress, Jed Martin breaks with that practice of realistic backgrounds which had characterised his work all through the period of the 'Professions'. He has trouble breaking with it, and you can sense that this break comes with much effort, that he strives through various artifices to maintain the illusion of a possible realistic background as much as possible. In the painting, Houellebecq is standing in front of a desk covered with written or half-written pages. Behind him, at a distance of some five metres, the white wall is entirely papered with handwritten pages stuck to one another, without any interstices whatsoever. Ironically, those art historians stress, Jed Martin seems in this work to accord an enormous importance to the text, and focuses on it detached from any real referent.
>
> (Houellebecq 2011: 119)

'Detached from any real referent'. Here Houellebecq turns Borges's story 'The Map and the Territory' upside down: 'there is nothing left but a map (the virtual abstraction of the territory), and on this map some fragments of the real are still floating and drifting' (Baudrillard 2000: 63). As such, the 'map' is no longer an abstraction, doubling or mirroring; it is the generation of the hyper-real, a real without reality or origin:

> The territory no longer precedes the map, nor does it survive it. It is nevertheless the map that precedes the territory ... and if one must return to the fable, today it is the territory whose shreds slowly rot across the extent of the map. It is the real, and not the map, whose vestiges persist here and there in the deserts that are no longer those of the Empire, but ours. *The desert of the real itself.*
>
> (Baudrillard 1994: 1)

Simulacrum is what Jed cannot avoid even though he tries to maintain the 'illusion' of realism. Consequently, Houellebecq is painted 'in the middle of a universe of paper', without any statement about realism in literature, nor, for that matter, about any formalist position. He is 'possessed' by a 'fury' described as 'demonic' (Houellebecq 2011: 119). And in this perspective, the murder of Houellebecq can be interpreted as the aesthetic triumph of the mediocre (Jed), which is contrasted to the demonic (Houellebecq). Nihilism, after all, signifies the triumph of the mediocre, also aesthetically. But is it possible to interpret the fictive murder of Houellebecq by the author (real Houellebecq) in line with the 'demonic' anger above, as an act of symbolic terror (against Jed's realism, to be sure, but also against the surrounding society)?

Indeed, for all the discontinuities between Houellebecq's previous novels and *The Map and the Territory* (less sex, more focus on artistic commitment and on artists ...), there is a visible continuity with respect to 'fury'. Nothing seems to obsess Houellebecq more than destruction and disappearance. Thus, *Platform* ends with a terrorist attack on a tourist camp in Thailand. In *The Possibility of an Island* we witness the disappearance of the species in a post-apocalyptic, pro-fascist world. Similarly, *Lanzarote*'s is literally a post-volcanic, 'burned-out' topology. The 'murder' of Houellebecq by Houellebecq must be placed in this series.

The paradox of his fictive self-destruction is that it invests destruction itself with desire. In this respect Houellebecq follows a long tradition of misanthropic social satire in literature that goes back to Roman, Juvenal tradition. As Bernstein (1992) shows, the 'abject hero' is in fact a character that originated in the carnival, in Saturnalian dialogues, in which the roles of the master and the slave are reversed. Crucially, the structure of the dialogues has a deeply bitter and negative strand that has survived throughout modern times. In contemporary culture, the abject hero remains a socially peripheral but symbolically central figure who refuses to conform to the society which he despises. Almost all Houellebecq's characters adopt the discourse of the abject hero in this sense. Thus they can denigrate themselves in order to be able to denigrate the society. There is therefore in Houellebecq an uncanny echo of Horace's satires:

> All right, I admit I'm easily led by my belly, my nostrils twitch at a savoury smell, I'm weak, spineless – if you like, a glutton into the bargain, but you are exactly the same, if not worse.
>
> (Horace 2005: 67–68)

Houellebecq's characters are always already prepared to debase themselves, to accept their misery. In *The Possibility of an Island*, for instance, Daniel, the protagonist, who is a stand-up comedian, admits that he is 'cynical', that he is a 'clown'. One should not, however, be misled by this 'modesty' for this move only serves the argument that the society that surrounds him is even more cynical, for instance, when he tells jokes like:

> 'Do you know what they call the fat stuff around the vagina?'
> 'No'
> 'The woman'
>
> (Houellebecq 2005: 11)

He is quick to add, however: 'Strangely, I managed to throw in that kind of thing, whilst still getting good reviews in *Elle* and *Télérama*' (Ibid.). I am bad, but you are worse. In *The Map and the Territory*, the comedian is replaced with the comic Houellebecq, who knows how to belittle himself, but does so in order to criticize the late capitalist consumer society.

How about the 'real' Houellebecq? Certainly, as a character in *The Map and the Territory,* he is 'detached from any real referent' and we are left 'with a collection of ideas that don't really stick to anything, because the relation between ideas and consequences has been so offhandedly obliterated' (Kipnis 2012). But, as is well known, Houellebecq often refers to his fictive characters, edits life, and mixes fictive and real figures in real life as well. It is therefore interesting that his non-fiction is similar to his fiction in spirit. Perhaps the best place to look for it is *Public Enemies*: in the beginning of the book, which is conceived together with Bernard-Henri Lévy, Houellebecq presents himself as a 'contemptible' individual, as a 'nihilist, reactionary, cynic, racist, shameless misogynist' (Houellebecq in Houellebecq & Lévy 2011: 3–4). Shortly after, 'provocative' ideas follow. For instance, Houellebecq describes himself as an 'absolute atheist' – 'not simply religious ... but political' atheist (Ibid. 164). Elsewhere:

> I don't believe much in the influence of politics on history. I think that the major factors are technological and sometimes, not often, religious. I don't think politicians can really have a true historical importance, except when they provoke major catastrophes Napoleon-style, but that's about it. I also don't believe individual psychology has any effect on social movements. You will find this belief expressed in all my novels.
>
> (Houellebecq in Hunnewell 2011)

He grounds his 'lack of political commitment' in 'consensus' politics (Houellebecq in Houellebecq & Lévy 2011: 82). This critique of post-politics is difficult to disagree with. But then what seems to be critical reverts to its opposite: 'I've always had the sense of living in a sort of technocracy, though without necessarily feeling that this was a bad thing' (Ibid. 83). So, there are 'honest engineers who build railway viaducts and office buildings; and bloodthirsty clowns who seize on any pretext, ideological or religious, in order to destroy them' (Ibid. 87).

> Is this, then, the core of my beliefs? Is it as simplistic as this? Sadly, I fear it is. I have always felt the deepest mistrust for those who take up arms in the name of whatever cause. I have always felt there was something deeply unwholesome about warmongers, troublemakers, rabble-rousers. What is a war or a revolution, in the end, but a hobby fuelled by spite, a bloody, cruel sport?
>
> (Ibid. 88)

Did we then reach the end of history, a point of no return, where capitalism has become a religion and the technocrats continue the work of angels? To be sure, Houellebecq gives a convincing account of the world, but his 'despondency and defeatism' vindicate Fukuyama's verdict (Bauman 2012: 23). The problem, however, is not only related to 'politicians' and 'individual psychology' – it is a political problem:

> The yawning gap between the grandiosity of the pressures and the meagreness of the defences is bound to go on feeding and beefing up sentiments of impotence as long as it persists. That gap, however, is *not* bound to persist: the gap looks unbridgeable only when the future is extrapolated as 'more of the same' as present trends – and the belief that the point of no return has already been reached adds credibility to such an extrapolation without necessarily rendering it correct. It happens time and again that dystopias turn into self-refuting prophecies, as the fate of Zamyatin's and Orwell's visions at least suggests …
>
> (Ibid. 24)

Not surprisingly, therefore, Houellebecq politically comes across as a nihilist. But his nihilism is about simulation, even of himself. Whereas previous forms of nihilism addressed the destruction of the imaginary (e.g. the moral, philosophical illusions) or the destruction of the symbolic order (e.g. meaning or ideology), contemporary nihilism is realized through simulation. For it, 'the apocalypse is finished' (Baudrillard 1994: 160). Consequently, Houellebecq's characters inhabit a world that has lost illusions – a world without values, utopias, ideals, a depressed and depressive world. The very proliferation of neutrality and indifference is therefore itself a source of fascination. Ours is, after all, a system that cancels out differences, upon which politics is based: an obscene system in which dialectical polarity no longer exists, a simulacrum, where acts disappear without consequences in indifferent 'zero-sum signs' (Ibid. 16, 32). Houellebecq's fiction, too, is contemporary in this sense; its 'fury' is a product of indifferent forces rather than political antagonisms. It emanates in the form of metastasis, bringing with it transparency (disappearance), a flattening process characterized by the exacerbation of indifference and the indefinite mutation of social domains (Baudrillard 1990: 7, 50). Hence the obscene indistinction between Hirst and Koons, Gates and Jobs, Jed and Houellebecq.

All Houellebecq fiction takes nihilism as a given, without being able to detect any crack, any line of flight, in the world it depicts. His fiction is a nihilistic portrayal of nihilism from inside, trapped within the triangle it mocks: religious nihilism (the idea of transcendence), passive nihilism (life without values), and radical nihilism (values without life). There is, to be sure, a fourth type of nihilism that, on the basis of the idea of immanence, opposes all these three forms of nihilism: Nietzsche's 'perfect nihilism', a nihilism that seeks its own limits, turns against itself and destroys itself, to create immanent values. Which involves profanation. And it is precisely this, the attempt at profanation, that Houellebecq mocks in the sociologist Comte who sought to replace religion with sociology:

> Comte ... failed; failed totally and miserably. A religion with no God may be possible (or a philosophy, if you prefer; something that carries in its wake, like so many delightful corollaries, a code of ethics, a sense of 'human dignity', maybe even a political theory, *if compatible*). But none of this seems to me to be conceivable without a belief in eternal life. ... Comte wasn't offering anything like that; all he proposed was one's theoretically living on in the memory of mankind. He gave the concept a slightly more high-blown twist, something like 'incorporation into the Great Being,' but it didn't change the fact that what he was offering was a theoretical perpetuation in the memory of mankind. Well, that just didn't cut it. Nobody gives a shit about living on in the memory of mankind (not even me, and I write books).
> (Houellebecq in Houellebecq & Lévy 2011: 166).

Comte's religious project is an 'easy-to-satirize' failure (see Wernick 2001: 5). Perhaps Durkheim's sociology of religion, which, similarly, found a 'higher reality' in the social, could have been a better target (see Durkheim 2001: 18). Or, going back to the origins, we could recall Spinoza's profanation of religious categories such as the soul, immortality, salvation, and blessedness. Yet, as Spinoza would remind us, reason can lead us to truth but cannot lead us to obey him – that is a political problem, not philosophical. It is herein that Houellebecq's political nihilism becomes significant. At any rate, profanation is what is at stake in Houellebecq's work. The problem is that he reduces the attempt at profanation to the sacralization of the social, that is, to secularization. Therefore one must insist that theology itself has always been political, that behind moral ideals that repress, negate life, there is always hidden a will to power.

Instead of conclusion
From four religions to four truth procedures

To end with, let us relate two different styles of profanation, Spinoza's and Badiou's. Notwithstanding the significant differences between the two philosophers, their shared desire for profanation testifies to an interesting convergence which is illustrative for our discussion. Here I want to deal with this convergence in divergence as a case of disjunctive synthesis through a comparison of the different understandings of religion in Spinoza and Badiou's truth procedures.

We have in previous chapters discussed four different understandings of religion. First, there is religion as 'superstition', which reduces faith to a sign perceived as the property of a single prophet or people. The second form of religion is the 'universal faith', still based on imagination but not reducible to superstition. It is open to all, universalist in orientation. Third, with the move from imagination to reason, we arrived at Spinoza's 'true religion', which is still common to all but, in contrast to both superstition and universal faith, corresponds to the second and third kinds of knowledge. We have added to Spinoza's original scheme a fourth form of religion, capitalism as religion, which signifies the perversion of reason into instrumental reason, and which constitutes a paradoxical form of religion by turning profanation (capitalism) itself into religion.

The following diagram illustrates the relationship between the four religions and their political implications.

As a hermeneutical 'fiction', the diagram enables the interpretation of the dynamics and the relations suggested by the four understandings of religion without being captured within their own schemas. Its intention is not to 'position' as such but to discuss the different constellations of religion, focusing on the intensities and tendencies the different perceptions of religions produce. Regarding the use of diagrams to illustrate relations and to structure thought, I draw on Mullarkey (2006: 176), viewing the diagram 'metaphilosophically and immanently, as thinking for itself, relating seemingly disparate philosophies through its intrinsic ability to outline thought'.

The diagram is cross-formed and based on two orthogonal axes: a vertical continuum between imagination and reason and a horizontal continuum between property and commons. The inspiration here is rooted in one of Engels' claims regarding religion: 'only lack of illusions in the head of workers

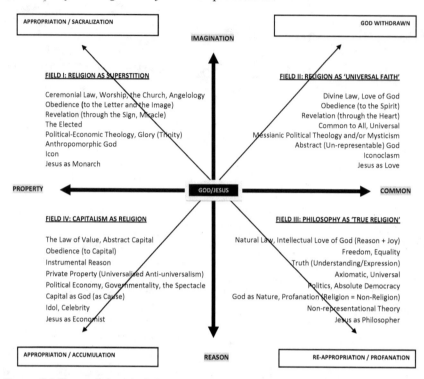

Figure C.1 Four religions in Spinoza

could correspond to their lack of property' (Engels 1957: 270). Notwithstanding the impossibility of getting rid of illusion, contra Engels' hope, the relationship between illusion and property is fruitful. Thus, following this insight in a Spinozist framework, the diagram aims at constructing a social theoretical perspective on religion by illustrating a dynamic field of forces. It assumes an a priori understanding of religion as separation and mediation between two poles: property (appropriation/sacralization) and the commons (re-appropriation/profanation). The same logic applies to the second axis, that of imagination and reason, where the relationship between them is that of a continuum, or, to use Spinoza's expression, 'perfection'. In other words, the relationship between the two poles is not given in advance but must be thought of in processual terms. Hence the differentiation between 'superstition', 'universal faith', and 'true religion' on the one hand, and between reason and instrumental reason on the other: faith is not identical to religion as superstition just as reason is not reducible to instrumental reason. At the same time, the intellectual love of God is related but not identical or reducible to love of God. This double differentiation also shows that it is naïve to oppose reason and religion as, for instance, is the case with the contemporary 'atheist' critique of religion launched in several best-selling books such as *The God Delusion* (Dawkins 2006) and *God Is Not Great* (Hitchens 2007).

'Property' in the horizontal axis signifies that which 'moves free use into a separate sphere and converts it into a right' (Agamben 2007: 83). Debt, which has played a central role in my discussion of religion and economy in *Chapters 1* and *4*, is a relationship based on property (see Nietzsche 1996: 68). In general, religion is a relation (religio) of property: we belong to God; we are his creations and our essential drive is to return to the master who made us. 'Salvation' is our return, as property, to God's *oikos*. The principle of formation or the telos of the religious system is based on property: God made us, we return to God.

Significantly in this respect, the state of nature in Spinoza excludes property; there cannot be 'anything in nature which can be said to belong to this man and not to that, but all things belong to all men' (Spinoza 1993a: 166). It is the social contract that introduces private property to the state of nature: since in the state of nature men are 'liable to emotions' (Ibid. 165), the social contract institutes a rationality into it by establishing sanctions and threats based on emotions stronger than the emotions it seeks to check (for instance it institutes fear to deter attacks on property). But this does not mean that the social contract is an ideal state to live in; it is only better than the state of nature: 'since we must do wrong, it is better to do wrong in that respect' (Ibid. 174). The social contract, in other words, is far from the true model for unification, which is free association or friendship: 'friends have all things in common, as in the state of nature' (Brown 1991: 139). Crucially, Spinoza's individual self is not a self-contained monad, a 'kingdom within a kingdom' (Spinoza 1993a: 82); rather, it is part of a whole (God or Nature), connected with other individuals that also are expressions, modifications, of the same substance, albeit to differing degrees and intensities. Indeed, human beings need for their preservation 'many other bodies' from which they are 'continually regenerated' (Ibid. 53). Thus, interpreted politically, Spinoza's monism takes us from the idea of private property to that of commons, or, communism.

> It is above all things useful to men that they join together in companionship and bind themselves together with such bonds by which they can most easily make one being of them all, and absolutely to do those things which serve for the purpose of confirming friendship.
>
> (Ibid. 189)

Against this background, within *Field I* of the diagram, we are dealing with superstition, the Biblical God which is anthropomorphic and monarchic. This understanding of religion, which is determined by the images of creation, free will, revelation, and chosen people, has the status of an affective 'fiction' or 'illusion'. However, it must not be dismissed for it is through fiction that God is 'known in the modality of the unknown', in the modality of 'ignorance' (Balibar 2012: 32).

The notion of universal faith within *Field II* incorporates universality or commonality to religious imagination, although love of God here is orientated towards theology (revelation) rather than reason and calls for obedience. Hence, as is the case with *Field I*, within *Field II*, also, the idea of God remains the focal point of voluntary servitude. Here the divine is not identified with an anthropomorphic Legislator but with the Law, and the idea of God signifies the imaginary space from which the Law is communicated indeterminately, a place 'towards which humans orient their desire to obey' (Balibar 2012: 33). In this context the concept of mysticism, which signifies unmediated love of God and excludes economy, is particularly relevant (see *Excursus 2*). In general, the 'universal faith' is a heterogeneous notion that combines both reason and imagination, existing only in an inconsistent state of metamorphosis, which can push it towards either *Field I* or *Field III*.

Within *Field III* we are confronted with a parallax view of 'God or Nature'. Here the distinction between transcendence and immanence tends to be dissolved. With the intellectual love of God, true religion and non-religion (atheism) come to coincide. The source of this procedure is profanation. Insofar as religion is a matter of untying the commons via sacralization, including them within an economy of glorification, the idea of profanation here relates to the idea of communism. (In this regard the difference between socialism and communism is relevant. While in socialism property is maintained in the form of public property, communism signifies the absence of property as such. Hence the idea of socialism could be placed on the borderline between *Field III* and *Field IV*.)

Finally, within *Field IV*, we can speak of capitalism as a cult religion and liberal democracy as a rational order based on property and (instrumental) reason. Here the conception of rationality is positivist and utilitarian. The logic of *Field IV* emerges in the form of a revised Spinozism in the framework of which perversion of democracy leads to liberal democracy and universalism to the logic of God-capital. Here 'common' and 'profane' do not coincide. On the contrary, something profane (capitalism) is elevated to the level of the sacred.

Importantly, even though they are conceptually differentiated here, these four understandings of religion can re-enter one another, or, repeat themselves in one another (for instance, other understandings of God can be present in a capitalist social formation in spite of the dominance of the capitalist cult). In this sense the diagram can claim a validity for it can 're-enter' itself (Spencer-Brown 1969), or, repeat itself within its different fields like a fractal structure in which one can recognize the same pattern in the overall system as well as in its parts (Borch 2000: 112; Kauffman 1987: 63–65). Thus, what is significant in the diagram is how the four conceptions of religion relate to and differ from each other. This is also why Spinoza himself is interested in passages and transformations between the different kinds of knowledge and between imagination and reason. The basic movement and thus the basic antagonism made visible by the diagram pertains to the two poles of sacralization and profanation (which are illustrated in the diagram as the vanishing points of *Field I* and *Field III*). Further, it allows for making two differentiations. First, in spite of the relations of perfection, there is a significant contradiction in this framework between imagination and reason. Second, there is a crucial difference between reason and instrumental reason, or, between intellectual love of God as passion (as love) and the denunciation of passion in the cynicism of instrumental reason.

Badiou and profanation: four truth procedures

Although the diagram is Spinozist in orientation, it can be modified to relate to different contemporary philosophies. To demonstrate this through an example let us turn to Badiou's philosophy. In relation to the so-called 'return' of religion into the political arena, Badiou insists that God is dead: 'I am a strict Nietzschean on this question. I really think that God is dead' (Badiou 2013: 30). The 'return of religion' is merely a screen for the processes of de-politicization characteristic of late modernity. But why does Badiou's philosophy itself often acquire a quasi-transcendental aspect? Despite his philosophy being radically a-theological, or, immanent, Badiou insists on making use of categories which are fundamentally theological categories. In this respect, regarding the use of the theological lexicon, there is an interesting similarity between Spinoza's and Badiou's philosophies.

As I demonstrated through a discussion of his work on Paul in *Chapter 2*, Badiou's re-appropriation of transcendental language seeks to open up the religious imagination to reason, to 'perfect' its imaginary truths by 'accommodating' them in philosophical discourse. Through this movement, Badiou also re-inscribes the promisory aspects of religion in the framework of politics. Certainly, this relation of appropriation/accommodation always runs both ways. Therefore Badiou assumes as a starting point that religion itself is an apparatus of capture. He emphasizes that 'love', for instance, is in its origin an impulse towards an idea of the common, towards universality. In love, one experiences the world from the perspective of the difference of the other, and 'constructs', together with the other, a new 'world' from a decentered point of view (Badiou 2012a: 16–17, 25–26). In this sense love is originally an immanent event. Religion captures and sacralizes it. In Christianity, for example, in which love is one of the most central concepts, the power of love is appropriated and used in order to articulate a transcendent universality:

> Christianity grasped perfectly that there is an element in the apparent contingency of love that can't be reduced to that contingency. But it immediately raised it to the level of transcendence, and that is the root of the problem. The universal element I too recognize in love is immanent.
> (Ibid.65)

Badiou's, like Spinoza's, is an atheistic theory that can do without theology; the truth-event is not transcendent to the situation but emerges as its immanent 'supplement', as a 'cut' in the continuum of becoming (Badiou 2009a: 384). However, while both philosophies unite in the idea of immanence, they diverge in their understandings of immanence. Thus, on the one hand, in a Spinozist perspective it might seem that Badiou wants to think 'transcendence within the immanent', expecting a 'breach' from immanence (see Deleuze and Guattari 1994: 47; Smith 2004: 640; Phelps 2013: 151). It is this breach that materializes Badiou's four truth procedures (politics, science, love, art). But in a Spinozist perspective there can be no 'supplementary' dimension to immanence. 'Immanence is immanent only to itself and consequently captures everything, absorbs All-One, and leaves nothing remaining to which it could be immanent' (Deleuze and Guattari 1994: 45).On the other hand, however, the Spinozist radical immanence itself tends to become a transcendent category (Albertsen 1995: 136). Thus Badiou sees the Spinozist event as 'the becoming (-One) of (unlimited) becoming' (Badiou 2009c: 382). He can neither accept the idea that the event is co-extensive with the actual nor settle with an interpretation of the event as a single Event, as the eternal recurrence of the same.

'Immanent transcendence' versus 'transcendent immanence'. This disagreement in agreement, disjunction in relation, means that the polarity here is not a neat polarity but rather a continuum based on the concept of immanence. In this sense, the relation between Spinoza's and Badiou's anti-theologies can be characterized as a disjunctive synthesis, a relation in which the two sides of the relation are not antagonistic enemies but agonistic adversaries who share a common ground (profanation). They have a common enemy (theology) and shared aspirations (thinking of the event without a transcendent God). Both resist theology, engage with practical politics, and value the role of the formal logic of mathematics, linking reason and passion together.

What I am primarily interested in at this point is the way in which the two philosophies paradoxically converge on some common aspirations (e.g. the idea of infinity) and unite against common enemies (e.g. theology). Regarding the convergences Badiou himself stresses the 'exceptional', mathematical form of Spinoza's *Ethics*, in which arguments are 'proved in geometrical order' (2011a: 41). Spinoza's style is based on the movement 'from a mathematics of being to a mathematics of eternal love and intellectual blessedness' (Ibid.). Since freedom is based on understanding necessity, logical proof plays a crucial role in Spinoza. Thus, the radical Spinozist act does not take place in disorder but 'within the cold quietness of the stars', while the actor has to persist in the most positive affect or passion: the intellectual love of God (see Ibid. 40, 49). In Badiou, too, the mathematical ontology is coupled with an emphasis on the role of passions such as fidelity and love. Further, in Badiou, as in Spinoza, 'life' is not reducible to the co-ordinates of empirical time and space but is an experience linked to the idea of infinity (see 2009c: 510). Following this, in both perspectives the truth is untimely and transcends the given reality. Thus, while for Spinoza philosophy is about perceiving reality *sub specie aeternitatis*, for Badiou the aim of philosophy is to make it possible to live 'like immortals'.

To be sure, there are significant disjunctions, too, especially regarding the conception of attributes, of event, and of the subject. Most importantly perhaps, in Badiou's perspective, Spinoza's philosophy 'forecloses the void' (2006: 113). In Badiou the void is a central category and signifies an inherent source of instability in every situation. To deal with this potential danger, which originates in its own structure, the situation needs to be doubled. Thus, every situation is 'structured twice', by its own structure and by the metastructure, also called the 'state of the situation' (Ibid. 94). While the initial structure guarantees belonging, the metastructure holds for inclusion (Ibid. 97).

But Spinoza makes attempts at identifying structure (Nature) and meta-structure (God), assigning the function of counting-as-one directly to the state of the situation, thus de-differentiating belonging and inclusion. Consequently, presentation (the situation) and representation (the state of the situation) become identical. In other words, Spinoza can only perceive 'normal' terms, overlooking the possibility of presentation without representation (singularity) and of representation without presentation (excrescence). The price for the equation of God and Nature is thus the 'ontological eradication of the void' (Ibid. 120). And since the event is a relation to the void, this is also to say that the event (in Badiou's sense) is missing in Spinoza's system.

Interestingly, however, the event in Badiou can take four forms: political, artistic, amorous, and scientific. These are also the four truth procedures in Badiou. Just as in Spinoza we humans cannot comprehend the infinity of God but can only know the two attributes through which God expresses himself, thought and extension, that is, we can only reach two kinds of truths while an infinity of truths exists, in Badiou, it is possible to reach the truth in four ways: politics, art, love, and science (see Badiou 2009c: 71). What I want to point out in this respect is the structural resemblance between Spinoza's four religions and Badiou's four truth procedures: thus, if we re-construct the previous diagram by incorporating into it Badiou's four truth procedures, it would look like this:

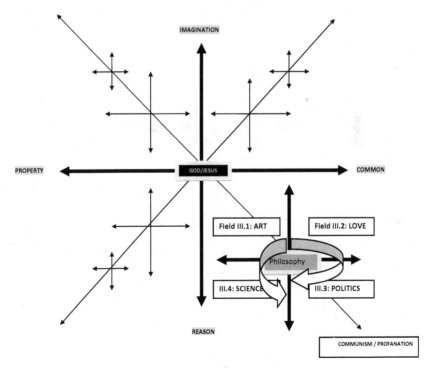

Figure C.2 Four truth procedures as a moment of re-entry

The diagram is constituted through the previous Spinozist diagram's re-entering itself within its third field. The concept of 're-entry' designates the re-entering of a distinction into the distinction itself, thereby splitting the originary distinction into two parts, one being traversed and one marked by another distinction (see Baecker 2006: 124). In this sense what is inserted into *Field III* of the first diagram is not a different diagram that merely bears some structural analogy with the first. What is at issue is rather the reinsertion of the whole (the relation between the four religions in Spinoza) into a part of itself (the third religion, that is, philosophy). Through this movement, which combines self-referentiality with coupling and allows for reflection, the formal similarity between Spinoza's religions and Badiou's truth procedures becomes visible. This of course also sets up a series of logical questions and paradoxes around recursion, self-reference and infinite regress which I should acknowledge. But within these limits the diagram can claim a validity insofar as it enables one to visualize an actual solution to a virtual problem (see Mullarkey 2006: 162 on the use of diagram as a 'problem solver').

Within *Field III.1*, art (fiction) as a truth procedure displaces or takes the place of religion as superstition in Spinoza. As discussed in *Chapter 1*, the critique of illusion does not mean that a world totally devoid of illusions is possible or desirable. Just as imagination (illusion) is necessary for Spinoza, for Badiou art is a truth procedure that enables us to *think* history and the event. Thought in art is indistinguishable from the sensible, an 'unthinkable thought' (Badiou 2005b: 19). However, art is not mimesis (Ibid. 21). In particular, modern art identifies itself as 'a form of thought', which makes it difficult to oppose the image and the idea (Ibid.). Rather, seen in the prism of philosophy, poetry is a truth procedure.

> And in fact I believe that the most difficult problem of our time is the problem of fiction. We must distinguish between fiction and ideology. Because, generally speaking, ideology is opposed to science, to truth or to reality. But, as we have known since Lacan, truth itself is in a structure of fiction. The process of truth is also the process of a new fiction.
> (Badiou 2012b: 77)

Within *Field III.2* we have (profane, profaned) 'love' which Badiou defines as 'the possible transition from the pure randomness of chance to a state that has universal value' (2012a: 16). In contrast to the romantic understanding of love as the ecstasy of a chance encounter, or to the commercial–legalistic perception of love as a contract, or to the 'sceptical attitude which only detects an illusion in love', for Badiou, love is a truth procedure, a 'quest for truth' (Ibid. 22).

Within *Field III.3* we have the third truth procedure: politics. For Badiou, the state of the situation is always in excess of the situation itself, and this excess, which expresses itself as repression and alienation in empirical situations, is not measurable in itself. Only in exceptional situations does the political truth-event 'prescribe' a measure to this excess 'through the emergence of the subject' (Badiou 2005a: 146). Thus, it is when an event occurs that the state really 'reveals itself' (Ibid. 145). What is revealed is not only the excrescent nature of the state, its excessive power or its repression, but also a measure for this excess. 'Politics puts the State at a distance, in the distance of its measure' (Ibid.). As such, politics for Badiou exists paradoxically, as a self-founding event which creates its own subject. It can only originate in an event, not in the actual situation. Only after an event, retroactively, does the political act come to appear as a presupposed element of such constitution (Badiou 2006: 345).

Finally, within *Field III.4*, we have science as a truth procedure. Mathematics, especially, is 'the thought of the multiple as such' (Badiou 2013: 102). Just as geometry reveals eternal truths in Spinoza (the sum of the angles of a triangle is always and everywhere 180), for Badiou, 'mathematics is sufficiently absolute for us to be able to discuss it with God' (Ibid. 101). However, the event itself cannot be determined by numbers. 'Number itself cannot get its measure' (Badiou 2006: 354). The reduction of truth to numbers would mean obscuring the event. Thus for Badiou a contemporary paradox relates to the accommodation of science by capitalism: 'we live in the era of number's despotism' (Badiou 2008: 1). Today social bonds are increasingly linked to numbers, ratings determine crucial moments of formation, the opinion polls increasingly empty out the content of real democracy, and so on; today even our souls are informed by number in the sense that existence is increasingly reduced to giving a 'favorable account of oneself' (Ibid. 2–3). The background for this 'banalisation' is capitalism and its reduction of value (truth) to number. In capitalism, number 'underlies everything of value' (Ibid. 213). Thus, against the law of capital, Badiou asserts that '*nothing* made into number is of value' (Ibid. 213). Scientific truth is indifferent to numericality (Ibid. 214). In fact, all truth-events become accessible only when they can escape the play of the sheer number, for instance, a political truth transpires only when it is subtracted from the framework of voting (Badiou 2006: 353–54).

Let us, to conclude, read the two diagrams together:

First, the existence of superstition does not justify the negation of imagination as such. The problem is not imagination, but taking what is imagined for truth. And the illusion that knows that it is an illusion is the artistic fiction. Art tells the truth of the social world in the guise of fiction. This is why in Badiou's theory we often see a double movement that seeks to place art in the place of religion, recognizing, at the same time, the differences between art and philosophy.

Second, even if the scientific truth is obscured by capitalism, capitalism as religion is not the last word on science. Despite the fact that science can be accommodated by capitalism, reducing reason to instrumental reason, this does not justify the denigration of science or reason as such.

Third, the love of God which is still 'accommodated' by Spinoza (*Field II* of the first diagram) is in Badiou totally profaned as a truth procedure (as love).

Fourth, while we have within *Field III* of the first diagram both 'philosophy' and 'politics' – possibly reflecting the fact that Spinoza took a break from *Ethics* in order to write on politics – in the second diagram philosophy and politics are clearly differentiated and *Field III.3* is exclusively preserved for politics (which is, interestingly, in line with Spinoza's own tendency; see Negri 2004). Philosophy, in turn, becomes what enables thinking together the truths emerging from the four different procedures, their 'compossibility' (Badiou 1999: 44; 2012a: xx).

Insofar as the second diagram is constituted on the basis of the first diagram's re-entry into itself, it takes the first diagram to its logical extremes by repeating its logic. It is also in this movement that philosophy profanes, and seeks to take the place of, religion.

References

Adorno, TW (1967) *Prisms*. Cambridge: The MIT Press.
Agamben, G (1995) *Idea of Prose*. New York: SUNY.
——(1998) *Homo Sacer. Sovereign Power and Bare Life*. Stanford: Stanford University Press.
——(1999) *Potentialities. Collected Essays in Philosophy*. Stanford: Stanford University Press.
——(2000) *Means without End. Notes on Politics*. Minneapolis: University of Minnesota Press.
——(2003) 'The State of Emergency'. Available online at www.generation-online.org/p/fpagambenschmitt.htm.
——(2005) *The State of Exception*. Chicago: The University of Chicago Press.
——(2007) *Profanations*. New York: Zone Books.
——(2008) 'The Lost Dress of Paradise'. Available online at http://notesforthecomingcommunity.blogspot.co.uk/2008/04/lost-dress-of-paradise.html.
——(2011a) *The Kingdom and the Glory. For a Theological Genealogy of Economy and Government*. Stanford: Stanford University Press.
——(2011b) *Nudities*. Stanford: Stanford University Press.
——(2014) 'Dios no murió. Se transformó en dinero', P Savà's interview with Agamben. Available online at www.rebelion.org/noticia.php?id=180570.
Ahearne, J (1995) *Michel de Certeau: Interpretation and Its Other*. London: Polity.
Albertsen, N (1995) 'Kunstværket, en sansningsblok under evighedens synsvinkel. Spinoza, Wittgenstein, Deleuze', in Lehmann, N & Madsen, C (eds) *Deleuze og det æstetiske. Æstetikstudier II*. Århus: Aarhus Universitetsforlag, pp. 135–62.
——(2002) 'RetfaerdiggoerelseiByen', *Distinktion* 4, pp. 45–61.
——(2005) 'From Calvin to Spinoza', *Distinktion* 11, pp. 171–86.
——(2006) 'Concepts Reasonably Contested. Rereading Gallie'. Paper presented at the conference *Normative Implications of the Conceptual Turn*, Roskilde University, 1–2 March.
——(2012) 'Kapitalismens krematistiske varieté: Gamle og nye numre', in Raffnsøe-Møller, Morten, Thorup, Mikkel, Vinther Larsen, Thomas & Hansen, Ejvind (eds) *Kapitalismens ansigter*. Aarhus: Philosophia, pp. 11–30.
Althusser, L (2008) *On Ideology*. London: Verso.
Appelbaum, R (2011) 'Voltaire and the Fanati-system'. Paper presented at the workshop *The Fanatic*, Lancaster University, 11 September.
Aristotle (1995) *Politics*. London: Oxford World's Classics.
Atatürk, MK (2004) *Söylev. Cilt I-II*. Istanbul: Cumhuriyet Kitapları.

Badiou, A (1999) *Manifesto for Philosophy*. New York: SUNY Press.
——(2001) *Ethics. An Essay on the Understanding of Evil*. London: Verso.
——(2003) *Saint Paul. The Foundation of Universalism*. Stanford: Stanford University Press.
——(2005a) *Metapolitics*. London: Verso.
——(2005b) *Handbook of Inaesthetics*. Stanford: Stanford University Press.
——(2006) *Being and Event*. New York: Continuum.
——(2008) *Number and Numbers*. London: Polity.
——(2009a) *Theory of the Subject*. New York: Continuum.
——(2009b) *Pocket Pantheon. Figures of Postwar Philosophy*. London: Verso.
——(2009c) *Logics of Worlds. Being and Event, 2*. New York: Continuum.
——(2011) 'Tunisie, Egypte: quand un vent d'est balaie l'arrogance de l'Occident'. Available online at www.versobooks.com/blogs/394-alain-badiou-tunisie,-egypte-quand-un-vent-d'est-balaie-l'arrogance-de-l'occident.
——(2012a) *In Praise of Love*. London: Serpent's Tale.
——(2012b) *Philosophy for Militants*. London: Verso.
——(2013) *Philosophy and the Event*. Interviews by Fabien Tarby. London: Polity.
Balibar, E (1998) *Spinoza and Politics*. London: Verso.
——(2012) 'Spinoza's Three Gods and the Modes of Communication', *European Journal of Philosophy* 20(1), pp. 26–49.
Baudrillard, J (1990) *Fatal Strategies*. Paris: Semiotext(e)/Pluto.
——(1994) *Simulacra and Simulation*. Ann Arbor: The University of Michigan Press.
——(1999) *Fatal Strategies*. London: Pluto.
——(2000) *Vital Illusion*. New York: Columbia University Press.
Bauman, Z (1998) 'What Prospects of Morality in Times of Uncertainty', *Theory, Society & Culture*, 15(1), pp. 11–22.
——(1999) *In Search of Politics*. London: Polity.
——(2012) *This Is Not a Diary*. London: Polity.
Baecker, D (2006) 'The Form of the Firm', *Organization*, 13(1), pp. 109–42.
Bellah, RN (1974) 'Civil Religion in America', in Richey, RE & Jones, DG (eds) *American Civil Religion*. New York: Harper & Row, pp. 21–44.
Benjamin, W (1979) 'Divine Violence', in *One-Way Street*. London: Verso, pp. 132–54.
——(1996) 'Capitalism as Religion', in Bullock, M & Jennings, MW (eds) *Selected Writings. Vol. 1, 1913–1926*. Massachusetts: Harvard University Press, pp. 288–91.
——(1999) *Illuminations*. London: Pimlico.
Benslama, F (2004) *Islamin Psikanalizi*. Istanbul: Iletisim.
Bernauer, J (2004) 'Michel Foucault's Philosophy of Religion: an Introduction to the Non-Fascist Life', in Bernauer, J & Carrette, J (eds) *Michel Foucault and Theology. The Politics of Religious Experience*. Aldershot: Ashgate, pp. 77–98.
Bernstein, MA (1992) *Bitter Carnival. Ressentiment and the Abject Hero*. Princeton: Princeton University Press.
Bettridge, T (2012) 'Michel Houellebecq's *The Map and the Territory*', *The Columbia Journal of Literary Criticism*, X, pp. 6–9. Available online at http://english.columbia.edu/files/english/content/FINAL%20JOURNAL%20FINAL.pdf.
Boer, IE (1996) 'Despotism from under the Veil: Masculine and Feminine Readings of the Despot and the Harem', *Cultural Critique* 32(1): pp. 43–73.
Boltanski, L & Chiapello, E (2007) *The New Spirit of Capitalism*. London: Verso.
Borch, C (2000) 'Former, der kommer i form – om Luhmann og Spencer-Brown', *Distinktion* 1, pp. 105–22.

Borges, JL (1998) 'On Exactitude in Science', in *Collected Fictions*. London: Penguin Books, p. 325.
Bradley, A & Fletcher, P (2010) 'The Politics to Come: A History of Futurity', in Bradley, A & Fletcher, P (eds) *The Politics To Come*. New York: Continuum, pp. 1–12.
Brown, NO (1991) *Apocalypse and/or Metamorphosis*. Berkeley: University of California Press.
Canetti, E (1962) *Crowds and Power*. London: Phoenix.
Certeau, M de (1996) *The Possession at Loudun*. Chicago: The University of Chicago Press.
Chamayou, G (2012) *Manhunts. A Philosophical History*. Princeton: Princeton University Press.
Colas, D (1997) *Civil Society and Fanaticism. Conjoined Histories*. Stanford: Stanford University Press.
Connolly, WE (1993) 'Beyond Good and Evil: The Ethical Sensibility of Michel Foucault', *Political Theory* 21(3), pp. 365–89.
——(1999) *Why I Am Not a Secularist*. Minneapolis and London: University of Minnesota Press.
——(2002) *Neuropolitics. Thinking, Culture, Speed*. Minneapolis and London: University of Minnesota Press.
——(2005) *Pluralism*. London: Duke University Press.
Dawkins, R (2006) *The God Delusion*. London: Bantam Press.
Debord, G (1983) *Society of the Spectacle*. Detroit: Black & Red.
Deleuze, G (1983) *Nietzsche & Philosophy*. New York: Columbia University Press.
——(1988) *Spinoza. Practical Philosophy*. San Fransisco: City Lights Books.
——(1989) *Cinema 2. The Time-Image*. London: The Athlone Press.
——(1990) *Logic of Sense*. New York: Columbia University Press.
——(1992) *Expressionism in Philosophy: Spinoza*. New York: Zone.
——(1994) *Difference & Repetition*. London: The Athlone Press.
——(1995) *Negotiations*. New York: Columbia University Press.
——(1998) 'Nietzsche and Saint Paul, Lawrence and John of Patmos', in *Essays Critical and Clinical*. London: Verso, pp. 36–52.
Deleuze, G & Guattari, F (1983) *Anti-Oedipus. Capitalism and Schizophrenia*. Minneapolis: University of Minnesota Press.
——(1987) *A Thousand Plateaus. Capitalism and Schizophrenia II*. Minneapolis & London: University of Minnesota Press.
——(1994) *What is Philosophy?* London: Verso.
Denike, M (2003) 'The Devil's Insatiable Sex: A Genealogy of Evil Incarnate', *Hypatia* 18(1), pp. 10–43.
Derrida, J (1994) *Specters of Marx*. London: Routledge.
——(1995) *On the Name*. Stanford: Stanford University Press.
——(2001) 'Above All, No Journalists', in Vries, H & Weber, S (eds) *Religion and Media*. Stanford: Stanford University Press, pp. 56–93.
——(2002) *Acts of Religion*. London: Routledge.
——(2004) 'For a Justice to Come', Lieven De Cauter's interview with Derrida. Available online at http://archive.indymedia.be/news/2004/04/83123.html.
——(2005) *Rogues. Two Essays on Reason*. Stanford: Stanford University Press.
Dillon, M (2008) 'Lethal Freedom: Divine Violence and the Machiavellian Moment'. *Theory and Event* 11(2), pp. 1–22. Available online at http://muse.jhu.edu/login?uri=/journals/theory_and_event/v011/11.2.dillon.html.

——(2011) 'Specters of Biopolitics: Finitude, Eschaton and Katechon', *The South Atlantic Quarterly* 110(1), pp. 782–94.
——(2012) 'The Political Legitimacy of the Modern Age'. Working paper, Lancaster University.
Durkheim, E (2001) *The Elementary Forms of Religious Life*. London: Oxford University Press.
Engels, F (1957) 'Juristic Socialism', in Marx, K & Engels, F *On Religion*. Moscow: Foreign Languages Publishing House, pp. 267–70.
Erdoğan, T (2013a) 'O sözlerimden rahatsız olan varsa özür de dilerim'. Available online at www.haberturk.com/gundem/haber/849466-o-sozlerimden-rahatsiz-olan-varsa-ozur-de-dilerim.
——(2013b) 'Biz ne diyoruz; Durmak yok yola devam.Onlar ne diyor; Duran adam!'. Available online at https://twitter.com/RT_Erdogan/status/348058441094406144.
——(2013c) 'Ne yaparsınız yapın kararı işleyeceğiz'. Available online at http://siyaset.milliyet.com.tr/basbakan-erdogan-taksim-gezi/siyaset/detay/1715767/default.htm.
Ergun, AF (2011) *Isyan Yazilari*. Istanbul: Ozan.
Feuerbach, L (1972) *The Fiery Brook: Selected Writings of Feuerbach*. New York: Garden City.
——(1989) *The Essence of Christianity*. New York: Prometheus.
Forsyth, N (1987) *Old Enemy: Satan and the Combat Myth*. Princeton: Princeton University Press.
Foucault, M (1977) *Discipline and Punish*. London: Penguin.
Foucault, M (1982) 'Afterward: The Subject and Power', in Dreyfus, HL & Rabinow, P (1982) *Michel Foucault. Beyond Structuralism and Hermeneutics*. New York: Harvester Wheatsheaf, pp. 208–26.
——(1983) 'Preface', in Deleuze, G and Guattari, F *Anti-Oedipus. Capitalism and Schizophrenia*. Minneapolis: University of Minnesota Press, pp. xi–xiv.
——(1991) 'Governmentality', in Burchell, G, Gordon, C & Miller, P (eds) *The Foucault Effect*. Chicago: The University of Chicago Press, pp. 87–104.
——(1997) 'What is Enlightenment?', in Rabinow, P (ed) *Michel Foucault. Ethics. Essential Works of Foucault 1954–1984*. London: Penguin, pp. 303–20.
——(2001) *Fearless Speech*. Los Angeles: Semiotext(e).
——(2002) *Power. Essential Works of Foucault 1954–84*. London: Penguin.
——(2005) 'Is it Useless to Revolt?', in Afary, J & Anbersaon KB *Foucault and the Iranian Revolution*. Chicago: The University of Chicago Press, pp. 263–67.
Fukuyama, F (1992) *The End of History and the Last Man*. New York: The Free Press.
Gallie, WB (1964) 'Essentially Contested Concepts', in *Philosophy and the Historical Understanding*. London: Chatto & Windus, pp. 157–91.
Girard, R (1986) *The Scapegoat*. Baltimore: The University of John Hopkins Press.
Göle, N (2013) 'Gezi: Bir Kamusal Meydan Hareketinin Anatomisi'. Available online at http://t24.com.tr/yazi/gezi-bir-kamusal-meydan-hareketinin-anatomisi/6824.
Goodchild, P (2005) 'Capital and Kingdom: An Eschatological Ontology', in Davis, C, Žižek, S & Milbank, J (eds) *Theology and the Political*. Durham: Duke University Press.
Greenblatt, S (1996) 'Foreword', in Certeau, M. de (1996) *The Possession at Loudun*. Chicago: The University of Chicago Press, pp. ix–xi.
Grosrichard, A (1998) *The Sultan's Court*. London: Verso.
Güngörmez, B (2013) 'Modern mesihler: Gezi hadisesinin politik teolojisi' (1) (2), *YeniSafak* 13–14 Aralik.

Hamacher, W (2002) 'Guilt History. Benjamin's Sketch "Capitalism as Religion"', *Diacritics* 32(3–4), pp. 81–106.
Harvey, D (1996) *Justice, Nature and Geography of Difference*. Oxford: Blackwell.
Hass, J (1982) *Illusionens filosofi. Studier i Nietzsches firser manuskripter*. Copenhagen: Nyt Nordisk Forlag.
Hitchens, C (2007) *God Is Not Great*. New York: Twelve.
Hobbes, T (1985) *Leviathan*. London: Penguin.
Horace (2005) *Satires and Epistles*. London: Penguin.
Houellebecq, M (1998) *Whatever*. London: Paul Hammond.
——(2001) *Atomised*. London: Vintage.
——(2005) *The Possibility of an Island*. London: Weidenfeld & Nicolson.
——(2011) *The Map and the Territory*. London: William Heinemann.
Houellebecq, M & Lévy, B-H (2011) *Public Enemies*. London: Atlantic Books.
Hunnewell, S (2011) 'Michel Houellebecq', interview with M Houellebecq: The Art of Fiction No. 206. Available online at www.theparisreview.org/.
Huxley, A (2005) *The Devils of Loudun*. London: Vintage.
Illuminati, A (2003) 'Postfordisten Spinoza', *Agora* 2(3), pp. 317–29.
James, S (2012) *Spinoza on Philosophy, Religion and Politics. The Theologico-Political Treatise*. London: Oxford.
Jonas, H (1958) *The Gnostic Religion*. Boston: Beacon Press.
Kantarowicz, E (1985) *The King's Two Bodies. A Study in Medieval Political Theology*. Princeton: Princeton University Press.
Kauffman, L (1987) 'Self-reference and Recursive Forms', *Journal of Social and Biological Structures* 10(1), pp. 53–72.
Kipnis, L (2012) 'Death by Self-Parody', *Bookforum*. Available online at www.bookforum.com/inprint/018_04/8584.
Kongar, E & Küçükkaya, A (2013) *Gezi Direnisi – Türkiye'yi Sarsan 30 Gün*. Istanbul: Cumhuriyet Kitaplari.
Kouvelakis, S (2003) *Philosophy and Revolution. From Kant to Marx*. London: Verso.
La Boétie, É (1942) *Discourse on Voluntary Servitude*. New York: Columbia University Press. Available online at www.constitution.org/la_boetie/serv_vol.htm.
Latour, B (1988) *The Pasteurization of France*. Massachusetts: Harvard University Press.
Laustsen, CB (2003) 'Det uhæmmede begær – Vestens fantasier om Orienten'. Working paper, University of Aarhus, Institute for Political Sciences.
——(2011) 'Religion of Politik. Fire Tilgangetil et Forskningsfelt', *Politica* 43(2), pp. 143–62.
Lawrence, DH (1931) *Apocalypse*. London: Penguin.
Lazzarato, M (2011) *The Making of the Indebted Man*. Cambridge: Semiotext(e).
Levinas, E (1985) *Ethics and Infinity*. Pittsburgh: Duquesne University Press.
Lloyd, V (2009) 'Michel Houellebecq and the Theological Virtues', *Literature & Theology* 23(1), pp. 84–98.
Marx, K (1844) 'Comments on James Mill'. Available online at www.marxists.org/archive/marx/works/1844/james-mill/.
——(1847) 'The Communism of the Paper Rheinischer Beobachter'. Available online at https://marxists.anu.edu.au/archive/marx/works/1847/09/12.htm.
——(1957) 'Contribution to the Critique of Hegel's Philosophy of Right. Introduction', in Marx, K & Engels, F *On Religion*. Moscow: Foreign Languages Publishing House, pp. 41–58.

―― (1970) *Critique of Hegel's 'Philosophy of Right'*. London: Cambridge University Press.
―― (1976) *Capital. Volume I*. London: Penguin.
―― (1977) *The Eighteenth Brumaire of Louis Bonaparte*. Moscow: Progress Publishers.
―― (1993) *Grundrisse*. London: Penguin.
―― (2007) *Economic and Philosophic Manuscripts of 1844*. New York: Dover.
Marx, K & Engels, F (1998) *The German Ideology*. New York: Prometheus Books.
―― (2002) *The Communist Manifesto*. London: Penguin.
Melville, H (1998) *Moby Dick*. Oxford: Oxford World's Classics.
Mondzain, M-J (2005) *Image, Icon, Economy. The Byzantine Origins of the Contemporary Imaginary*. Stanford: Stanford University Press.
Mouffe, C (2000) *The Democratic Paradox*. London: Verso.
―― (2005) *On the Political*. London: Routledge.
Mullarkey, J (2006) *Post-Continental Philosophy: An Outline*. New York: Continuum.
Negri, A (2004) *Subversive Spinoza*. Manchester: Manchester University Press.
Nietzsche, F (1960) *Joyful Wisdom*. New York: Frederick Ungar Publishers Co.
―― (1961) *Thus Spoke Zarathustra*. London: Penguin.
―― (1967) *The Will to Power*. New York: Vintage.
―― (1969) *Twilight of Idols. The Anti-Christ*. London: Penguin, pp. 1–112; 113–99.
―― (1972) *Beyond Good and Evil*. London: Penguin.
―― (1974) *The Gay Science*. London: Vintage.
―― (1995) *The Birth of Tragedy*. London: Dover.
―― (1996) *On the Genealogy of Morals*. London: Oxford University Press.
―― (2006) 'On Truth and Lies in a Nonmoral Sense', in Pearson, KA & Large, D (eds) *The Nietzsche Reader*. London: Blackwell, pp. 114–23.
―― (2008) *Human, All Too Human*. London: Wordsworth.
Peterson, E (2011) *Theological Tractates*. Stanford: Stanford University Press.
Phelps, H (2013) *Alain Badiou. Between Theology and Anti-Theology*. Bristol: Acumen.
Prozorov, S (2011) 'Pornography and Profanation in the Political Philosophy of Giorgio Agamben', *Theory, Culture & Society* 28(4): 71–95.
Rancière, J (1999) *Disagreement*. Minnesota: University of Minnesota Press.
―― (2010) *Dissensus*. New York: Continuum.
Ratmoko, D (2009) 'Preface' in Taubes, J (2009) *Occidental Eschatology*. Stanford: Stanford University Press.
Reginster, B (2006) *The Affirmation of Life. Nietzsche on Overcoming Nihilism*. Cambridge & Massachusetts: Harvard University Press.
Salecl, R (1998) *(Per)versions of Love and Hate*. London: Verso.
Schmitt, C (1985) *Political Theology. Four Chapters on the Concept of Sovereignty*. Chicago: The University of Chicago Press.
―― (2007) *The Concept of the Political*. Chicago: The University of Chicago Press.
―― (2009) *Hamlet or Hecuba*. New York: Telos.
Schopenhauer, A (1957) *The World as Will and Idea (Volume II)*. London: Routledge and Kegan Paul.
Sennett, R (1998) *The Corrosion of Character*. New York: W.W. Norton
Shakespeare, W (1970) *Timon of Athens*, in *The Complete Works of William Shakespeare*. London: Spring Books, pp. 660–83.
Simmel, G (1978) *The Philosophy of Money*. London: Routledge.
Smith, DW (2004) 'The Inverse Side of Structure: Žižek on Deleuze on Lacan'. *Criticism* 46(4), pp. 635–50.

Spencer-Brown, G (1969) *Laws of Form*. London: George Allen and Unwin.
Spinoza, B (1671) 'Letter XLIX. Spinoza to Isaac Orobio'. Available online at www.yesselman.com/letters.htm#TableOfLetters.
——(1951a) *A Theologico-Political Treatise*. London: Dover.
——(1951b) 'A Political Treatise', in Spinoza, B (1951) *A Theologico-Political Treatise*. London: Dover, pp. 279–387.
——(1993a) *Ethics*. London: Everyman.
——(1993b) *Treatise on the Correction of the Intellect*, in Spinoza, B (1993) *Ethics*. London: Everyman, pp. 221–59.
Taubes, J (2009) *Occidental Eschatology*. Stanford: Stanford University Press.
Toscano, A (2010) *Fanaticism*. London: Verso.
Virno, P (2004) *A Grammar of the Multitude*. Los Angeles: Semiotext(e).
Voltaire, M (1742) 'To His Majesty the King of Prussia', Rotterdam, January 20, in Voltaire, *Mahomet*, Kindle Locations 48–51.
——(1824) 'Alcoran', entry in *A Philosophical Dictionary*. London: J & HL Hunt. Available online at http://books.google.co.uk/books?id=3XANAAAAYAAJ&print sec=frontcover&redir_esc=y%20%20v=onepage&q=Alcoran&f=false#v=snippet&q= Alcoran&f=false.
——(2010) *God & Human Beings*. New York: Prometheus Books.
——(2011) *A Philosophical Dictionary*. London: Oxford University Press.
Vries, H de (2005) 'The Two Sources of the "Theological Machine": Jacques Derrida and Henri Bergson on Religion, Technicity, War, and Terror', in Davis, C, Milbank, J & Žižek, S (eds) *Theology and the Political*. USA: Duke University Press, pp. 336–91.
Warren, M (1988) *Nietzsche and Political Thought*. Cambridge: The MIT Press.
Weber, M (2003) *The Protestant Ethic and the Spirit of Capitalism*. New York: Dover.
Wernick, A (2001) *August Comte and the Religion of Humanity: The Post-theistic Program of French Social Theory*. London: Cambridge University Press.
Žižek, S (1999) *The Ticklish Subject. The Absent Center of Political Ontology*. London: Verso.
——(2000) *The Fragile Absolute*. London: Verso.
——(2002a) *Welcome to the Desert of the Real*. London: Verso.
——(2002b) 'Introduction: Between the Two Revolutions', in Introduction to Lenin (2002) *Revolution at the Gates. Selected Writings of Lenin from 1917*. London: Verso, pp. 1–14.
——(2002c) 'Afterword: Lenin's Choice', in Introduction to Lenin (2002) *Revolution at the Gates. Selected Writings of Lenin from 1917*. London: Verso, pp. 165–336.
——(2008a) *Violence*. London: Profile Books.
——(2008b) 'Masturbation, or Sexuality in the Atonal World'. Available online at www.lacan.com/symptom/?page_id=247.
——(2009) *First as Tragedy, Then as Farce*. London: Verso.
——(2013) 'Trouble in Paradise', *London Review of Books*. Available online at www. lrb.co.uk/2013/06/28/slavoj-zizek/trouble-in-paradise.

Index

Abraham 14, 60
Adorno, T.W. 84
Agamben, G. 25, 51, 56, 92, 94–5, 110–11, 120, 133
agonism 76–84
'agonistic respect' (Connolly) 77–8, 80, 83
AKP Party 89, 99
Alexander the Great 5–6
alienation, religious 109
Althusser, L. 22–4
angels, dual function of 55–6
Aristotle 24–5, 60, 98, 103–4
asceticism 6
'assemblages' (Deleuze and Guattari) 93
Atatürk, M.K. *see* Kemal, Mustafa
atheism 15, 20, 39
Augustine, St 54
auto-immunity 112–15

bad conscience 17–21
Badiou, A. 9, 11, 49–51, 84, 96, 101, 131, 135–40
Balibar, E. 44, 76, 134
Baudrillard, J. 40, 126, 129
Bauman, Z. 108–9, 115
Benjamin, Walter 2, 8, 93, 121
Bernstein, M.A. 127
Bettridge, T. 126
the Bible 60
'blessedness' (Spinoza) 43, 47
Bodin, Jean 64
Boltanski, L. 116
Borges, J.L. 126
Brown, N.O. 133

capitalism 10–11, 113, 121, 123; and 'banalisation' 139; new spirit of 116–17; as religion 2, 103–11, 124, 131–4, 139
çapulcu movement 95–7

ceremonial practices 13–14
Certeau, M. de 62
Chamayou, G. 60–1
chrēmatistikē principle 103–4
Chiapello, E. 116
Christianity 1, 6, 19–20, 25, 36–7, 61, 85–6, 97–8, 113, 135
city, the: conflict in 76–80; *despotic* or *free* 70–1; and reason 71–4
civil religion 80–1
'compossibility' of different truths 140
Comte, A. 130
conatus 71–3
Connolly, W.E. 77–9
credit 105–7
Cynics 5–6

Dawkins, R. 132
Debord, G. 99, 110
debt 107–8, 133; *see also* credit
Deleuze, G. 1, 4, 7, 14, 20, 42, 48, 72–3, 93, 97, 101, 106, 136
democracy 72–6, 82–7
democratic perversion 84–7
Derrida, J. 84–5, 112–15
despotism 10, 19, 24–8, 33–8
The Devils (film) 9, 57–69
Dillon, M. 7
Diogenes 5–6
Divine Law 13–14
Durkheim, E. 3, 124, 130

Engels, F. 22, 100, 131–2
Enlightenment thought 4
Erdoğan, Recep Tayyip 88–9, 92–7
Ergun, A.F. 99–101
ethics 115–16
eunuchs 36–7

faith 114–15; *see also* 'universal faith'
fanaticism 34, 40
Femen group 94
Feuerbach, L. 14–17, 21, 47, 109
Foucault, M. 4–6, 37, 85, 99
France 121
free association and free speech 73–5
free will 17, 25
Fukuyama, F. 111–12, 129

Gallie, W.B. 78
Gates, Bill 122–4, 129
Gezi Park protests (2013) 90–101
Girard, R. 35
globalization 113
glory and glorification 25–6, 110
Gnosticism 52–3
God 12–24, 41–8, 82–3, 100, 108, 110, 133, 137; love of 42–8, 140
God-capital 105–9, 134
Göle, Nilüfer 91
government, true aim of 74
grace 50–1
Grosrichard, A. 27–8, 32–3, 38
Guattari, F. 4, 48, 93, 136
Gündüz, Erdem 92
Güngörmez, Bengül 97–8

Hebrew Republic 74–5
Hikmet, Nazim 101
Hirst, Damien 121, 129
Hitchens, C. 132
Hobbes, Thomas 23–4, 73
Horace 102, 127
Houellebecq, Michel 11, 117–30
Huxley, Aldous 57

idealism 78
imagination: as a level of knowledge 41–2; and reason 46–8
immanence 135–6
the Inquisition 61, 64
intellect 43
intuitive knowledge 41
Islam 8, 26, 32, 35–8, 90–1, 113
islamism 99–101

Jesus Christ 1, 39, 45–6
Jobs, Steve 122–4, 129
Jonas, H. 52
Judaism 54, 113
Judas 2

Kafka, Franz 92
kairos concept 7–8, 53, 69, 106
Kaya, Ahmet 101
Kemal, Mustafa 89–90
khora concept 115
Kipnis, L. 126, 128
Koons, Jeff 121, 129
the Koran 39, 100

Lacan, J. 96
Latour, B. 116
Laustsen, C.B. 80
Lawrence, D.H. 1–2
Lazzarato, M. 106
Levinas, E. 115–16
Lévy, Bernard-Henri 128
liberalism and liberal democracy 85–6, 112, 134
Lincoln, Abraham 81

McDonald's 100
Mahomet (play) 8, 29–40
Malleus Maleficarum 64
The Map and the Territory (novel) 11, 128
Martin, Jed 122–9
Marx, K. (and Marxism) 3, 7–8, 21–2, 40, 83–4, 94, 98–110
mathematical thought 139
messianicity and *messianism* 114–15
Microsoft (company) 123
monarchy 83–4
money, role of 103–6
Moses 45, 110
Mouffe, C. 76
Mullarkey, J. 131
mysticism 9, 63, 134

nakedness, symbolism of 94–5
natural rights 71–5
Nazism 81
Negri, A. 75, 101
networking 116–17
Nietzsche, F. 1–2, 7–8, 10, 12, 16–21, 41, 85–7, 96, 98, 111–12, 130
nihilism 127–30
Nimrod 60

oikonomia 24–6, 55, 63, 104, 110, 112
Orientalism 26–7, 32–3
'original sin' 19
Orwell, George 129
Ottoman Empire 90

parrhesia 5–6, 68, 99
passions 70
Paul, St 11, 49–51, 71
Peterson, Erik 54–6
'phantoms of imagination' (Spinoza) 41
Plato 98, 115
political theology 70, 81, 98, 105
politics *versus* religion 80–4
pornography 119–21
possession 62–3, 67
post-Fordism 117
power, theory of 2
profanation 3–4, 48–51, 111, 115, 130–1, 134, 136, 140
Protestant ethic 104

Rancière, J. 84, 94
reason 41–8; and the city 71–4; and imagination 46–8; as a level of knowledge 41–2
relativism 80
religion 13–22, 38–9, 42, 49, 79–84, 100, 108–16; core of 15; different conceptions of 2, 131–4; organized 39; origin of 16, 18; 'return' of 2, 7, 113, 135; sources of 114–15; *versus* politics 80–4; *see also* 'true religion'
religious freedom 82
ressentiment 17–21, 84–6
revolution, concept of 101
Russell, Ken 9, 57

sacralization 3, 15–16, 115, 134; of the social 130
salvation 47, 51
Schmitt, Carl 2, 51–3, 56, 68, 81, 97
Schopenhauer, A. 16
secularization 51–6, 130
Sennett, R. 123
Shakespeare, William 5, 103
Simmel, G. 105
slave morality 86

social contract 72–4, 133
socialism 134
sovereignty 75, 80
Spinoza, B. (and Spinozism) 2, 4, 8–14, 18, 20, 32, 37–51, 70–83, 93, 105, 116–17, 130–40
spirituality, political 4–5, 68
state of nature 71–3, 80, 82, 133
Strauss, Leo 77
Su, Ruhi 101
Sungur, Ceyda 91
superstition 12–14, 38, 41–2, 131–2, 139
surplus-value concept 104–5

Taksim Square protests (2013) 92, 96, 98
Taubes, J. 2, 52–3
theism 40
theology 2; *see also* political theology
tolerance 79
totalitarianism 85
transcendence 3
Trinitarian dogma 54–6
'true religion' 2, 9–10, 38, 42–8, 70, 80, 83, 100, 131–2
Turkey 10, 88–102

United States 80–1
'universal faith' (Spinoza) 13, 39, 42, 80–3, 90, 131–4

Verne, Jules 124
Virno, P. 117
viziers 27–8
Voltaire 8, 29, 32–40

Washington, George 81
Weber, M. 52, 104
Whiting, John 57
witchcraft 63–4

Zarathustra 110–11
Žižek, S. 84, 91, 97, 101, 108